THE MADNESS OF PRINCE HAMLET
&
Other Extraordinary States of Mind

THE MADNESS OF PRINCE HAMLET
&
Other Extraordinary States of Mind

Robert M. Youngson

Carroll & Graf Publishers, Inc.
NEW YORK

Carroll & Graf Publishers, Inc.
19 West 21st Street
New York
NY 10010–6805

First published in the UK by Robinson Publishing Ltd 1999

ISBN 0-7867-06244

Printed and bound in the United Kingdom

Contents

Contents

To Muriel Cornes

Who has tried for years to persuade me that,
in both senses of the phrase,
there is more to mind than matter.

Preface

The purpose of this book is to entertain and amuse — and perhaps stimulate and surprise — those who share my particular, slightly cynical view of the world and my interest in the extraordinary mental processes of many of its inhabitants. While it will comfortably massage the prejudices of those of my particular persuasion, it will, necessarily, infuriate those who do not share my views. I do not think that a bad thing. The massaging of prejudices is pleasant but unenlightening; the prompting of disagreement can be fruitful.

This is not a textbook of psychiatry or philosophy, but an account of some of the more bizarre reaches of human psychology, written for people who enjoy thoughtful literature and who require assertions to be properly supported. There are many things in this book that the reader will find hard to believe; but nothing has been claimed without respectable authority. These extraordinary things do happen or have happened. The interpretation and explanations of them are, however, often contentious and controversial. Because of my impatience with nonsense, I have occasionally referred to some of the solemnly expressed opinions on these phenomena in less than complimentary terms. This may be painful to those whose cherished notions are treated with scant respect, but a book that fails to express strongly held beliefs can hardly expect to be taken seriously. So one of my underlying purposes is to stir things up a bit and to irritate readers whose natural cast of mind differs markedly from that of my own. I justify this ungentlemanly conduct on the grounds that, by analogy with the oyster, mental irritability can sometimes generate pearls of understanding.

Angry readers will, I trust, discover all sorts of reasons for dismissing my assertions. To assist them in this I would mention that several of the essays herein may, with gratifying precision, be applied to me. In particular, they may find the chapter entitled **Universal self-delusion** especially apposite and useful. Others, who feel themselves abused, might like to elaborate, preferably in their own minds, on the premise that it is presumptuous for a mere Grub Street hack to dilate on such a wide range of subjects spread over so many different disciplines. This is one of these situations in which, inevitably, someone will be prompted to apply Pope's celebrated (and usually misquoted) warning:

> A little learning is a dangerous thing;
> Drink deep, or taste not the Pierian spring:
> There shallow draughts intoxicate the brain,
> And drinking largely sobers us again.

Fair enough. But I am going to be even more presumptuous and suggest that Pope was wrong to apply the dictum with such sweeping universality. The truth is that, other than for someone professionally engaged in the exercise of a discipline, a little learning is a delightful thing and not in the least dangerous. Clearly the poet was not to be deterred from expressing his original and elegantly expressed conceit by such minor considerations as the need for complete accuracy. Incidentally, I had thought to call this book *Shallow Draughts* but this did not find favour with the publisher, so I present this wonderful name for a book gratuitously to any reader, friendly or otherwise, who has paid for this one.

There is, of course, no end to the 'proper study', however superficial, of the reach of the human mind and its vagaries. The subject is much too large for me to treat with the Olympian detachment that it merits. The difficulty is further compounded by the fact that humanity is divided into two classes – those who regard the mind as a discrete entity with transcendental characteristics; and those, like myself, who see the mind as an epiphenomenon of the brain. So, ever slothful, I have chosen a limited objective – to try to see how far I can cover the subject, writing from only one vantage point, but avoiding too deep an involvement in the eternal debate about the nature of the mind and its relationship to the brain. One's philosophy, of course, colours one's every thought.

Two notable advantages of this polarized approach are that one can write with intellectual honesty and that one is absolved from the necessity to be fair-minded and to indulge the other side's point of view. As La Rochefoucauld probably said (or, if he didn't, should have): 'A man who is unable to repress the exercise of his natural censoriousness will invariably find a way to disguise it as a virtue.' I have assured my publisher that this narrowing of my perspective will not mean losing half his potential customers at a stroke; my reasoning being that those who detest my views will, having dipped into the book, inevitably be so caught up in their outrage as to be forced to go on reading it to the bitter end.

The study of the extraordinary variety of mental states is immensely interesting and the revelation of each new facet adds to the fascination. This study has received an unprecedented boost by recent scientific developments. One of the major advances in thought of the second half of the twentieth century has been the recognition that the interaction between disciplines normally considered wholly unconnected can be highly fruitful. Barriers have been tumbling. Today, physiologists are talking to electronic engineers; theologians are talking to astronomers; painters are talking to computer gurus; and politicians are talking to everyone. Few interactions can have been more fruitful than that between modern neurophysiology and psychology and between neurophysiology and philosophy. For some psychologists squeezed between the two, the interaction has been distinctly uncomfortable. Some of the philosophers, too, have had a hard time, and many have had to come to terms with what may seem distressingly materialistic developments.

Psychiatry, too, has suffered, as the status of, and vogue for, speculative and imaginative assertion by quasi-religious leaders like Freud and his 'disciples' have faded under the assault of more hard-headed approaches to mental disorder. No one can yet claim to know what causes the commonest psychotic disorder – schizophrenia – or the commonest neurotic disorder – anxiety, in all its protean manifestations. But psychopharmacology and behaviour therapy have at least made it possible for society to be relieved of many of the embarrassments and florid disturbances caused by these misfortunes. Whether such treatment has done much good for the victims themselves is another matter, as a perusal of this book will show. One thing we can be sure of is that neither of these extraordinary states of mind is susceptible to treatment by Freudian psychoanalysis.

Knocking Freud, now an almost too easy activity, has become a major industry. These days, Freud is an irresistible, if rather soft, target, and I, too, have been unable to leave him alone. In common with many others, I think it important to attack assertions, made in the name of science and widely accepted, which have been shown either to be meaningless or simply not true. The best that the psychoanalysts can do in response to such attacks is a kind of *argumentum ad hominem* in which the critics are, one and all, accused of having an unresolved Oedipus complex. But in our enthusiasm to dismiss Freud as a scientist, it is easy to forget his importance as a literary man – an importance possibly higher than that of any other twentieth-century writer. I hope I have made this point in the book. Unfortunately, by insisting that Freud was a scientist and that psychoanalysis works, his partisans have made it harder for their opponents to acknowledge his greatness.

The mind, of course, interfaces with everything, and this is reflected in the diversity of subjects touched on in this book – saintliness, sadism and syphilis; spiders, schizophrenia and satyriasis; wine, witches and wombs; crime, castration and the corpus callosum; music, mania, masochism; morning sickness, Münchhausen and the *malleus maleficarum*; demons, dancing and delirium; love, lying and liquor; genitals, geology and Ganser syndrome; etc. etc. This is an *embarras de richesse* and, of course, a stimulus to self-indulgence which I have strenuously embraced.

Now that the book is finished and I read through it, I begin to wonder if I am quite as sceptical of the opposition party as I have long thought myself to be, for I find that, here and there, I have come close to being guilty of heresy. Although I recognize the impossibility of constructing a bridge over the troubled water between the two extreme camps in the eternal war between the 'body people' and the 'soul people', I am encouraged by this eclecticism. It seems that my mind may not be entirely closed to the possibility that I could be wrong about all kinds of things. Writing a book of this kind is a salutary experience and I find, on finishing it, that I am not quite the same person I was when I started.

Mind-modification of this kind, whether in the direction of Truth or a recognition of doubt, is generally regarded as a healthy experience – a prophylaxis against mental ankylosis (joint-stiffening). Fixation of the mind, like fixation of the joints, is remarkably disabling, but harder to recognize. So let us hope that some of my exasperated, but generous and open-minded, readers may share my experience. I believe that only a provocative and occasionally abusive book of this kind is likely to prompt readers into the kind of furious mental activity that can end in a paradigm shift. If the book does have any such effect, it may have done something more than merely entertain, something that is all too rare in these days of mass publication – it may have served a useful purpose.

Robert M. Youngson
Blandford Forum, 1998

The madness of Prince Hamlet

There has been much debate among Shakespearean scholars as to whether Hamlet was mad or not. I suggest that Hamlet was suffering from a condition known as Ganser syndrome. Moreover, as Hamlet shared Shakespeare's supreme intelligence and sensitivity, he made a far better job of it than any of his successors in the long line of people who simulate madness.

The unfortunate, much-maligned, yet much-quoted Polonius – who was a far more perceptive man that he is usually given credit for – was the first to cotton on to this: 'Though this be madness, yet there is method in't,' he said, thereby putting his finger on the salient point of this chapter. Ganser syndrome – the voluntary production of psychiatric symptoms, sometimes known as the 'syndrome of the almost correct answer', or the 'balderdash syndrome' – was first described in 1898 by J. S. Ganser in the German *Archives of Psychiatry and Nervous Diseases*.

The syndrome nearly always affects men. It sometimes occurs in people in fugue situations (see **Seeking a better life**) or those with amnesia, and it occasionally occurs in disorders such as schizophrenia, general paralysis of the insane (GPI), alcoholism and depression. However, it is commoner in those who are apparently free from psychiatric disorder and have something notable to gain from being thought mad: so it may occur among people in prison and occasionally among people in the armed forces.

So far as psychiatrists are concerned, Ganser syndrome provides good news and bad news: The good news is that, for a psychiatrist, Ganser syndrome is easy to spot. Very few people outside medicine have more than the most sketchy idea of how mad people really think or behave. As a result, the attempt to simulate madness is usually so feebly inept that the fact that it is a try-on is immediately apparent. The condition has also been called 'the syndrome of approximate answers' because, characteristically, the subject will usually get things *almost* right. On being asked 'What is the sum of five and five?' he will reply 'Nine and a half.' On being asked to count up to ten, the subject will say something like: '1, 3, 7, 9, 2, 1, 8, 9, 7, 10.' 'Who is the Prime Minister?' 'Benjamin Disraeli.' or 'What did you have for breakfast?' 'Roast beef and Yorkshire pudding.' Questions are always answered wrongly but the answers make it clear that the question has been fully understood.

Behaviour is in accordance with the subject's conception of madness. On being asked to use an object such as a pencil, the subject will try to write with the unsharpened end. On being given a plate, he will try to eat it. Sometimes the person will attempt to simulate dementia, but it is hard to do this in a consistent manner. Dementia is loss of mind, most obviously shown by loss of memory with 'confabulation' to fill in the gaps. Demented people usually talk a lot and repeat themselves, replaying well-worn tapes. People with this version of Ganser syndrome invariably rely on a vacant expression, an open, drooling mouth and conversation limited to 'Uh...' In other words, they simulate severe mental defect rather than dementia. In fact, Hamlet himself admits to his deception when he confides in his friend Guildenstern:

> I am but mad north-north-west;
> when the wind is southerly,
> I know a hawk from a handsaw.
>
> (Act 2, Scene 2)

A madman's moods were thought to be influenced by the weather; and here Hamlet is intimating that he has not completely lost his senses, for he can tell the difference between a hawk and a handsaw (another bird of prey).

The bad news for the psychiatrists is that it is hard for them to make up their minds as to whether Ganser syndrome is a genuine psychiatric entity or just another all-too-human ploy in the battle for personal survival in a hostile world. American psychiatrists respond to this question by admitting that the syndrome does not fall into any recognized psychiatric category. They therefore classify it as a dissociative disorder 'that does not meet the criteria for one of the specified dissociative disorders' described in the official manual.

It would probably be less trouble just to call it 'trying it on'.

Of love: delusional psychosis

Psychotic disorder is far commoner than most people realize. This is not the same as saying that psychotic *abnormality* is very common, for a disorder that affects nearly all of us at one time or another can hardly be said to be abnormal. But if we are to define a psychosis as any form of severe mental disorder in which the individual's contact with reality becomes highly distorted, and in which there are major delusions and often hallucinations, then being in love certainly qualifies as a state of madness. Nor is it necessarily a harmless form of madness, as the history of humankind has amply shown.

The reason why love has such a good reputation as compared with other forms of insanity is that one of its principal features − another common criterion of psychosis − is extreme elevation of mood. This pathological euphoria is manifested by excessive elation, talkativeness, inflated self-esteem, expansiveness and flight of ideas and is, of course, very pleasant and enjoyable. Unfortunately, it is often only part of a bipolar process (see **Of elation, sadness and the Amish**) that is liable to swing to the opposite extreme of depression, sadness, loss of self-esteem, hopeless misery and sometimes even suicide.

People in love suffer from a number of notable delusions (a delusion is a sustained belief that cannot be justified by reason). They have an unshakable belief, for instance, that their love will last for ever. This is a remarkable delusion that is not in the least disturbed by recollection of past experience or by the enormous amount of available evidence to the contrary. It is the delusion that sustains the much-married denizens of Hollywood and other haunts of the glamorous in their conviction that each successive marriage is for ever. Another delusion relates to the personal qualities of the beloved.

However commonplace he or she may be, the lover is convinced that the other possesses virtues and attributes of the highest superiority. This delusion is retained for as long as the state of love persists. When it is over, reality is once again accessible. Perhaps the most remarkable delusion of all is that other people who fail to recognize these alleged qualities are suffering from a severe defect of perception.

It could be argued that love is not madness because the love delusion differs from other delusions in that it refers only to a single object, is not global, and is thus of a fundamentally different kind. There is no substance in this argument. Many psychotic states are based on a single fixed delusion. This type of condition is so common that it has its own title – the systematized delusion. In all other respects the person with this disorder is completely normal. The feature of the systematized delusion is that if one allows that the original premise – the delusion – is true, everything else follows logically and reasonably. Of course, the original premise is usually something beyond reason – that, for instance, there is an invisible flying saucer floating over the subject's house from which little green men are watching his every action (see **Alien abduction**).

A person in love also shows serious defects of judgment, which are sometimes difficult to distinguish from delusions. These defects are manifest not only in relation to the beloved but also in relation to the person's own life. As well as completely misjudging the qualities and abilities of the beloved, the lover will commonly misjudge his or her own capacity. A young man in love will be convinced that, inspired by the beloved, he can achieve almost anything. He will try to obtain a mortgage on a house that he could never possibly afford to service. He will register for educational courses far beyond his intellectual level. Or he will talk endlessly, but often quite unrealistically, about his prospects for advancement in his present job.

The other common criterion of psychosis is the hallucination. This is not the same as a delusion. A hallucination is a sensory perception in the absence of the normal stimulus – seeing things that are not there, for instance. People in love commonly have a hallucinatory perception of the physical beauty of the beloved when, by any objective standards, the person concerned is devoid of any aesthetic advantage whatsoever. The presence of this hallucination is the reason for the frequency with which one hears such comments as 'I can't think what he sees in her.' This is not the only hallucination suffered by people in love. Another is the perception that one is seeing the beloved – usually from behind – when one is actually looking at a complete stranger. It might be argued that this is a simple illusion – a mistake in perception – rather than a hallucination, but often the conviction is so strong as to be pathological. In addition, the subject of the hallucination commonly bears so little real resemblance to the beloved that, for the mistake to have occurred, a genuinely hallucinatory element must have been present.

Paranoia and pathological jealousy are other common elements in this particular form of psychosis. The lover formulates elaborate schemes of persecution in which others – usually perfectly innocent persons – are attempting to seduce the beloved away. Invitations to parties are interpreted as sinister plots; conversations between the beloved and others are taken as evidence of infidelity; and the worst possible interpretation is placed on any unexplained absences. It is hardly necessary to give examples of pathological jealousy, but for an account of the most extreme cases the reader is referred to the chapter on the **Othello syndrome**.

The love psychosis is commonly an acute and recurrent disorder. Some people suffer from it many times. The incidence is highest in adolescence and early adult life, but in some cases new attacks occur at intervals throughout life. In most cases, however, a degree of immunity is acquired and the mature years may be relatively undisturbed. Occasionally, quite rarely, a single attack of the psychosis may persist throughout life.

There is one feature that seems to be unique to this particular psychosis – it has a biological, or at least a social, value. This is not to suggest that, without it, the human race would die out. But it seems probable that, in the absence of the delusory element, couples would probably not be willing to remain in each other's company for such long periods as they currently do.

It is hardly necessary to add that the love psychosis is a feature of sexual infatuation, and that the word 'love' has a much wider meaning. In its mature and best aspects, it encompasses some of the finest and most sane of all human states of mind.

Of ghosts and genitals: koro

At certain times of the year in certain parts of south-east Asia and China, men will tie heavy stones to their penises with a length of string. Some men, determined to retain secure attachment, come what may, will even pass a safety-pin through the foreskin or glans so that the string and stone will not come adrift. Others, motivated in the same way, will persuade friends, working in relays, to hang on grimly to the inoffensive organ. Why should they do such an extraordinary thing? Why, because they are, one and all, convinced that the penis is shrinking and terrified that it may disappear altogether.

The human penis is a remarkably variable organ. This is not so much a reference to degrees of erection, as to the variability of the size of the *flaccid* member. Even in the absence of sexual interest the penis will expand in the warmth and close down to pitiable dimensions in the cold. In *Ulysses*, James Joyce writes of the 'snot-green sea. The scrotumtightening sea', but this well-known effect of cold on the dartos muscle that corrugates and lifts the skin of the scrotum, is nothing to the changes that cold and the emotion of fear can effect in the penis itself. Consider the change in the dimensions of a large sponge, tightly squeezed in the palm of the hand into negligible bulk, and you will have the general idea. The penis is a column of three 'sponges' — the two corpora cavernosa and the single, central corpus spongiosum — and these will, when deprived of their tumescent blood, shrink down, both in length and in lateral bulk, almost to nothing.

We who are privy to this information know, of course, that, however impressively it may be attenuated by cold or other influences, the human penis will always retain some real identity. 'It may be a poor thing,' the enlightened Western man will say to himself, 'but it is mine own, and, God willing, it will again be great.' But we must remember that this information is not widely disseminated and that there are many who do not share our vaunted scientific paradigm. In a less mechanistic culture there have to be different explanations for phenomena of this kind, and in Malaya there are still many for whom the only plausible explanation involves what we, in our superior wisdom, might call magic.

Koro – the local, and medically adopted, term for this phenomenon – is what the psychiatrists call a delusional disorder. It is prevalent in south-east Asia and some parts of China, affects males and sometimes occurs in epidemics, especially during spells of unusually cold weather. The suffering man, observing the physiological changes in the dimension of his penis, becomes obsessed with the conviction that it is inexorably shrinking and will eventually disappear into his body. When it does so, he will die. To prevent this, he will, of course, go to any lengths – hence the string, the stone, the safety-pin. As in all systematized delusions, there is method in this madness. It is deeply embedded in this culture that ghosts have no genitalia. Ghosts are the spirits of the dead. So the disappearance of the penis must be fatal. It's obvious.

We smile. Such an idea is, of course, ridiculous. But when one cultural tradition smiles at what may seem one of the more peculiar manifestations of another, is the smile always justified – or fair? Might it not, perhaps, as in this case, imply a lack of awareness of the basis of the manifestation? Or even a lack of awareness of the role of illogic in all our lives?

Some of our most profound beliefs are induced in childhood when we have no grounds for rejecting them and no logical equipment to question them. Our elders are, in this respect, always our betters, and their *ex cathedra* statements become built into our neural physiology and are very hard to shift. Early notions, impinging on a mind avid for information and some kind of explanation of the world, make a deeper impression than do later and more sophisticated data. They are displaced only with difficulty and, unless we are faced with very convincing later reasons for countering them, will remain for a lifetime, modulating much of our thought. There is not much scientific education around, and even less training in logic. In societies devoid of such concerns, early beliefs remain unchallenged.

Other beliefs, especially those about ourselves, are cherished because they are essential to us for our comfort of mind. They are items in the long catalogue of defence mechanisms (see **Universal self-delusion**). Whether they are true or not is of secondary importance. A scientific training is no defence against illusory beliefs. A man or woman may be rigorous in his or her logic as it is applied to a scientific problem or a piece of research, but at the same time hold beliefs that, to objective examination, may be seen to be obviously untrue. Science and logic can enable us, later in life, to dispose of early beliefs on matters, covered by science, which we can jettison with little cost to our psyche. But they are liable to have little or no effect on data that we need, or think we need, for our spiritual comfort.

So extraordinary states of mind are not restricted to those we call insane, or to those who live on the basis of primitive magical thinking: they are the day-to-day characteristics of us all.

The shaking horrors: delirium tremens *d*

Probably the best description of the terrifying ordeal of *delirium tremens* is to be found in Charles Jackson's remarkable novel *The Lost Weekend*, published in 1944. The film of the novel, released the following year, was also outstandingly good, and starred Ray Milland as the alcoholic failed writer Don Birnam. Directed by Billy Wilder, who specialized in subjects not previously considered suitable for motion pictures, it earned the actor a well-deserved Academy Award and a quite undeserved, world-wide reputation as an uncontrolled drinker.

Delirium tremens (or DTs) – the shaking delirium – is no joke. Stories of pink elephants are all very well but the reality is shocking and serious. Delirium tremens is the result of alcohol withdrawal. It affects mainly people in their thirties or forties and seldom occurs until the person concerned has been drinking heavily for at least five years. Most victims have been drinking excessively for up to 15 years. It tends to occur in binge drinkers rather than in those whose intake is large but steady. The syndrome follows within a week after stopping drinking – most commonly on the third day after the last drink. It comes after a long period of heavy drinking and starts with shaking tremors, exaggerated sensitivity to any stimulus, a rapid heart rate, sweating, nausea and often vomiting. It is most likely to occur in people who are unduly fatigued, poorly nourished (as are many alcoholics, who get all the calories they need from the alcohol), dehydrated from vomiting or other cause, and physically ill. There is gross trembling, severe agitation, often epileptic seizures followed by horrifying hallucinations, which may be visual or auditory or both, paranoid delusions of various kinds, severe disorientation for time and

11

place, and extreme terror. This unpleasant and dangerous state may persist for up to 10 days and quite commonly results in death. In fact, if delirium tremens is not expertly treated, the death rate is about 20 per cent.

In delirium tremens, the behaviour of the affected person is quite unpredictable and he or she is commonly a danger to others or to self. There may be maniacal fury, and anything within reach may be smashed to pieces. Restraint is dangerous as this adds to the terror and distress and will be fought to the point of exhaustion. This really is a case for a padded cell, but skilled medical management is important. Delirium tremens can be avoided if strong withdrawal symptoms are noted early and suitable sedative medication given.

Studies of the mind of the alcoholic, and the reasons for excessive drinking, have preoccupied experts for years. Many different theories of alcoholism have been evolved. Even the definition of alcoholism seems to be in doubt: most experts would agree that there is no absolute definition. Attitudes to alcohol are strongly culturally based. Behaviour that in one culture would unequivocally define alcoholism may not do so in another culture. Some definitions rely on the proposition that excessive intake of alcohol causes harm to the drinker. These definitions run into the problem of defining harm. This may vary with the point of view of the definer, and may range from the one extreme of regarding all indulgence in alcohol, however minor, as bad and dangerous, to the other in which alcohol is regarded as one of humankind's greatest blessings, to be enjoyed as a daily habit even at some expense to health.

It is interesting, in this context, to note that in the professional medical press, although smoking is universally and roundly condemned, any hint that alcohol might have health benefits seems to meet with warm approval. Many papers are published showing the value of alcohol – or of some of the constituents of alcoholic drinks, such as bioflavonoids – in reducing the incidence of arterial diseases and coronary heart disorders. Much attention has been give to the so-called 'French paradox' – the fact that, in spite of a diet traditionally high in saturated fats, the French enjoy a far lower prevalence of coronary heart disease than the diet-conscious British and Americans. The favourite explanatory theory seems to be that the French intake of red wine, with its high content of antioxidant flavonoids, reduces the oxidative processes that seem to be necessary for the laying down of cholesterol in the walls of the coronary, and other, arteries. All this may be important information, or it may be no more than a systematized rationalization (see **Universal self-delusion**) on the part of wine-loving doctors. But it does not help when one is searching for formal definitions of alcoholism.

A widely accepted earlier medical definition simply described alcoholism as a disease caused by persistent excessive drinking. Few experts would now agree with this. The concept of harmful drinking, however, seems to be a reasonable one, and there can be no question that excessive drinking can cause harm of various kinds – harm to the body, to the mental processes, to the social integrity and to the pocket. If this is accepted, it is easier to lean in the direction of regarding alcoholism as a disease. Implicit in so doing is the idea that the person concerned is aware of the damage, and its cause, and would cut down on drinking if this were possible. The failure to do so seems to imply either that some form of addiction is involved or that alcohol offers the person some advantage that outweighs the disadvantages.

Some commentators try to draw a close analogy between alcoholism and addiction to other drugs, pointing out that ever-increasing doses are needed to produce the desired effects and that withdrawal symptoms occur when drinking is stopped. The comparison, however, is inept. Long-term drinking by no means necessarily leads to addiction; habituation to alcohol does not lead to the taking of doses considerably greater than the normally lethal dose, as in the case of some narcotics; and withdrawal symptoms occur inconsistently and, in some very heavy drinkers, not at all. Delirium tremens is the unhappy fate of only about one severe alcoholic in twenty.

It seems likely, from studies of the behaviour of drinkers, that the disinhibiting effects of alcohol offer some people an enormous and badly needed personal, social or inter-personal benefit. Alcohol provides us all with a more optimistic view of ourselves and it promotes easy access to social (to say nothing of sexual) intercourse. It may be that most alcoholics depend on this effect to reduce psychological discomfort to a tolerable level. This advantage may, for some, be so great that the drug becomes irresistible. Unfortunately, disinhibition applies also to the ability to exercise moderation, and the result is overuse with all its attendant damage. It may be significant that many modern alcoholism therapists do not make it their aim to achieve complete avoidance of alcohol for their patients, but simply aim for complete avoidance of more than moderate drinking. As Cleobulus of Lindos, who died in 579 BC and was one of the seven wise men of Greece, insisted, 'Moderation in everything.'

That so many drinkers are ready to risk immoderation, and the attendant horrors of possible delirium tremens, in their quest for the softening of a destructive self-view or to allow freedom in social relationships, testifies to the central importance of these things to us all.

Destruction of a personality: general paralysis of the insane

The Italian composer Gaetano Donizetti (1797–1848), whose numerous operas – he wrote some sixty of them – include *Lucia di Lammermoor*, *La Fille du régiment*, *Lucrezia Borgia*, *Don Pasquale* and *La Favorita*, was one of the most popular and outstanding opera composers of the early nineteenth century. He was also immensely popular as a person. He was amusing, generous, friendly, good-natured and handsome, and, unlike most of his fellow artists, was never envious of the successes of others. His father had hoped he would become a major composer of church music, but, to one of his cheerful and outgoing temperament, his natural inclination was always for the theatre. Donizetti was immensely hard-working and talented and had an enthusiastic public following. He was appointed official composer to the Emperor Ferdinand I and was greatly supported by Rossini, who had reciprocated his friendship by always generously promoting his works in Paris.

Donizetti fell deeply in love with Virginia Vasseli, the sister of a close friend, and soon married her. She became pregnant three times but, each time, the baby was born dead. Soon after the stillbirth of the third, Virginia died and Donizetti was inconsolable. His last important opera, *Don Sébastien*, with a libretto by Scribe, was produced at the Paris Opéra in 1843. It was during the rehearsals for this work that his friends began to notice an extraordinary change in the state of his mind, and some strange eccentricities of behaviour. He became irritable, querulous and difficult, and quite unlike his usual self. It was as if he had become a different person. From this time onwards he was guilty of serious behavioural, even criminal, lapses. He was soon in trouble with the Paris police. Those friends who had loved him for his good humour and evenness of temper were astonished and horrified at the change in him. The few years that remained to him were characterized by rapid degeneration of personality, eccentricity of behaviour, a radical change to moroseness and black moods, constant complaints of headaches, loss of speech and physical control, incarceration in a private asylum near Paris, progressive dementia and eventual death in a state of hopeless insanity.

There was a link between the stillbirths of his children and the tragic end of his own life. That link was *Treponema pallidum*, the spirochaete that causes syphilis, which Donizetti had acquired, it is believed, in the course of a single disastrous sexual adventure as a young man. Spirochaetes had settled in his body, multiplied unchecked, spread to every part, including his brain, damaged brain cells by their toxins, damaged small blood vessels so that the vital blood supply to his brain was prejudiced, and led, after many years, to the dreaded condition of general paralysis of the insane (GPI).

Today, because of antibiotics, syphilis is almost a trivial disorder, except in people with immune deficiency. Anyone with knowledge of medical history will agree that the conquest of this otherwise terrible disease is one of the greatest boons conferred by antibiotics. Before there was an effective remedy for syphilis, one third of all cases went on to the tertiary stage and about 8 per cent developed syphilis of the nervous system – neurosyphilis. The worst of these cases were those in which the spirochaetes caused diffuse inflammation of the brain – encephalitis. Characteristically, the damage was worst in the frontal lobes, those parts concerned with personality. It was because of this that such an extraordinary change in the state of mind occurred.

The victims of GPI first complained of severe headaches and poor ability to concentrate. Work began to become more difficult and the quality fell off. There was irritability and forgetfulness. Soon the behaviour became unacceptable. Dress became slovenly, personal hygiene deteriorated, and delusions occurred. These might be of any kind but sometimes took the form of a conviction of a sudden rise in social status and wealth. Those affected would manifest contempt for those less fortunate, and would engage in reckless spending and wild and extravagant living. Classical textbook accounts of the cases emphasized the feature of delusions of grandeur but it now appears that, because the most bizarre cases were the most fully publicized, it came to be thought that these were necessary features of the condition. In fact, many unfortunate victims simply sank gradually into dementia and a state of gross personal neglect without showing such dramatic changes.

During the early stages, however, it was common for people with neurosyphilis to lose many of their former inhibitions and to behave accordingly. Life-long ascetics and temperance fanatics would take to alcohol and would shock their friends by their sudden taste for, and indulgence in, sexual promiscuity. As the damage to the brain progressed, motor as well as intellectual functions were affected and, by the time insanity was obvious, there would usually also be a widespread paralysis with loss of speech, incontinence, inability to walk, widespread tremors, loss of sensation and an expressionless face.

This kind of outcome presented an irresistible opportunity for the moralists to talk of the wages of sin – just as, today, some use the example of AIDS. This was the fate of the excellent and talented Gaetano Donizetti, of whom biographers of the time, with characteristic censoriousness, wrote of 'symptoms of mental decay, arising chiefly from habits of intemperance'. There is a sad photograph of the demented and paralysed husk of destroyed humanity wrapped in tartan rugs. There is, for the 'holier than thou' fraternity, a peculiar satisfaction in the contemplation of the mental, moral and psychological downfall of the sinner. The disproportion between the 'sin' and the 'wages of sin', as in this case, are brushed aside as irrelevant. The real concern is with the gratification of feeling superior.

Happily, the memory of what Donizetti had been, remained with some of his relatives, friends and acquaintances. Verdi was deeply moved by the fate of his friend and, for the rest of his life, reproached himself for his cowardly failure to visit Donizetti during the final

17

stages of the disease. Donizetti's nephew tended him devotedly throughout his illness and even took him from the mental hospital in Paris to stay with him in his home in Bergamo. His brothers erected a monument to his memory in his native city.

Of sexual insatiability:
satyriasis and nymphomania

Nymphomania exerts a peculiar fascination for many adolescents and young men, who, in the natural course of events, devote a considerable proportion of their mental time to thinking about sexual intercourse. The idea of nymphomania seems to imply ready sexual access – a circumstance understandably attractive to young animals pacing their social cages largely under the influence of testosterone. But there is more to the popular concept of nymphomania than copulation on demand. The term, of course, refers only to the female sex and invariably incorporates a pejorative element that can furnish the male with a pleasant sense of moral superiority. Regrettably, many young males are only too ready to enjoy the erotic pleasures provided by the female while still being determined to enjoy their awareness of her degradation.

This interesting example of the double standard is compounded by the fact that whereas everyone has heard of nymphomania, that is, insatiable sexual desire by a woman, hardly anyone outside the medical profession has ever heard of the male equivalent, satyriasis. Perhaps the truth of the matter is that satyriasis is the normal condition of young men, so need not be dignified by a medical label. In the case of women, on the other hand, extreme sexual interest is deemed, at least by some men, to be so shocking as to be abnormal.

The idea of nymphomania, like the male sense of superiority, goes back a long way. The following account, taken from the third edition of the *Encyclopaedia Britannica* (1788), was inspired by the writings of the celebrated Greek philosopher Aristotle (384–322 BC):

> The *furor uterinus* is in most instances either a species of madness or a high degree of hysterics. Its immediate cause is a preternatural irritability of the womb and pudenda of women (to whom the disorder is proper), or an unusual acrimony of the fluids in these parts. Its presence is known by the wanton behaviour of the patient: she speaks and acts with unrestrained obscenity; and as the disorder increases, she scolds, cries, and laughs, by turns. While reason is retained, she is silent and seems melancholy, but her eyes discover an unusual wantonness. The symptoms fare better and worse until the greatest degree of the condition approaches, and then by every word and action her condition is only too manifest. In the beginning a cure may be hoped for; but if it continue, it degenerates into a mania... When the delirium is at the height, give opiates to compose. Injections of barley-water, with a small quantity of hemlock-juice, may be frequently thrown up into the uterus; but matrimony, if possible, should be preferred.

Note the chauvinist implication that a strong, lusty husband will do the trick. There is, in fact, much to be said for the view that 'nymphomania' is a male fiction generated by a process of wish-fulfilment. This is to be expected in definitions formulated during earlier male-dominated periods. So let us take a look at the contemporary 'official' definitions of nymphomania. A highly respected current dictionary, in its latest CD-ROM edition, defines nymphomania as 'a neurotic condition in women in which the symptoms are a compulsion to have sexual intercourse with as many men as possible and an inability to have lasting relationships with them'. The latest *Encyclopaedia Britannica* is a little more cautious. A computer search of the entire work shows that the word appears only once, in a reference to the work of the Polish novelist and playwright Michal Choromanski who wrote stories about the more unusual aspects of sexuality. The word is not defined.

A major textbook of clinical psychiatry states, merely, that 'nymphomania' signifies excessive or pathological desire for coitus in a woman. Other modern textbooks, such as the *Oxford Textbook of Psychiatry*, make no reference to it. The second edition of the *Oxford Medical Companion*, however, seems quite interested in nymphomania and defines it as 'intense sexual excitement in a woman, indiscriminately directed at any man and unrelieved by orgasm.' This is more in keeping with conventional male ideas of the condition. The article goes on to state, however, that nymphomania should be distinguished from 'female hypersexuality, which is simply one end of a normal distribution curve.' Clearly, the authors wish to be thought broad-minded and, at the same time, to indicate that nymphomania is a 'disease'. But there is a male chauvinistic give-away in the paradoxical statement that female *hyper*sexuality is normal.

Surprisingly, it seems that there have been very few scientific studies of the matter and that the few cases that have been reported were of women who had problems in achieving orgasms or had a strong fear of losing love. There is even the statement that women suffering from this 'disorder' are trying to satisfy their need for dependency rather than to gratify their erotic desires.

The history of the word is found in the *Oxford English Dictionary*, where it is defined as 'a feminine disease characterized by morbid and uncontrollable sexual desire.' As usual, the OED comes up with some wonderful philological gems. We find that the first reference to the word the compilers could find was in a book, published in 1775 and called *Nymphomania, or, a Dissertation Concerning the Furor Uterinus*. We learn that in 1860 it was taught that in a few rare cases, psychiatric disorder of pregnancy 'has degenerated into nymphomania.' In 1861, in his *Hints on Insanity*, J. Millar stated that 'nymphomaniac symptoms are constantly present when young females are insane'. In 1876 the case was reported of a girl without a cerebellum who suffered from nymphomania. The cerebellum, of course, has nothing to do with personality, instincts, emotions or sex.

In 1905, in a book on diseases of cattle, it was stated that 'nymphomania may be considered as almost invariably the result of a genital lesion'. It seems that the term was widely used by veterinary surgeons and that this reference is to animals, not humans. The same year Dr Henry Maudsley (1835–1918) reported in the *Journal of Physiology of the Mind*, 'She, though ultimately married, was a regular nymphomaniac.' Maudsley, incidentally, was pathologically averse to the idea of women engaging in sexual activity and advocated that women caught masturbating should have their clitorides cut off (see also **So near and yet so far**). In 1899, Allbutt, in his *System of Medicine*, refers to 'The furious nymphomaniac who embraces every man she can get at.'

There are then references to the works of James Joyce and Aldous Huxley and to a few more veterinary instances. This is followed by a jump to 1962, not, presumably because of paucity of material but probably because of superabundance. Selections at this point in the evolution of the word must have been somewhat arbitrary, but we learn that in the *Textbook of Psychosexual Disorders* by C. Allen, it is stated: 'Since writers... have become fascinated with the concept of nymphomania... it might be as well here to state that it is clinically very rare.' In 1969 the same author, in the second edition of the same book, refers to 'Nymphomaniacs who have a compulsion due to brain lesions, hormonal imbalance or other physical abnormalities.' The last reference is from 1973 and is a quotation from the novel *Hungarian Game* by R. Hayes: 'From different sources I'd heard that she was nymphomaniacal or homosexual or frigid.'

It begins to look as if the medical profession is getting wise to the absurdity of the idea of nymphomania. Psychiatrists have a sort of bible called *Diagnostic and Statistical Manual of Mental Disorders* (DSM), published by the American Psychiatric Association. This work, now in its fourth edition, is used all over the world and is immensely influential on psychiatric thought. It is good to be able to record that, so far as the authors of this distinguished work are concerned, there appears to be no such thing as nymphomania.

Since men have had their fun with nymphomania it is only fair to the women to include a short reference to satyriasis. Today, this is generally taken to mean no more than excessive sexual activity by a male, usually with the implication of promiscuity. In other words, it is what many people would regard as normal male behaviour. In the past the word has sometimes been regarded as synonymous with priapism which, today, is confined in its meaning to the dangerous condition of an abnormally sustained penile erection that persists after sexual interest has fled. Priapism is dangerous because, unless treated within a very few hours, the blood will clot in the corpora cavernosa and spongiosum of the penis, leading to permanent damage. Treatment is by simple drainage of the blood through a wide-bore needle.

Ironically, priapism, which was named after the god Priapus – who was only interested in copulation and is usually depicted in a fully erect state – is painful, embarrassing and humiliating and could hardly be less appropriately equated with satyriasis. In 1897, the Sydenham Medical Society decreed that the two were the same. Nowadays we know better.

Of the diversity of schizophrenia:
flexibilitas cerea *et al.*

There was a time, not so long ago, when the common public perception of a mad person was one who claimed to be Jesus Christ, Napoleon Bonaparte, Lloyd George, Albert Einstein, Mrs Thatcher, or a teapot (note the historic sequence). Being a teapot was boring but the schizophrenic often had plenty of patience. The popularity of the teapot was mainly due to medical staff wishing to demonstrate the phenomenon of flexibilitas cerea, which was once a common feature of schizophrenia. It is a condition in which the limbs can be slowly and passively bent into bizarre positions which they will maintain for long periods. It used to be said that the posture would be maintained indefinitely but this was a typical medical exaggeration.

Fashions in schizophrenia change with the times and this once common manifestation is now almost unknown. The behaviour of many schizophrenic people seems also to change with what they perceive to be expected of them. So writers of textbooks of psychiatry have a problem in describing the 'symptoms' of schizophrenia and an even bigger problem in describing the state of mind of the schizophrenic. There is no single sign or symptoms that can be said to be diagnostic of schizophrenia. Moreover, the manifestations, in any one case, may change with time. In different people, the indications vary with their cultural, educational and intellectual status.

People in this situation may withdraw from society and shut themselves off in a silent world of their own, or they may be restless, gregarious, noisy or violent. They may behave in an apparently perfectly normal manner or they may show extremes of eccentricity. Their mood may be flattened to the point where they seem incapable of any emotional reaction, or it may be exaggerated, elated, angry or anxious. Often, the mood seems inappropriate to the prevailing circumstances. Tragedy may promote laughter; while humour may bring tears.

The behaviour and statements of a person with schizophrenia may suggest that thinking is disordered. The person may appear to hold unreasonable or ridiculous beliefs. Some are attracted to religious cults; others openly defy God. They may claim to be hearing voices coming from nowhere, or to see things that do not exist, to feel touch when not touched, or to smell non-existent smells. These sensory disturbances are called hallucinations. The explanations patients offer to account for these things often seem ridiculous. For example, they may say: 'The voices are commanding me to take certain actions because there is a world-wide conspiracy against me,' or 'People are constantly watching me out of the corners of their eyes,' or 'Invisible people are constantly touching me so as to ensure that I cannot escape them,' or 'My body has been contaminated with poisons so that it is becoming diseased and smelly.'

The response to questioning and conversation, however, indicates that the memory is perfectly normal, as are awareness of present time and place. The person may seem not to be particularly interested in being interrogated. The psychiatrists call this 'attention deficit'. The affected person will invariably insist that he or she is perfectly sane. This is what psychiatrists call 'loss of insight'.

Schizophrenic people often behave and speak as if they held delusional beliefs. These commonly relate to expressed ideas of persecution. They may, however, express quite different ideas – those implying feelings of grandeur, social and intellectual status, wealth, and political power. Sometimes they will express ideas of extreme religiosity. Sometimes they will indicate the belief that their bodies have become distorted or are rotting away. Many seem to have an intense preoccupation with philosophical speculation, symbolism and abstract and esoteric ideas. They will often write endless letters justifying these beliefs and expressing these preoccupations.

It is important to appreciate that when the psychiatrist writes down what are taken to be positive diagnostic features of psychosis — such as mood changes, thinking disorders, hallucinations, attention deficit, lack of insight and delusions — the information on which these diagnostic points is based is entirely inferential. None of it is objective, and there is simply no way of knowing what is happening in the mind of the 'patient'. None of it is of the kind that would be allowed as evidence in a court of law. Things are easier for the psychiatrist if the person accused of being schizophrenic reacts by becoming violent. Such objective manifestations will sometimes justify the accusation of schizophrenia; it will justify restraint, which may also have to be violent, and it will also justify the use of powerful sedatives given by injection.

Since no one but the 'patient' has any idea of what is going on in his or her mind, there are several possible explanations for this strange state of affairs. At one time, it was almost universally accounted for by the entry into the body of evil spirits — possession, as it was called. Few people currently subscribe to that hypothesis, but if the present increase in irrational ideas and superstition in the Western world continues, that idea might soon make an effective come-back. Another possible explanation is a biochemical abnormality affecting some of the neurotransmitters in the brain, especially dopamine. This sounds intellectually more respectable and few doctors would be ashamed to be thought to subscribe to such a hypothesis. Unfortunately, in spite of the remarkable advances in our understanding of neurophysiology, there is no evidence that schizophrenia is caused in this way.

Could a genetic abnormality be the cause? Genes code for proteins, including enzymes, which do most of the chemical work that keeps our bodies and brains functioning. However, there is no evidence for a genetic defect. Psychiatrists point out that schizophrenia is commoner in the families of schizophrenic people than in the general population, but this is equally consistent with the view that family problems may cause schizophrenia. If one identical twin has schizophrenia, there is a 50:50 chance that the other will have it too. Since identical twins are so identical in their responses to environmental influences, this is exactly what one would expect. The observation that, if such twins were separated from their natural parents early in life, the probability of becoming schizophrenic remained the same, has been taken as evidence that there is genetic predisposition to schizophrenia. However, this fails to take into account the possibility that the trauma of separation of small children from their parents, not to mention the trauma of separation of identical twins from each other, could cause the problem, rather than any genetic defect.

Another interesting possibility at least has the merit of plausibility. Suppose a young person, growing up and becoming aware of the manifold difficulties and problems of life – such as conflicts with parents; irreconcilable differences between parental demands and peer pressures; conflicts between instinctive personal values and social forces; career conflicts; educational problems; anxieties about sexuality; strong feelings of inferiority; or whatever – gets to the stage at which the whole thing becomes too difficult to cope with. Suppose such a person is so oppressed that the only real choice is between suicide or finding a more acceptable paradigm than 'real life'. This is not a fantastic suggestion. Suicide in adolescents is endemic in our society. For some young people – and schizophrenia is a young person's condition – the move into a new world in which these problems do not have to be faced may appear to be an effective way out. To ask whether this is a deliberate, conscious choice is to ask a question to which no positive answer is possible. Human motivation is largely unconscious and, on an issue as major as this, repression would be highly probable.

This alternative world, in which personal failure and shortcomings are clearly explained – perhaps by persecution – and in which there is a free choice to be, for instance, a profound philosophical thinker, a world statesperson, a great religious leader or a saint, may be, for many, a highly attractive alternative to the miseries of the 'real world'. When looked at in this way, all the manifestations of schizophrenia — it is hardly appropriate to call them symptoms — seem reasonable and plausible, as do other features of the condition such as the resentment of incarceration and the violent resistance to drugs and other treatment. 'Lack of insight' now takes on a new significance.

Whether or not this condition is 'chosen', society does not like it. Schizophrenics often do not work and do not earn. They become a drain on society and are a great and expensive nuisance. They are also less pleasant to live with and can, occasionally, be dangerous. Formerly the easiest way to deal with them was simply to lock them up in a secure place where they could be forgotten about. Many people spent all their adult lives as patients in 'mental hospitals'. But such institutions have become too expensive, so another, much cheaper, solution has had to be found.

This solution started in the 1950s with the drug chlorpromazine (Largactil). This remarkable substance, which produces life-threatening adverse effects in over 1 per cent of people taking it and adverse reactions in over 12 per cent, becomes widely distributed in the body and ends up in a higher concentration in the brain than in the blood. It has a profoundly depressing effect on the central nervous system. Initially it acts as a strong sedative but people taking it soon adapt to this and remain awake during the day. Largactil interferes with the action of dopamine — one of the many neurotransmitters that allow the brain to function normally. The drug controls excitement, agitation and aggression, it suppresses spontaneous movements and complex behaviour, it reduces initiative and interest in the environment without affecting intellectual function. The effect of all this is that, over the course of a few days, the person taking the drug ceases to have hallucinations and delusions and starts to think in what most would call a 'rational' manner.

This effect proved so convenient for society generally, and so potentially profitable to the pharmaceutical industry, that an enormous research effort was put into developing similar but better drugs. Soon hundreds were produced, all with much the same effect. Everyone was immensely grateful – except the people who had to take them. Millions returned to the community to try to make the best of a life in the real world.

Society's reaction to madness predicates that it is an illness. Doctors and lay people talk, quite casually, of 'mental illness', the implication being that conditions like schizophrenia are much the same as conditions like tuberculosis or meningitis. In fact, they are not. Mental disorders have hardly anything in common with organic physical disease. We know the causes of nearly all organic disorders and we know what they do to the body. The mechanisms by which organic disease cause their effects and symptoms are generally well understood, and the effects of these diseases on different people tend to be, qualitatively at least, always the same. Schizophrenia does not have this uniform character. What the different forms have in common, is not a formal and recognizable complex of signs and symptoms as in organic disease, but, I suggest, a common motivation – to find a more acceptable paradigm.

The observable changes occurring in the body – including the brain – in the course of organic disease are called pathology. So far as current research can demonstrate, there are no corresponding organic changes causing schizophrenia. Terms like 'mental pathology' or 'mental disease' are in fact metaphors, but have been used so often that the metaphors have acquired solidity. But it is still a category error of the type described by the philosopher Gilbert Ryle (see **Human as machine**). It is, however, convenient for society to subscribe to this bit of intellectual dishonesty because it justifies the actions society wants to take to cope with this problem.

Although British psychiatrists must be medically qualified before they can practice their specialty, when they are doing so they are not doctors in the sense that orthopaedic surgeons, gastroenterologists and dermatologists are doctors. Rather, I contend, they are valued agents of society who carry out a tidying-up function much more closely equated with that of the police and the judiciary than with that of the medical profession. Is there really any difference between what

29

happened in Russia, when political dissidents were deemed to be mad and were incarcerated in mental hospitals, and what happens in Britain and America when people who do not conform to current social mores are legally certified and locked up. The notion of 'voluntary admission' is a piece of disingenuous face-saving. All concerned are aware that if the 'patient' decides not to volunteer, he or she will be arrested, probably by the police, and the end result will be the same.

The most vocal proponent of these heretical views has been Thomas Szasz, a maverick Professor of Psychiatry at the State University of New York Upstate Medical Center at Syracuse, New York. His books *The Myth of Mental Illness* (1961), *The Manufacture of Madness* (1971) and *Ideology and Insanity* (1974), and others, have persuasively and eloquently argued this case. That they have, apparently, had no effect on medical opinion on the matter is a commentary on the importance to the medical establishment, and to society as a whole, of maintaining the *status quo* – even if it should actually be an ingenious and convenient fiction about a state of the mind.

Character assassination:
Raspe and Münchhausen's syndrome

Karl Friedrich Hieronymus, Freiherr (Baron) von Münchhausen, widely reputed to be one of the great liars of all time, was born on 11 May 1720, at Bodenwerder, in Hanover, Germany. He was a notable sportsman, hunter and military gentleman who joined the Russian army to fight against the Turks. He retired to his country estates at the age of 50 and was soon well known in the Hanover region as a splendid after-dinner raconteur. It seems likely that his stories, as originally told by him, were either true or at least based on fact with a little judicious embellishment. There is no reason to suppose that Münchhausen was other than the soul of honour, and the full extent of his reputation as a teller of tall tales came not from him, but from others. Between 1781 and 1783, a series of tales, attributed to Münchhausen, appeared in the magazine *Vademecum für lustige Leute* (Handbook for lively people) and, even then, the Baron's reputation was being swelled by apocrypha, for several of these tales can be traced to earlier sources.

Münchhausen owes his international fame as a liar to a thoroughly nasty contemporary, the German scientist, scholar and petty criminal Rudolf Erich Raspe (1737–94), who had known the Baron in Göttingen and had heard some of his stories. In 1785 Raspe published, in London, a 42-page pamphlet entitled *Baron Münchhausen's Narrative of His Marvellous Travels and Campaigns in Russia*. Most of this work was Raspe's invention and it paints an unsavoury picture of an egocentric, swashbuckling braggart and pathological liar. But the stories were undeniably lively and they started a vogue for outrageous tall tales. In 1786 and 1788, the poet G. A. Bürger translated Raspe's stories into German and added his own contributions, greatly enlarging the book.

Bürger's versions quickly became famous and were translated into many languages.

In some respects, Raspe was a more interesting person than Münchhausen, and it is intriguing to speculate on how far his interest in stories that are economical of the truth, and in other literary frauds, reflects on his own character. After reading science and philology at the Universities of Göttingen and Leipzig, Raspe published, at the age of 26, a substantial book on geology which earned him an international reputation. Sir Charles Lyell (see **Of faith and fossils**) strongly commended this book many years later. Raspe then took up library work and, at the age of 30, was appointed librarian and Professor of Antiquity to Frederick II, the Landgrave of Hesse-Kassel. This job also involved custody of a valuable collection of gems, medals and coins.

Raspe was assiduous in his work and made a detailed catalogue of the Landgrave's collections, finding hundreds of items that had escaped notice. He was also an energetic bookman and was one of the first to draw critical attention to the important collection of old poems and ballads, Percy's *Reliques of Ancient English Poetry*, popularly known as Percy's *Reliques*. He was also well ahead of the field in his study of the collection of epic poems claimed to have been discovered by the Scottish poet James Macpherson (1736–96) and purporting to be translations of work by Ossian, the third-century Irish warrior poet. These remarkable poems aroused enormous interest all over Europe and were accepted as genuine by most people. They did not fool discriminating people like the great Dr Johnson or the philosopher David Hume, however, and by the end of the nineteenth century it was known that they were literary forgeries and the work of Macpherson.

Raspe's scientific and literary studies earned him a considerable reputation as a scholar and he was elected a Fellow of the Royal Society of London in 1769. An incorrigible spender, he was soon deeply in debt to the moneylenders. So he married the daughter of a rich Berlin doctor and, for a time, kept his creditors at bay. Unfortunately he did not amend his habits and, in the end, the temptation of the Landgrave's valuable medals became too much for him. Some of them found their way into his pockets and thence to the pawnbroker.

In 1774 he was offered a diplomatic job with excellent prospects and, greatly relieved, he at once accepted. But nemesis awaited him when, before leaving, he was required to account for the Landgrave's possessions. Ironically, the very scrupulousness of his own inventory was his undoing. His peculations were uncovered and, to escape arrest, he had to flee to England, where he was promptly drummed out of the Royal Society. It was while living secretly as a fugitive and desperate for money that, in 1785, he wrote and sold the manuscript of the Münchhausen stories to an Oxford printer. It must have been distressing to him to have to produce this work anonymously, but he could not risk being identified, and had no choice.

Raspe then became involved in a Scottish mining swindle and, in 1791, again had to flee the country to escape prosecution. This time he went to Ireland, where, in Muckross, County Kerry, he died three years later. His authorship of the Münchhausen book was eventually revealed, more than 50 years after his death, in a biography of Bürger by Heinrich Döring.

Raspe's greatest crime, in the opinion of some commentators, was to ruin the evening of Münchhausen's life. The international fame of the stories spread to Bodenwerder where the old man's declining years were made miserable by inquisitive sightseers and by an acquisitive harridan of a wife whom he had lately married in the hope of some consolation. He outlived by three years the man who had ruined his reputation for all time and died in 1797.

By the mid-twentieth century the tall tales of Baron Münchhausen were so well known that when the distinguished medical writer Richard Asher was looking for a name for a syndrome he was describing in the *Lancet* in 1951, the Baron's name at once occurred to him. In this germinal paper, Asher described the condition as:

a common syndrome which most doctors have seen, but about which little has been written. Like the famous Baron von Münchhausen, the persons affected have always travelled widely; and their stories, like those attributed to him, are both dramatic and untruthful. Accordingly, the syndrome is respectfully dedicated to the Baron, and named after him.

Münchhausen's syndrome, now commonly spelled with only one 'h' and without the umlaut, is classified as a 'factitious disorder' and it undeniably demonstrates an extraordinary state of mind. The name, however, is not a very happy one as it tends to perpetuate the quite unjustified reputation of the original Münchhausen conferred on him by the unpleasant Raspe. In addition, it is a condition from which Münchhausen most certainly did not suffer, nor, of course was it described by him. So it is neither commemorative nor eponymous. It is, however, now so firmly established that there is no chance of a change in nomenclature.

The condition is rare, occurs more often in men than in women and usually starts before middle age. It may, however, persist for many years. It manifests itself by the repeated desire for medical consultation and medical treatment. To this end, the person concerned simulates a variety of diseases – the more serious and dramatic, the better. The preference is for conditions calling for urgent surgical treatment and the history, symptoms and even physical signs are often extremely convincing. The natural prey of these patients is the young and inexperienced doctor, still excited at the making of a diagnosis. In many cases the patient will know more about the putative condition than the doctor, for these people are avid students of medical textbooks and are often ingenious in their simulations. They will usually time their arrival in the hospital Accident and Emergency Department so as to ensure that they are seen when the senior staff are off duty. Commonly they present themselves in the middle of the night.

They will give a detailed and circumstantial history; add blood or sugar to a urine sample, as appropriate; inflict injuries on themselves; ingest foreign bodies; promote fevers and abscesses by rubbing faeces into deep wounds; produce various forms of dermatitis by physical means; organize amputations of various parts; and claim to be experiencing all kinds of symptoms. Some have even taken the anticoagulant warfarin (a rat poison) to produce blood in the urine, and there are cases in which deliberate blood-letting to the point of profound anaemia have occurred. The essential difference between this form of malingering and straight hypochondriasis (see **Of the deadly dread of disease**) is that the history, symptoms and signs will almost always point to a particular disorder that will require hospital treatment.

It is typical of the condition that the 'patient' has been admitted, often for the same complaint, to numerous widely separated hospitals. The 'patient' will invariably use false names and addresses and will deny previous hospital admissions. If the person 'specializes' in surgical disorders, however, he or she is likely to bear numerous operation scars. The commonest complaint is of severe abdominal pain, often associated with an alleged history of vomiting blood or of bleeding *per rectum*. The pain is usually said to be so severe as to justify begging for powerful painkillers or narcotics. In this way emotional pressure is put on the doctor to help. Some of these people ingeniously simulate rare neurological disorders so as to excite the interest of the experts, who may often be carried away by their enthusiasm to confirm an exotic diagnosis. In such cases, heads have been opened and brains explored. Common to all is the rapidity with which the 'patients' will discharge themselves from hospital as soon as it becomes apparent that they are suspected.

Some of the manifestations of Munchausen's syndrome are remarkable. A young woman with a strong French accent appeared in a well-known teaching hospital with a history of a leg injury, said to have been sustained in a motor-cycle accident in Paris, two weeks before. She informed the doctors that this injury had been complicated by the 'flesh-eating' bacterial infection necrotizing fasciitis and required immediate radical surgery and skin grafting. The leg was undeniably inflamed and the area of inflammation was already twice what her GP had described. Accordingly, she was taken to theatre for immediate removal of all involved tissue (this is the only possible treatment for this dreadful condition). Surprisingly, the muscle under the affected area was normal and the problem appeared to be limited to a black, necrotic skin graft with surrounding inflammation. Swabs and tissue samples were sent for bacterial culture and skin was taken for a later graft. The woman was given antibiotics. A day or two later the graft was applied but by then the bacteriologists had reported that no organisms had been cultured. The woman complained, however, of excruciating pain and developed a fever of 39°C; although the graft took well, the 'patient' developed a further area of inflammation and underwent further surgery. Again no pathological organisms were cultured and microscopic examination of the specimens showed no features of necrotizing fasciitis. Five days later there was yet another area of leg inflammation with terrible pain and the 'patient' was given special treatment in a high-pressure oxygen chamber. This was followed by a fourth episode of inflammation. At this point the woman was challenged with the suggestion that her injury was self-inflicted, and at this, she immediately stated that the original injury had not been caused by a road accident but that she had been struck by shrapnel in Bosnia. She had, in fact, had treatment for the alleged fasciitis in four other hospitals. At this point she discharged herself. Further enquiries elicited that she was not French but was an English nurse. Her photograph and a letter were sent to all appropriate medical units in the UK.

What are we to make of the extraordinary state of mind of a person who can behave in this kind of way? They are, of course, pathological liars and are usually of a restless, aggressive disposition. Most of them find it very difficult to form close relationships. In many cases, questioning suggests that they have had a seriously disturbed childhood, often with parental abuse. Unfortunately, since it is part of their stock-in-trade to mislead about the past history, it is very difficult to know whether these histories can be believed. Proper investigation by the social services, however, will often confirm them.

Offer of help with social problems is usually refused though, and psychiatric treatment is seldom possible because the suggestion is immediately followed by the disappearance of the patient.

The motivation behind Munchausen's syndrome remains largely mysterious. Some have suggested that there is a deep, unsatisfied need to experience the concern of others and to be looked after. Some, less sympathetically, perhaps, suggest that it is no more than a desire for free board and lodging. There is no real indication that these people are primarily concerned to obtain narcotics; few of them are addicted to drugs. Whatever the motivation, it is certainly powerful enough to drive them to undergo repeated major surgical operations. It is possible that a motive for such behaviour may simply be excitement of the competition with the doctors and the emotional intensity of the experience when they are exposed.

There is a further and more sinister aspect to the Munchausen syndrome. Increasingly, in recent years, cases have occurred in which parents or others with care of children falsify a child's medical history and deliberately produce symptoms or signs of serious illness. This is called Munchausen's syndrome by proxy. The commonest effects produced are bleeding, rash, coma, weak and shallow breathing, diarrhoea, vomiting and epileptic fits. Sometimes blood from elsewhere is smeared on the child or bleeding is produced by anticoagulants. Coma and weak breathing are produced by poisons or drugs such as insulin or antidepressants, or by pressing on the major neck arteries. Laxatives and emetics produce diarrhoea and vomiting. Skin rashes may be caused mechanically or by caustics. Severe emaciation may be produced by withholding food. About one in ten of such children die from the assault, and the parent may exhibit all the manifestations of severe grief.

The perpetrator in these cases is nearly always the mother. There is more to this than simple child abuse. The parent will, typically, bring the child repeatedly for medical investigation and treatment. She will commonly allege that the child is allergic to all kinds of foods and other things but will otherwise deny any knowledge of the cause of the illness. Separation of the child from the mother will usually lead to the child's recovery. Again, investigation will often show that the perpetrator was, herself, abused and unhappy as a child.

Doctors have become greatly concerned about this development and have, in some cases, resorted to covert surveillance by hidden video cameras in order to prove what is happening. This has been condemned by some as unethical and likely to lead to further and worse abuse. There is general agreement that such surveillance should be avoided unless there is very strong suspicion and the belief that no other way of confirming the diagnosis is possible.

Compulsive coprolalia:
Gilles de la Tourette syndrome

Coprolalia is the involuntary uttering of obscene and filthy words or phrases — a remarkable state of mind that occurs in Gilles de la Tourette syndrome. This is an extraordinary disorder which begins in childhood with simple, involuntary, uncontrollable body movements such as shrugs, twitches, blinks, nods, jerks or sniffs. Such movements are called tics and are very common in children but rarely persist. When children are affected by them, the condition is nearly always short-lived and eventually disappears spontaneously. But in this syndrome the tics progress to a repertoire of ever more extensive and grotesque manifestations.

Initially, these are complex bodily movements only, and they may be severe. A simple twitch may become progressively more extensive, involving an ever wider range of muscles. Movements around the mouth may extend to involve the chin, then the neck and then shoulders. They are worse when the affected person is relaxed and may disappear altogether when the person is concentrating on a difficult job. This, the first stage in the progress of the disorder, may, in itself, be severely embarrassing and disabling. But there is worse to come.

In the next stage the sufferer begins to emit noises, at first minor grunts, coughs or barks. These then progress to loud grunts, squeals, or yelps. Finally the manifestations take the form of compulsive utterances, usually of an obscene nature, such as common swear-words. There is also a common tendency to 'echolalia', that is, the compulsion to echo or repeat words of sentences that have just been spoken by another person. Some victims also exhibit 'copropraxia', the compulsion to make obscene gestures. Some are unable to restrain themselves from repeating their own words or noises.

Coprolalia occurs in about half the cases so that the condition becomes a severe social disability. The organic basis of the disorder is uncertain (see below) but there is a strong genetic basis; its effects, however, are strongly psychological. The tics and the coprolalia are of a kind. Pressure builds up that can be relieved only by giving way to the physical reaction or verbal utterance. Often in the most unsuitable surroundings, such as a church or public platform, the victim contemplates the awfulness of saying something obscene. There is never any question of a desire to shock or distress – that is the last thing the sufferer wants to do. It is just that once the thought has occurred, the effort to inhibit or control the impulse has to become ever stronger. In the end, it fails and the victim has the humiliation of making a public spectacle of himself. Once fully established, the condition lasts for a lifetime.

Georges Gilles de la Tourette was a pupil of Charcot at the famous Salpétrière hospital in Paris. It was there that, in 1885, he published an account of the condition in a paper entitled *Étude sur une affection nerveuse caractérisée par l'incoordination motrice accompagnée d'écholalie et de coprolalie*. Tourette was not the first to describe the extraordinary condition but, as is usual, the one who makes the most stir gets the credit. The syndrome runs in families, with dominant inheritance, but appears in various degrees of severity. It often starts in childhood – sometimes as early as the age of five – but occasionally as late as early adult life.

The organic cause of the syndrome is presumed to result from some defect in the basal ganglia – the large nerve cell masses in the base of the brain. The entirely different condition of sleeping sickness (encephalitis lethargica) has many features in common with Gilles de la Tourette syndrome and certain drugs, known as neuroleptics, which act on the basal ganglia, have a remarkably calming effect on the syndrome. One major feature of the disorder is that sufferers from it nearly always have an obsessive–compulsive neurosis. They feel compelled to carry out certain actions, such as touching every second post on a fence as they walk along, or avoiding walking on cracks in the pavement.

There is a famous literary figure noted for behaving in this way and also for his 'grotesque gesticulations', and occasionally for emitting inappropriate grunts and noises. Dr Samuel Johnson's massive figure was made grotesque by a strange infirmity. Madame d'Arblay talks of his 'vast body in constant agitation'. Miss Reynolds describes his seemingly unconscious 'antics,' especially when entering a building. Sometimes when he was reading a book in the fields a mob would gather to stare at his strange gestures. He had queer tricks of touching posts and carefully counting steps, even when on horseback. He was constantly talking or muttering prayers to himself.

Happily, if the Great Cham did suffer from Tourette syndrome, it must have been in a very mild form. Nothing could have been more unsuitable than for the great Dr Johnson, whose moral consciousness is justifiably legendary, to engage in coprolalia.

So near and yet so far: frotteurism

Nubile women who travel in crowded public transport may find themselves the recipients of undesired attention in the form of 'frottage'. This is a form of fully clothed surrogate sexuality, involving rubbing of the penis against the buttocks or other parts of an unconsenting and sometimes unaware female. Such dubious delights are probably limited to a fairly small number of men, but it is impossible to obtain reliable figures as many women in this situation are unaware of what is happening.

What are we to make of the state of mind of men who habitually engage in such a practice? Frotteurism is said to be a compulsive paraphilia – a mental disorder characterized by sexual deviation. However, many frottage episodes must have occurred for no more sinister reason than the chance close juxtaposition of male and female in a crowded place. Most healthy young males are polysexual and, on finding themselves pressed tightly against an attractive woman, would find it hard to remain entirely indifferent. In such a situation, a man of reasonably gentlemanly instincts will, of course, strive to remain aloofly neutral and will make every effort to turn away. But there are some who see no need to exercise such consideration and who look on such a situation with satisfaction as one to be exploited to the full. This is hardly sexual aberration – more a matter of lack of normal respect, courtesy and proper standards of behaviour. To exploit the situation in the interests of a cheap sexual thrill is to behave disgracefully, and, as would become apparent were a woman to have the courage to bring charges, is to engage in a criminal indecent assault.

Habitual and sought-out frotteurism is a slightly different matter and can become a compulsive state, although still criminal. Men with this compelling need will use trains and lifts for this purpose only. They engage in frottage to achieve sexual stimulation, erection and, if possible, orgasm. If the act fails to culminate in an orgasm, the man concerned proceeds to masturbation. Some frotteurs have admitted that they feel profoundly guilty if detected in the act, even if the woman's protest is no more than a silent look of disgust or a sudden movement away. Some also state that the orgasm, however induced, is also followed by strong guilt feelings and that the whole business leads to serious unhappiness. Many habitual frotteurs admit that they are passive and isolated and that frottage is their only source of sexual gratification.

All this suggests that the habitual frotteur may be a sexually or socially inadequate person, incapable, for reasons of personality defect, of forming a mature social and sexual relationship. But this may be no more than a pejorative response to the contemplation of a distasteful activity. Psychiatrists who react in this way and who write books are liable to allow their prejudices to harden into categorical assertions. These, in turn, acquire the authority of print and are perpetuated from one book to another.

A good deal of 'received wisdom' originates in this way. An excellent case in point is the English psychiatrist Henry Maudsley (1835–1918) after whom the psychiatric hospital in Denmark Hill, London was named. Maudsley, influenced, no doubt, by childhood religious and parental pressures, had developed an almost hysterical aversion to the very idea of masturbation. In the *Journal of Mental Science* in 1868 he published a paper on masturbation in which he wrote of '...the high-pitched and absurd sentiments professed by these degraded beings...' and 'a mind enervated by vicious practices, dwelling continuously on sexual subjects. It is curious that to such a state of moral degradation have patients of this class come, that they will actually defend their vice on some pretence or other.' Maudsley was convinced that masturbation caused insanity. The thought of female masturbation was more than he could bear and he strongly advocated the surgical removal of the clitoris in women guilty of this appalling vice.

So it behoves us all to be wary of accepting the *ex cathedra* assertions of all medical authors, especially psychiatrists, and certainly not excluding those of the begetter of the book you now hold in your hands.

The mind of the offended:
punishment for crime

On the question of punishment for crime, the view generally held to be most respectable is that it should act as a deterrent to further crime. Many people, however, if pressed, will admit that they believe that punishment is justified as a retribution by society. They will agree that, in response to a particularly savage or horrifying crime, punishment such as flogging or execution is appropriate and justified. These views have been almost universally held from the earliest times, often in an extreme form. As a result, penal systems have often been barbarously cruel. Long sentences of incarceration in dungeons and manacles, flogging to the limits of endurance, branding, blinding, amputation and torture of all kinds have been commonplace. The practice of execution, by decapitation, strangulation, burning, hanging or crucifixion, was widespread.

English justice was capable of brutal savagery in the medieval period, when the sentence for treason was public hanging, drawing and quartering, in which, after partial strangulation, the victim, while still alive, was disembowelled, the intestines burned and the body hacked into four parts. The explicit justification for such punishments – that they would be a deterrent – was based on the assumptions that potential offenders would act rationally to avoid pain and would contemplate the consequences of their actions. History has shown that these assumptions are seldom justified. The fear of severe punishment does not necessarily deter. The crowds watching such a spectacle would always contain many criminals engaged in the exercise of their profession.

An enlightened and humane early writer on the subject of

punishment was the Italian jurist Cesare Bonesana Marchesi di Beccaria (1738–94). In his book *An Essay on Crimes and Punishments*, published in 1764, Beccaria argued that a state should legislate for a scale of crimes ranging from those most harmful to the state to those causing the least harm to the individual. The state should also legislate for an appropriate scale of punishments whose function was not retributive but was purely to deter. Punishment should therefore have the greatest deterrent effect consistent with the least harm to the offender. It should be certain, quick and consistent. Punishments found not to deter should be abandoned and others tried. The laws should be clear and known to all.

Beccaria's book was one of the most widely read and influential works of the time both in Europe and in Britain and prompted much thought and argument on penal reform. Voltaire gave it his support and attempts were made to incorporate its ideas into the French penal code of 1791. The English philosopher Jeremy Bentham (1748–1832) took Beccaria's ideas further and pointed out, among other things, that excessively severe punishment defeated its own object because the offender could argue that he or she 'might as well be hanged for a sheep as for a lamb' – the offender may as well commit a more serious crime since the punishment would be the same.

In modern society, imprisonment is an effective deterrent for most first offenders. About three-quarters who are imprisoned for the first time do not offend again. But of those who do, and who are again imprisoned, the rate of habitual relapse into crime (recidivism) rises steadily. Overcrowded long-stay prisons often simply promote further crime by reinforcing criminal tendencies through contact with other criminals. Prisons act as schools for criminals. It would seem that, once the real damage has been done to the mind, it is too late to undo it.

Infectious insanity: *folie à deux*

In 1877, two French psychiatrists, C. Lasège and J. Falret, published a paper in the Paris *Annals of Psychological Medicine* entitled 'La Folie à deux, ou folie communiquée'. This paper described seven cases in each of which a dominant mad person had recruited a submissive normal person who entered willingly into, and fully participated in, his or her insane world. This was not the first report of this strange phenomenon, but the name given to it by these two doctors caught on and the condition has been known ever since under their title. *Folie à deux* is a well-established, although fairly rare, psychiatric condition.

The name suggests that the condition affects only two people; although 95 per cent of cases do involve only two people, usually members of the same family, this is not necessarily so. Numerous instances have been reported of multiple cases. These have been described as *folie à trois, folie à quatre, folie à cinque* and so on up to one recorded case of *folie à douze*. The essence of the condition is that two or more people are living in a very close association in which one or more are dependent on one particular person who is suffering from a paranoid schizophrenic disorder. The delusory ideas that are transmitted to the dependent person or persons are usually persecutory, grandiose or hypochondriacal, and they are, at least ostensibly, fully accepted by the dependant.

The cooperation of the dependent members is remarkable. Not only do they acquiesce freely in the completely delusional beliefs of the dominant person, but they also actively reinforce these delusions by word and deed, often supporting them quite unnecessarily. Such associations may persist for many years. The delusions are usually at least moderately plausible so that the dependent member or members need not unduly strain credulity. They may relate to the alleged social or financial status of the dominant member or they may be of the more usual persecutory type.

It is noteworthy that the submissive person is often younger then the dominator and is in one respect or another inferior. The condition affects women more often than men and the commonest combination is of two women, often two sisters. In about a third of the cases, however, a husband and a wife are involved, and in rare cases the participants are a father and a child. In almost all cases the people concerned are relatively or severely isolated from the general community and there is almost always a notable advantage from the situation to all parties. The dependant receives support, approval and security, and the dominator receives comforting reinforcement of her delusions.

The most interesting question about this odd situation is how far the submissive person really is mad in any meaningful sense of the term. It also raises the problem of the definition of madness. This question is important as it may throw light on the proposition that psychiatric disorder is, at least sometimes, a matter of deliberate choice (see **Of the diversity of schizophrenia**). The choice of the kind of world one wants to live in – a world with values that are comfortable and acceptable to a person with a non-standard paradigm may, it is suggested, direct a person into a state defined by the psychiatrists as a psychosis. The psychiatric textbooks insist that the dependent person or persons 'unquestionably' accept the delusions of another person. One wonders how they can be sure of this. The dependant dare not suggest otherwise, for to do so would be to hazard a wanted life situation.

It is not without significance that, if the members of a case of *folie à deux* are separated, the dependent person usually experiences a rapid and dramatic disappearance of his or her delusory symptoms. In cases in which this does not occur, the victim is, sooner or later, labelled as a delusional schizophrenic (in which case, of course, the original diagnosis of *folie à deux* was, by definition, wrong).

All gone: Cotard syndrome

Some people think that anyone who claims to be a nihilist must be mad. Be that as it may, there is certainly a form of madness in which nihilism is the central feature. In 1880 and 1882 the French psychiatrist J. Cotard described a syndrome, which he called *délire de négation*, and in which the sufferer was convinced that he had lost his friends, family, money possessions, heart, lungs, brain, intestines and anything else he could think of. The whole outside world was also reduced to nothing, and it was all entirely his own fault.

Cotard syndrome received its eponymous name, and became well known, in 1897 when J. Séglas wrote a book giving a highly detailed account of it. It is a total nihilistic delusion, in which the sufferer believes that their own unworthiness, sinfulness and loathsomeness have brought about the destruction of the world. It is associated with profound depression. There are often precipitating factors, usually of a type that may readily give rise to a strong sense of guilt.

Some psychiatrists deny that Cotard syndrome is a distinct clinical entity and claim that it is just one more of the great catalogue of delusions from which schizophrenic people suffer. Others, however, consider this state to be a special one that can exist in a pure form. When it does, it may last for only a few days or a week or two. The condition commonly starts with a delusional belief that a part of the sufferer's body is missing — usually an internal organ such as the heart or the stomach. Alternatively, the initial delusion may be of loss of money or possessions. As the condition progresses, so does the extent of the loss. More and more organs may disappear, as may more and more of the outside world. Some affected people are so disgusted with themselves that they express the wish to disappear altogether. Others, however, acquire a conviction of immortality so that they are left alone in a non-existent world.

Cotard syndrome has a special philosophic and neurophysiological interest as it has been shown that, although it may occur as a purely psychiatric disorder, it can often be of purely organic origin and arise from brain damage. Certain parts of the brain are concerned with conscious awareness of the existence of the body. It is common, for instance, after a stroke that damages the right side of the brain, for the victim to be convinced that the left half of his body does not exist. That damage to one half of the brain affects the other side of the body is a consequence of the fact that the nerves that carry sensation from each half of the body, cross over to the other side in the stem of the brain (see also **Divided brains**).

When the part of the brain that mediates vision is severely damaged, a very peculiar form of blindness occurs. This is called cortical blindness because it is caused by damage to part of the outer layer, or cortex, of the brain. The affected person is certainly blind, but he or she will invariably deny it and will produce various explanations, or rationalizations, to account for the disablement. 'My glasses need changing.' or 'The lights are not bright enough.' Neurologists recognize that there is an inherent tendency to deny loss of function of various kinds brought about by brain damage. This is not perversity but is a consequence of the complexity of the brain and of its ability to continue to operate in certain departments in spite of damage to others.

Part of the function of the brain is to provide us with a kind of sense of our structural and functional completeness as an organism; this is not necessarily abolished when a particular function is destroyed by local brain destruction. It may be that widespread but subtle organic damage to the brain can remove this sense of bodily integrity thereby causing Cotard syndrome. The awareness of so much damage would have to have its justification or rationalization, and this may account for the associated sense of sin or guilt. It may be argued that recovery from Cotard syndrome is quite common; it may also be argued that at least a degree of recovery of function after brain damage is the rule rather than the exception.

Metaphysical philosophers could have a great time working out the full implications of Cotard syndrome. If our sense of reality can be removed by brain malfunctioning, it seems to follow that our awareness of 'genuine' reality depends on proper functioning of our brains. This being so, how much confidence can we put in the reality of 'genuine' reality?

Of elation, sadness and the Amish: cyclothymic states

The manic–depressive disorder is a serious disturbance of the emotions. Sometimes the affected person shows only an abnormal elevation of mood (mania) or only extreme sadness (depression). This is called a unipolar disorder. If both phases occur, even if separated by long intervals, it is said to be a bipolar disorder. Until recently, the cause was unknown, but, as we shall see, there is now good evidence that hereditary factors are involved.

In the bipolar disorder the depressive phase usually comes first; about 10 per cent of people thought to be suffering from unipolar depression have a manic episode six to ten years later, usually in their early thirties. There is no real difference between the depressive phase of the manic–depressive disorder and psychotic depression generally. In the depressive phase there is mental and physical slowing; loss of interest and energy; loss of concentration; pessimism; self-doubt; self-blame; and thoughts of suicide. Untreated depressive episodes last for about six months to a year, and most affected people suffer five or six episodes over a 20-year period. Treated episodes usually clear in about three months, but if treatment is not continued for about three months, relapse is likely. The manic phase, if it occurs, usually comes after two to four depressive episodes.

The manic phase features constant elation or euphoria; speeding up of thought and speech; ever-changing flights of ideas; severely disordered judgment and mental reliability; inappropriate optimism; grandiose notions; and a gross overestimation of personal ability that tends to result in unrealistic plans and intentions and in socially and financially damaging or ruinous behaviour. The affected person sleeps poorly and may engage in an unusually high level of sexual activity. About three-quarters of those with this disorder are involved in threatening behaviour or personal assault, sometimes against people in prominent positions. They are notoriously unreliable and characteristically engage in deceit and lying. Both the mania and the depression may feature hallucinations and delusions. The spontaneous recovery rate in manic–depressive illness is very high – about 90 per cent recover. The relapse rate, however, is also high.

It has long been suspected that there was a genetic element in the causation of the bipolar disorder. The incidence in most populations is about 1 per cent. In families that contain a case, the incidence is about 5 per cent. It is five times as common for both identical twins to have the manic–depressive disorder than it is for both members of a pair of fraternal twins (who have different genes) to be affected. Identical twins have the same genes. The life-time risk of developing a bipolar disorder is ten times as high in first-degree relatives of people with the disorder as in people not so related.

In the first half of the eighteenth century about 30 married couples of a conservative Christian group, the Old Order Amish Mennonite Church, emigrated from Germany and settled in Lancaster County, Pennsylvania. These people, whose descendants now number some 12,500, were followers of Jakob Ammann, a tough-minded seventeenth-century holy man who had, by his teachings, disrupted the Mennonite religion and caused a major schism. Ammann insisted that anyone caught telling a lie should be excommunicated and anyone suffering this fate must be shunned. Church members should wear plain and severe uniform clothes fastened with hooks and eyes and with no buttons. Men should wear broad-brimmed hats. Beards should not be cut and moustaches should not be worn. Women must wear the kind of dress common at the time – bonnets, long plain dresses with shoulder capes and shawls and black shoes and stockings. All jewellery was prohibited. Members must never attend services in state churches, and their own services, which were held in each others' houses, must include washing of feet.

Following the spirit of this teaching, the present-day Amish dress in the manner of seventeenth-century Europe, do not use electricity or telephones, do not drink alcohol or take drugs, and use horses and horse transport instead of cars and farm machinery. Violence is unknown. They allow their children to attend primary schools but not secondary schools. This remarkable association of mode of dress with religious conviction might be thought by some to be an indication of an extraordinary state of mind, but that is not the reason for introducing the Amish phenomenon here, interesting though it may be in its own right. The principal interest in them for the present purpose is that the members of the colony in Lancaster County are descended exclusively from the 30 original settlers. Genetic mutations apart, the gene pool of all the Amish in this group is the same as came across the Atlantic more than 250 years ago. Because of their strict rules of sexual conduct, parental lineage is reliably known. Also, it was always possible to be sure of the diagnosis of the manic–depressive disorder, even in people long dead, because the behaviour of normal Amish people is so good. If the features of the manic phase occur, it has to be pathological; normal Amish people never behave like that. This made the study of Amish pedigrees of cyclothymic disorder much easier and family patterns could reliably be mapped out. The Amish believe that mental disorder is a scourge of God and have been very cooperative in genetic research into the condition. The prevalence of unipolar depression in the Amish is much lower than in other groups in America – only about one tenth. The prevalence of the manic–depressive disorder is the same.

In one extended Amish family of 81 people, 11 were diagnosed as having manic–depressive disorder and 62 were entirely normal (8 were not quite normal, and therefore excluded from study). The question was, what was the genetic difference between the 11 people with manic–depressive disorder and the 'normal' people? Research showed that there was a difference. Genetic studies showed that nearly all the people with manic–depressive disorder had two defective genes near the tip of the short arm of chromosome 11; the normal people did not. The affected genes are in a location for genes that code for brain neurotransmitter substances (hormones) called catecholamines. This group includes adrenaline, noradrenaline and the thyroid hormones.

There is also fairly strong independent evidence that the systems of the brain that use noradrenaline are concerned with the control of the emotions. Indeed a considerable amount of pharmacological research has strongly implicated noradrenaline and another amine hormone called serotonin in the production of depression. Excess of noradrenaline and serotonin can have the opposite effect. The anatomical organization of the noradrenaline and serotonin systems suggests that they perform important regulatory functions in the brain. They appear to be involved in setting the responsiveness of large areas of brain circuitry, determining the level of arousal and attention and degree of motivation. They also determine whether the attention is turned inwards or concentrated on external stimuli, and, in the latter case, whether or not stimuli are noted and the incoming data recording in memory.

The drug reserpine depletes neurons of noradrenaline and causes depression. Some of the antidepressant drugs act by preventing the breakdown of noradrenaline. The drug Prozac (fluoxetine) is a selective inhibitor of re-uptake of serotonin. This means that Prozac effectively increases the amount of serotonin available. Adverse reactions from Prozac include convulsions and mania.

Thus it begins to look as if the organic cause of at least one major psychotic condition is being elucidated. Like many other diseases, manic–depressive psychosis seems to have a genetic basis. It has nothing to do with the Oedipus complex or any other such mystical entity. It has nothing to do with childhood sexual abuse. It is just a matter of chemistry.

The celebrated Hahnemann delusion: homoeopathy

Biographies of Christian Friedrich Samuel Hahnemann, while probably mainly accurate, are remarkably variable in tone and theme. They paint a picture either of one of history's most notable benefactors, or of an unscrupulous charlatan and mountebank who cynically prostituted his talents for gain. This divergence is achieved by a simple process of selection of the desired features from the available biographical material, for Hahnemann was certainly a complex character with, as will shortly become apparent, a remarkably eclectic personality. What is of special interest about Hahnemann, however, is that he was responsible for a remarkable instance of what could be called mass delusional insanity. For nearly 200 years, millions of people have accepted, and acted on, a proposition that seems quite incredible.

Christian Friedrich Samuel Hahnemann was born at Meissen, in Saxony, on 10 April 1755. His father was a porcelain painter but so poor that he could not afford to have Samuel educated. Happily, the boy showed so much talent and determination to work that his schoolmasters at the Fürstenschule kept him on for free. In spite of all the difficulties of poverty, he determined to study medicine and was admitted as a poor student to the Medical College at Leipzig where he supported himself by teaching French and Greek and by translating English texts into German. In the course of translating William Cullen's lectures on materia medica into German, Hahnemann was struck by what he thought was the similarity of the symptoms produced by an overdose of quinine to those of the fevers that quinine was used to cure. This observation led him to formulate the theory that 'like cures like', or, in other words, that diseases are cured by those drugs that produce, in healthy persons, symptoms similar to the diseases.

There was no clinical teaching at Leipzig so, after two years, Hahnemann went to Vienna. While there he ran out of funds but managed to get a job as librarian to the Governor of Transylvania. After two years he was able to enrol at the University of Erlangen, from which he graduated MD in 1779. He worked as a general physician and as a doctor to an insane asylum where it is to his credit that he adopted the humanitarian, non-restraint principles that had recently been proposed by the French physician and psychiatric pioneer Philippe Pinel (1745–1826).

Although studious and highly conscientious, Hahnemann found he had little sympathy for the methods of medical practice of the time. Among other things, he recognized that the widespread practice of bloodletting killed more patients than it cured. Much of what his colleagues were doing would, he thought, be more likely to aggravate disease than to cure it, and he was right. So for a time he gave up medicine and turned to chemistry and writing. His energy was astonishing, and he showed himself indefatigable, producing no less than 58 volumes of original work. For all his good qualities, he was a difficult, arrogant man, unable to tolerate any hint of criticism of his ideas or assertions.

In 1810, having elaborated his cherished theory of 'like curing like', he published in his *Organon der Heilkunst* an account of his doctrine of homoeopathy. Hahnemann based this entirely new system of medicine solely on symptoms and regarded any investigation into their cause as a waste of time. Anatomy, physiology, pathology and scientifically observed drug action he brushed aside as irrelevant. In fairness to Hahnemann, it has to be admitted that this view, heretical as it may seem to scientific doctors of today, was unremarkable in its time. The distinction between symptoms and the underlying cause of them was by no means widely appreciated in those days. Doctors were constantly evolving new systems of medicine. The celebrated Edinburgh medical writer and lecturer John Brown was teaching that the whole subject could be reduced to two diseases only – sthenic (strong) and asthenic (weak). It followed that there were only two treatments – stimulant and sedative – for which Brown prescribed alcohol and opium respectively. These views were highly popular, were widely accepted and spread to Europe.

Hahnemann had a somewhat more elaborate theory. All diseases, he maintained, resulted either from conventional medical treatment or from three conditions – psora (the itch), syphilis, or the skin disease sycosis. Most chronic (persistent) diseases were caused by the itch being 'driven inwards'. In order to cure disease, a remedy must be given which would substitute an effect similar to the symptoms but weaker. To this end, Hahnemann studied the effects of many drugs on healthy people, selecting those which produced appropriate effects. But since medicines which simulate the symptoms of disease also aggravate them, they must, he appreciated, be used in small doses. This was a definite step forward at a time when elaborate prescriptions, containing large numbers of useless and sometimes dangerous substances, were all the rage.

Today, we have a well-documented and reliable knowledge of the full range of symptoms and signs of all known diseases. In Hahnemann's day, comparatively little was known of disease and many different conditions were lumped together into groups described as 'fever', 'colic', 'ophthalmia' or 'phlegm', and so on. These groups were not specific diseases and, naturally, their symptoms differed from those of the actual conditions. Some of Hahnemann's descriptions of the symptoms of the supposed diseases are far from accurate. This is an important point because the whole basis of his system depended on symptoms and he was often working on faulty data.

Not surprisingly, Hahnemann noted that the smaller the dose of his medication, the less severe were the symptoms caused. This seems to have impressed him strangely, for it was at this point that reason deserted him. He developed an extraordinary theory, dignified by the title of 'potentiation', by which, he claimed, medicines gained in strength by being diluted, so long as the dilution was accompanied by vigorous shaking or pounding. On this principle, he diluted his original tinctures to one fiftieth; these, in turn, to one fiftieth; and so on for 30 consecutive dilutions. This, the thirtieth consecutive dilution by 50, was his favourite, to which he ascribed the highest 'potentiality'.

If a solution is diluted as Hahnemann prescribed, it is impossible that it should contain even a single molecule of the original substance. But Hahnemann was not a man to be put off by such trifling detail. 'It is a therapeutic axiom,' he said, 'not to be refuted by all the experience in the world, that the best dose is always the smallest. He who does not walk on the same line with me is an apostate and a traitor.' In this he showed a characteristic common to many proponents of such systems – the belief a thing is true merely because they have said it. If homoeopathy is true, then the whole basis of scientific medicine is wrong. Indeed, the whole basis of science is wrong. If Hahnemann's 'discovery' is true, then there is a principle, far more wonderful than anything known to science – a principle that must revolutionize human thought.

Not content with homoeopathy, Hahnemann turned some of his other 'discoveries' to commercial advantage, advertising patent medicines, such as borax, which he sold at a high price under the name of 'pnoeum', and claiming it had great medical value. He tried to patent a secret remedy, which turned out to be belladonna (atropine), as a sure cure for scarlet fever. He also claimed that only the 'soluble mercury of Hahnemann' was any good in the treatment of venereal diseases. The hard-headed authorities in Leipzig barred him from practising homeopathy, but the French were more accommodating, and he settled in Paris where he eventually made a large fortune. He died in 1843.

What is far more remarkable than Hahnemann's ideas is that, in spite of all its manifest absurdities, the practice of homoeopathy should have persisted to this day. Notwithstanding that its principles run counter to common sense, homeopathy still enjoys a dubious respectability. Numerous textbooks have been written. Institutes of Homoeopathy have been set up. In France, about a quarter of the doctors prescribe homeopathic 'remedies'. The British public unthinkingly swallow millions of pounds' worth of homoeopathy every year, doubtless to the satisfaction of the private pharmaceutical industry. There are five homoeopathic, if eclectic, hospitals in Britain, and the National Health Service offers homoeopathic treatment, presumably on the principle that it is cheap and, of course, harmless. Homoeopathic 'remedies' are even given to sick animals.

Public acceptance of homoeopathy is, doubtless, largely based on ignorance. The homoeopathy industry blandly implies that all this nonsense is scientific and genuine. A great many people, with no notion of the principles of the subject, must assume that there is not much difference between scientifically derived and proved remedies and the similarly packaged substances on the next shelf in the pharmacy. When a respectable pharmacist with a degree in pharmacology purveys, and even seems to be promoting, homoeopathic 'remedies', what is the uninformed layperson to think?

Many people, observing that recovery from a disorder followed after they had taken a homoeopathic medicine, quite naturally assume that the treatment had cured them. This, the *post hoc ergo propter hoc* ('after this, therefore because of this') fallacy is one of the commonest errors in logic, and is probably responsible for much of the reputation of homoeopathy. It gives no credit to the remarkable power of the immune system and the adaptive powers of human physiology generally, in promoting recovery from all minor, and most major, illnesses.

The truth about homoeopathy has been known since Hahnemann's time. Indeed, he was roundly condemned by most of his professional colleagues for the sheer effrontery of his propositions, and doctors and scientists have been pointing out its absurdities ever since. That so many seemingly intelligent and sensible people — professional as well as lay — should continue to behave as if homoeopathy is beneficial, seems to scientists to reveal a truly extraordinary state of mind. Questions immediately arise. Are these people indifferent to reason? Do they believe in magic? Are the producers, advertisers and retailers of homoeopathic 'remedies' honest? Are they cynical? Or are they simply unconcerned so long as the profits continue to roll in? Whatever the reasons, to scientists all this provides a remarkable insight into the ease with which the mind can encompass and live with absurdity. Some profess to be alarmed at this indication of the persistence of superstition, but most are reassured by their belief in the protective power of plain common sense.

There is another side to this, and one which, to some extent, balances the equation as to which is the more extraordinary state of mind. In spite of its unscientific basis, alternative medicine, including homoeopathic practice, commands a great deal of public respect. This is partly because of the necessarily greater element of human interaction in it than is commonly experienced in orthodox medical consultations. There is also the public perception that alternative medical treatment is less dangerous than allopathic treatment. But perhaps most important of all is the element of mystery, perhaps even of magic, which is an ingredient for which much of humanity is always hungry. This element is, nowadays, notably absent from orthodox medicine, which is now seen as a rigidly mechanical process. People need the spiritual element — perhaps need it in a fundamental biological sense — and they are more likely to get it from an alternative practitioner than from a scientific doctor. Looked at from this point of view, which is the more remarkable state of mind?

Delusional double: Capgras' syndrome

William Cowper (1731–1800), who was to become one of the most popular poets of his generation, was a frail and unhappy child. When he was six his mother died and he was immediately sent to a public school where he was cruelly bullied. At ten he was sent to Westminster School where he stayed for eight years. Cowper's family was distinguished in the law — it had included a Lord Chancellor and a judge — and, as a result of family pressures, he was articled to a solicitor. He hated the work but, after three years, was prevailed upon to take chambers in the Middle Temple. While there, he fell in love with his beautiful and accomplished cousin Theodora, but his father forbade the match and Cowper had to give up all thoughts of marriage. He was called to the bar at the age of 23, but the thought of practising law was horrifying to him. So, living on a small income from his father, he passed his time in the company of poets and men of letters.

Nine years later, by family influence, he was offered a sinecure as a clerk in the House of Lords. Unfortunately, this required the formality of a public examination at the bar of the House, and the pathologically shy Cowper decided that death would be preferable. His catalogue of failures extended even to this attempt at suicide and he passed into a period of delusional insanity, the principal feature of which was the conviction that he had been abandoned by God and was irrevocably cut off from a state of grace in this world and the next. At the end of 1763 he entered a private mental asylum where he remained for a year and a half.

In 1765 he went to Huntingdon to be near his younger brother, who was then at Cambridge; while there, he was accepted, as a lodger, into the tranquil household of the Reverend Morley Unwin and his wife, Mary. Cowper was very happy there and gradually recovered his mental ease, expectations of salvation, and comfort of mind. In his own words:

> God moves in a mysterious way
> His wonders to perform;
> He plants his footsteps in the sea,
> And rides upon the storm.
>
> Judge not the Lord by feeble sense,
> But trust him for his grace;
> Behind a frowning providence
> He hides a smiling face.

Unfortunately, Mr Unwin suffered a fatal riding accident in 1767 and Mary moved, with Cowper and her children, to Olney in Buckinghamshire. The curate of Olney, one John Newton, was a morose man of gloomy and pessimistic evangelical piety and with the strongest possible views of religious duty. Having acquired a powerful influence over the unfortunate Cowper, he made it his business to see that the poet's mind was engaged as continuously as possible on religious matters. Newton was, apparently, either unaware of, or indifferent to, Cowper's precarious mental balance. As is often the case with religious fanatics, such considerations are allowed to weigh little when the fate of the soul is in question. This kind of pressure was the last thing that Cowper needed and, in spite of trying desperately to divert Newton from his endless preaching and praying by helping him to write a volume of hymns, he was soon driven mad again.

Interestingly, and perhaps significantly, one of the features of this bout of insanity — which lasted for nearly four years — was the conviction that the Reverend John Newton had, in fact, been replaced by an impostor who resembled him in every detailed particular. There was more than a little method in this madness and the delusion probably allowed Cowper to survive. He held strong religious convictions, which would normally persuade him that it would be gravely sinful to oppose the exhortations of the pious Newton – whom he had long professed to respect deeply for his sanctity. But, at the same time, his strong inclination was to devote himself to literature. Invariably, his psychiatric episodes were related to his spiritual state, suggesting that there was an underlying conflict between his inclinations and his sense of duty. By substituting a double for Newton, it may have been possible for him to express his dislike of some aspects of the man's personality without committing what he would regard as a sin.

Happily, Newton moved away from Olney and, under the kindness and soothing care of Mary Unwin, Cowper was gradually diverted from his gloomy condition to one of more positive health. He spent hours in gardening and carpentry, and in the taming of hares and studying their habits. Significantly, Cowper did not take this opportunity to rid himself of Newton's influence, but continued to correspond with him for a number of years. He invariably expressed his appreciation of Newton's spirituality and status as a theologian.

Mrs Unwin gently encouraged Cowper's poetic talent and there followed a period of high creativity during which he published two volumes of poems and began to acquire a reputation. Cowper seems to have been attractive to women, for another friend, Lady Austen, whom he had seen and admired from a distance and had asked Mary to invite to tea, now also took him in hand. Under her urging, he produced several long poems, a translation of Homer which occupied him for six years, a new edition of Milton's works and translations of Latin and Italian poems. Lady Austen, a sprightly widow, was greatly taken with the poet and moved to Olney to be nearer to him and Mrs Unwin. It was she who suggested the subject for Cowper's poem *John Gilpin*. The publication of his long poem *The Task* brought him fame and a crown pension of £300 a year. Unfortunately, just before the book appeared Lady Austen left Olney suddenly and Cowper never saw her again. The biographers pass over in silence the reasons for this unexpected event.

Cowper was now persuaded by another cousin, Lady Hesketh, to leave Olney and move to Weston. This was a mistake and soon he was again afflicted with madness. Lady Hesketh, however, contributed much to the comfort of his later years. In December 1796 Mary Unwin died and Cowper fell into a depressive decline. After three miserable years, he too died, in his sixty-ninth year.

Cowper's is by no means the only literary association with the extraordinary state of mind in which a close acquaintance is believed to have been replaced by an identical stranger. In his novel *The Possessed*, Dostoevsky includes an impressive account of the condition. The character Stravrogin is secretly married to the half-mad Marya Timofyevna. One day he urges her to forget that they are married and to consider him only as a close friend. A few days later, Marya takes matters further than he had expected. On meeting Stravrogin, she denies that he is the real person. She admits that the man she is talking to resembles Stravrogin and thinks he might be a relative, but insists that *her* Stravrogin is a 'prince and a bright falcon' and that he (the 'impostor') is a 'shopkeeper and an owl'. She then accuses her interlocutor of murdering Stravrogin.

This account is so characteristic of what is now known as Capgras' syndrome that it seems likely that Dostoevsky may have come across a case. If he had not, it is a remarkable feat of imagination.

The French psychiatrist J. M. J. Capgras, who with his colleague J. Reboul-Lachaux first produced a formal description of the condition, was too modest to claim an eponymous title for it. Drawing on classical literature, they called it *l'illusion des Sosies,* a reference to the play *Amphitryon* by the great Roman comic dramatist Plautus. Amphitryon was a popular subject in French and other literature. Indeed, when the ingenious and entertaining playwright Jean Giradoux produced his version in 1929 he initially called it *Amphitryon 38* – a joking reference to his claim that there had been 37 previous versions of the story.

Alcmene, the fabulously beautiful wife of Amphitryon, caught the fancy of Zeus, who determined to seduce her by impersonating her husband while he was away at the wars. To add to the deception, he enlisted the aid of Mercury and persuaded him to impersonate Amphitryon's servant, Socias (*Sosies* in French). Mercury, in this guise, was to go on ahead to Alcmene and announce her husband's imminent return. The plot worked well and Zeus had such a good time that he stopped the Sun's movement and extended one night into the length of three days. In due course, the real Amphitryon came back and Alcmene, still remembering the superior sexual performance of the chief of the gods, was somewhat disappointed by the apparent decline in his powers. Nine months later, however, she gave birth to Hercules.

In Capgras' syndrome, the temporary delusional conviction that a close relative or friend has been replaced by an exact double is so powerful that nothing will move it. Some instances occur in paranoid psychotic conditions, such as schizophrenia or, as in Cowper's case, manic–depressive psychosis. Others result from organic brain damage, either from disease or injury. In the psychotic cases the Capgras element usually becomes the principal feature and, often, the affected person is otherwise apparently sane and shows no intellectual deterioration or any clouding of consciousness. The implication may be that the decision to believe in the 'double' provides a satisfying solution to the powerful underlying psychological problem.

Interestingly and, perhaps, significantly, the delusion relates only to a close relative or spouse. When the condition affects a married person, the 'double' is *always* the spouse. Otherwise, he or she is a parent, brother or sister, lover or other close acquaintance. Invariably the person deemed to be impersonated is someone of central importance in the life of the patient. Various psychological explanations have been put forward, but none seem adequate to account for it. It has been suggested, for instance, that a seriously ambivalent attitude to a person may force someone to attribute the undesirable features to the 'impostor' while attributing the desired features to the 'real' person. This has the advantage of allowing the patient to express, as explicit aggression towards the 'double', his or her hatred of the disliked elements – a thing that would otherwise be impossible.

There is some similarity between Capgras' syndrome and the idea of the *doppelgänger*. This is a ghostly double, an exact but usually invisible replica of another person walking beside one. German folklore has it that every living creature has a *doppelgänger*, of whom there is normally no sign. To meet with one's *doppelgänger* is to be near one's death. The idea was once very popular with writers of gothic horror stories and was exploited to the full. One of the best *doppelgänger* stories is the novel *The Devil's Elixir* by the German composer, painter and story-teller E. T. A. Hoffmann (1776–1822), well known to opera buffs for his appearance in Offenbach's *Tales of Hoffmann*. Dostoevsky also wrote a *doppelgänger* tale, *The Double*. This concerns the pitiable clerk, Golyadkin, who is driven mad by failure, poverty and unrequited love. He sees his *doppelgänger*, who achieves everything that Golyadkin could not and, in the end, makes away with his original.

Of exorbitant empathy:
male morning sickness

It is well known that the loving husbands or partners of pregnant women often suffer vicariously with their wives or consorts. The literature on this is very large. What is not well known is the extent to which this empathy can be displayed. The commonest manifestation relates to the sickness of early pregnancy, usually known as 'morning sickness'. In pregnant women, nausea and vomiting in the morning (or, in fact at any other time of day), and occurring from about the sixth to the twelfth week, are so common as to be regarded as normal. Morning sickness sometimes occurs when the woman does not know that she is pregnant. It is more severe with twins than with single pregnancies. It is believed to be due to a rise in the levels of a hormone, chorionic gonadotrophin, that is necessary for the maintenance of the pregnancy in its early stages.

Awareness that husbands or partners of pregnant women can also suffer morning sickness goes back a long way. The English philosopher and essayist Francis Bacon (1561–1626) records:

> There is an Opinion abroad (whether Idle or no I cannot say) that loving and kinde Husbands have a Sense of their wives Breeding Childe by some Accident in their Owne Body.

In other words, certain devoted husbands so sympathize with their pregnant wives that some change occurs in their own bodies, so that, in a sense, they partake of the pregnancy. Bacon recognized the phenomenon without being able to account for it. Some early explanations proffered include: the desire by the man to be able to claim the child as his own or to claim it as a member of his own family; male vanity and female submissiveness; natural justice; sympathetic magic; the attempt to expiate a sense of original sin by the husband; and so on. The implication behind some of these theories is that the condition is fraudulently simulated by the man. This may sometimes have been the case, but there can be no doubting that the phenomenon is often genuine. There are some even more remarkable 'explanations' of the phenomenon, as we shall see.

In a mid-nineteenth-century lecture on nervous maladies, one Dr S. Weir Mitchell, said to have been a notable authority, reported an extraordinary case. A woman with two female children greatly desired a boy. Years passed without pregnancy. Then her periods stopped and, in the second month, morning sickness began, as had happened in her previous pregnancies. With the first appearance of this, her husband, too, suffered morning sickness. Meanwhile the woman's abdomen began to enlarge and, as time passed, the enlargement progressively increased. The husband, distressed by his own constant sickness, consulted his doctor who advised him to leave home. Remarkably, the husband took this advice and soon ceased to be affected. The wife's sickness, however, continued daily until the seventh month, as did the progressive increase in the size of her abdomen. At that point, menstruation started again and examination showed that she was not, and had not been, pregnant and that the abdominal enlargement was simply due to fat.

In an even more remarkable case, a husband is reported to have developed daily morning sickness two weeks after 'the appearance of' his wife's last menstrual period. It was not until the absence of the wife's next period that there was any objective indication that she was pregnant. Unfortunately, the record does not make it clear whether the husband started to vomit two weeks after the *beginning* or after the *end* of the last menstrual period. Nor does it state whether the period was a long or a short one. It would also have been interesting to know whether the wife had had any suspicion of pregnancy at the time the husband's sickness started. Some women claim to be able to tell that they are pregnant as early as this.

Ovulation occurs in the middle of the menstrual cycle, about two weeks before the start of the next period. So, assuming the usual 28 day cycle, conception cannot occur until about two weeks after the beginning of the last menstrual period. If the husband's vomiting started two weeks after the *beginning* of his wife's last period, it would have coincided closely with the time of conception and there would hardly have been time for any physiological changes to have occurred in the wife. If the man's sickness started two weeks after the *end* of the last menstrual period, the conceptus would have been no more than a week old. A more plausible explanation might be that the husband had not, for a long time, had the opportunity to try for a child and that sexual intercourse had then occurred. He might then *assume* that his wife would become pregnant.

Other reported cases show the exact coincidence of the sickness, which started and stopped simultaneously in both parties. There are also reports of the phenomenon occurring during every pregnancy and also during every pregnancy of the husband's parents. In one account, this is stated, rather quaintly, to 'prove an hereditary predisposition.'

While vicarious morning sickness seems to be fairly common, there is a further stage to the story of exorbitant empathy. This is called the couvade syndrome, and it is a condition in which the husband's identification with the wife during her pregnancy becomes so strong that during her labour he, too, suffers all her discomforts and pains. There have also been reports of cases in which the husband has suffered progressive enlargement of the abdomen along with the wife.

Most of the more modern 'explanations' of this strange phenomenon have come from psychoanalysts, who have found it a fertile ground for their speculations. There is, in fact, a substantial psychoanalytic literature on the subject. Freud suggested that it might be an unconscious desire on the part of the man to prove that he actually was the father of the child. An even more ingenious psychoanalytic suggestion is that the husband's seeming mimicry of the woman's function manifests the deep, life-long, male envy of the woman's ability to give birth to a baby. Even further out is the idea that the husband is actually taking a masochistic pleasure in his wife's suffering – a pleasure he must, of course, conceal. This can most convincingly be done by a dramatic show of sympathy. Others have gone so far as to suggest that vicarious morning sickness is a clear indication of latent homosexuality that is shown by 'unconscious feminine reproductive fantasies'. Some people might, perhaps unkindly, suggest that an 'unconscious fantasy' is a contradiction in terms.

The problem with psychoanalytic literature is that most of it is incapable of being either proved or disproved. While scientific theories put themselves forward to be tested and, if necessary, knocked down, psychoanalyst theorists merely imagine and assert. Vicarious pregnancy symptoms can be explained without going to the exorbitant lengths detailed above. Empathy is not just a high degree of sympathy. It is a close identification with the physical experiences and emotions of others that may be so strong that these are literally experienced in common. The physiological effects that accompany emotions are inseparable from them. Some psychologists suggest that the physiological effects *are* the emotions. Real rage, as distinct from a purely intellectual awareness of the reasons for rage, cannot be experienced without a fast pulse, rapid breathing, flushing of the face, widening of the nostrils, and so on. Real fear cannot be experienced without a strong sensation of stomach contractions that may be so intense as to lead to vomiting. If a man shares to the full the emotions felt by his beloved partner in early pregnancy, there need be no great surprise that he may also share her physiological reactions.

Phantom lover: erotomania

Erotomania is not, as is often thought, a generalized sex-madness or a kind of nymphomania. In fact, it is a rather sad form of delusional conviction, almost always affecting a woman, that someone – in most cases a well-known person or one of high social status – is madly in love with her. If the object of the woman's delusion is married, she will invariably believe that he is aware that he made a terrible mistake and that she is the one he ought to have chosen. The affected woman is convinced that the man knows he can never be happy without her but that some evil fate is keeping them apart. In the mind of the woman, the phantom lover is endowed with extraordinary powers which he will use for her benefit and to show his feelings. In many cases she will believe that her safety and protection from all dangers are ensured by the man's powers.

Part of the delusion is that the man cannot refrain from sending her subtle and secret signals indicating his deep affection. If, for instance, the selected man is a pop star, he will select songs especially for her, by which he conveys his adoration. Likewise if he is a disc-jockey. If he is a politician, he will make certain arcane remarks during a radio interview which are intended for her and which only she can understand. If he is a minister of religion or a priest, his sermons will contain unmistakable messages and he will be careful not to look too directly at her in case the congregation should rumble their secret. If he is a doctor, she will attend frequently, often with a complaint requiring examination.

To begin with, the woman will be content to remain quiet, buoyed up by the knowledge that she is loved. But, sooner or later, she will want a more intimate relationship and will begin to make a direct approach, usually in the form of letters, to the man. Prominent people are accustomed to receiving correspondence of this kind and few of them will ever respond. At first, failure of response is interpreted as simply a sign that there is a good reason, known to the man, for their failure to meet. The woman will often elaborate on her delusion to account for this. Eventually she may telephone or try to meet the man. Rebuffs, and sometimes even police intervention and a legal restraining order, may follow. This does not necessarily compound the woman's unhappiness. In many cases she will become convinced that, although the man gives every outward sign of disliking her, the reality is that he loves her. This conviction is at the root of the condition.

It is a feature of erotomania that it starts suddenly. It is a genuine case of 'love at first sight'. It is not, however, a short-term disorder but may go on for years as the woman's delusion becomes more and more systematized, while being centred always on the same object. Almost a whole lifetime may be devoted in this way to the adoration of a man to whom the whole affair is usually a great nuisance. But sometimes the woman is forced to accept that the man is genuinely determined to avoid her, and when this happens, love may turn to hate. This can be dangerous to the man, for there is no knowing in what direction the delusion may turn. Attempts at violence are, however, uncommon.

Erotomania is not, as may be thought, a disorder primarily of unattractive, sexually neglected or lonely elderly women. It is not essentially a form of 'old maid's insanity'. In fact, it is commoner among comparatively young women. It is, however, concerned with love in the widest and wildest sense of the word, and has no connection with so-called 'nymphomania'. You can read about this imaginary condition in the section entitled **Of sexual insatiability**.

The mind in the wrong body:
trans-sexualism

There are male minds and female minds, and, almost always, male minds occupy male bodies and female minds female bodies. But not always. Surprisingly, the inner conviction that one is a man or a woman does not always correspond to the bodily, or anatomical, sex or even to the chromosomal sex. This has nothing to do with homosexuality, or with transvestism or with perversion in any sense of the word.

In general, both the bodily configuration and the appropriate kind of mind are determined by the sex chromosomes. Apart from these chromosomes, all the other chromosomes are identifiably the same in both sexes. Males have a large X chromosome and a tiny Y chromosome in each cell, so their chromosomal sex pattern is said to be XY. Females have two X chromosomes and are known as XX people. In the enormous majority of cases, an XX person is in every sense female and an XY person is in every sense male, and neither has any doubt about it. In a tiny proportion, however, people with the chromosome pattern corresponding to their anatomical body have a profound inner conviction that their real gender is the opposite one. They feel as if they were imprisoned in an alien body and are constantly longing to have the matter put right.

A person's gender identity is the sex he or she feels is right and, in these few but extraordinary cases, the gender identity is not the same as the body's sexual configuration. Gender identity has been defined as:

a complex system of beliefs about oneself: a sense of one's masculinity and femininity, that implies nothing about the origins of that sense (e.g.

whether the person is structurally male or female). It has psychological connotations only.

It is, of course, the state of the mind that matters, and in these cases there is a fundamental conflict. This unhappy state of affairs is called trans-sexualism. Quite naturally, trans-sexuals will want to wear the kind of clothes corresponding to the gender they feel is their right one. They will want to wear these clothes permanently as a natural part of conforming to the dress patterns and fashions of their 'real' sex. Transvestites do not do cross-dress for the same reason: they cross-dress only on occasion, and usually hope to achieve sexual stimulation by doing it.

People in a trans-sexual situation are always very unhappy. Their state of mind is exactly what yours would be if you were forced, against your will, to dress and to behave in every way as if you were a member of the opposite sex. You would suffer persistent mental discomfort and a strong feeling of inappropriateness. But the matter goes far deeper than this. Trans-sexual people who are anatomically male are disgusted with their sexual organs and with their general male shape and long to be rid of these primary and secondary sexual characteristics. Trans-sexual people who are anatomically female feel that they look effeminate and unmanly, and long to assume the external characteristics of the other sex.

It is not clear why, but trans-sexualism is about three times as common in anatomical males as in anatomical females. It is by no means confined to Western societies, occurring in all ethnic groups. Fortunately, it is very rare. Neglecting those cases in which the expressed desire for a change of sex is due to psychiatric disorders and other non-genuine influences, only about one male in 30,000 and about one female in 100,000 are trans-sexual.

Much thought has been given to the possible causes of this extraordinary state of mind, and some research has been done. Early researchers assumed that it must have had something to do with the amount of male sex hormone present when the fetus was in the earliest stages of development. It has been known for a long time that high male sex hormone levels at 6 weeks of fetal life masculinize the brain, and determine whether the structure of the body will be that of a male or of a female. So it seemed likely that inappropriate levels of sex hormones during fetal life could cause gender identity problems. Surprisingly, there is no scientific evidence to support this view. There are also reasons for rejecting it. One of these is that when children are born with abnormalities of the external genitalia, so that the sex is uncertain, they are sometimes assumed to be of the sex other than the chromosomal sex and are reared as such. In such cases, the child often accepts the assigned sex and never questions or wishes to change it, even if, after puberty, the mistake becomes apparent.

This fact gives a clue to what some experts consider to be a principal cause of trans-sexualism, namely the way the child is treated, during the early months and years of life, whether as a boy or a girl. Associated with this is often an obvious desire on the part of the parents for a child of the other sex than the real sex of the baby – a desire which has not been concealed from the child. There is evidence that the sexual identity can be determined by this early conditioning, which appears to be able to override both genetic and hormonal influences. Other possible causes are said to include 'an over-close relationship' between boy babies and the mother, and an uncaring father; depression in the mother of girl babies together with an unsupportive father; the inability to mourn a dead parent; or a combination of these factors.

Trans-sexual people often have a bad time from other people, too, and that includes doctors. This is because there are many unstable people who, for one reason or another, decide they would like to join the opposite sex. No doctor is going to take a request for a sex change seriously until, for instance, the trans-sexual person has lived as a member of the other sex for at least two years. No surgeon will even contemplate sex-change surgery until he or she is completely satisfied that the patient is genuinely trans-sexual. There will first have to be detailed psychiatric investigation by an expert in the field. The psychiatrist will have to be satisfied that there is no question of schizophrenia or other mental disorder involving delusions or hallucinations. If the person passes this test and is accepted as genuine, he or she will then have to undergo a gender reassignment programme involving hormone therapy and dress and behaviour counselling. This programme does not involve anything irrevocable. Before any question of surgery arises, the gender reassignment team will have to be satisfied that there is no genetic abnormality or intersex problem. There is never any question of sex-change surgery before puberty, as such surgery is irreversible.

The first case in which doctors agreed to reassign the sex of an anatomical man, by hormone and surgical treatment, so that he (she) could live as a woman, occurred in Denmark over 30 years ago, in the face of much criticism and opposition. Since then, the procedure has been performed many times and about 70 per cent of those so treated remain satisfied with the result. Such surgery is never undertaken lightly, as an error in decision can be disastrous. Of those not satisfied with the results of the surgery, some have requested restoration and some committed suicide. These cases presumably represent the failure of the medical profession to distinguish between true gender mis-identity and people with severe psychiatric or other personality disorders and misguided transvestites.

In the best centres, strict guidelines have been developed for the management of trans-sexualism. The reasons for the request for the treatment must be fully and exhaustively investigated and all the implications – surgical, hormonal and emotional – must be clearly understood. In the case of genuinely trans-sexual people whose cases have been properly managed, both psychologically and physically, the outcome can be excellent, with full integration into the new gender role, and great personal satisfaction with the new body.

That trans-sexual people are willing and anxious to undergo the major surgery involved in sex change is an indication of the strength of the desire to feel normal. These people are, of course, fully informed of what the surgery will involve and about its limitations.

Many people have unrealistic expectations based on their fantasies. Sex-change surgery produces complete sterility and impotence; there is no question of having children. Male-to-female surgery involves amputation of all the external genitalia but with preservation of the penile and scrotal skin, which is invaginated and used to form an artificial vagina. The urine outlet tube, the urethra, has to be moved to its new position, and labia are formed from the skin of the two halves of the scrotum. There is a strong tendency for the artificial vagina to shrink and close off and this must be prevented by long-term wear of a glass mould until the skin lining has healed onto the deeper tissues. Oestrogen hormones will already have been given to promote female secondary sexual characteristics, but it is often necessary also to insert breast implants.

Female-to-male surgery involves equally radical surgery. There will be complete removal of all breast tissue and the surplus skin; total removal of the womb (hysterectomy) and of the ovaries and fallopian tubes. Plastic surgery to produce a simulated penis is very difficult and not particularly effective, even if an inflatable implant device is used. Most are satisfied with an artificial penis or a dildo. It is, however, a much easier matter to fashion a convincing scrotum from the skin of the labia majora and plastic prosthetic testicles can be inserted. Male sex hormones are used to produce a more masculine body configuration and hair distribution.

Many who have undergone this major ordeal find, for the first time in their conscious lives, that their state of mind can properly be described as normal.

Phantom pregnancy: pseudocyesis

This extraordinary state of mind, called pseudocyesis, is a remarkable example of how a mental state – in this case the overwhelming desire for a child, or, occasionally, the overwhelming fear of pregnancy – can affect the body. The phenomenon is best illustrated by describing one or two cases.

Perhaps the most celebrated case, and certainly a very embarrassing one, was that of Queen Mary of England (1516–58) also called Mary Tudor, or Bloody Mary. A daughter of Henry VIII, she was an intelligent, educated and courageous woman, who became the first queen to rule England in her own right. Once on the throne, she married the Catholic Philip II of Spain and, against the wishes of the people, formally restored Catholicism as the official religion of the country.

Mary was determined to ensure that there was a Catholic heir to the throne and prayed constantly to become pregnant. Finally, she ceased to menstruate, and suffered severely from morning sickness. Her breasts enlarged and the areolae around her nipples turned brown. This is one of the characteristic signs of pregnancy and is permanent. Then her abdomen began to enlarge. The whole court was aware that she was pregnant and there was much making of baby clothes. An ambassador was sent to the Vatican to inform the Pope that Mary had felt the movements of her baby.

Near the end of the ninth month, Mary went into labour. All London was awakened one night by a loud peal of bells announcing the new heir. The populace flocked to St Paul's cathedral to hear the Archbishop of Canterbury describe the new prince and give thanks to God for his safe delivery. There was a pause and then Mary's pains stopped. Doctors were summoned and, daringly, informed the Queen that there was no pregnancy. A violently hysterical scene followed. Philip, who was disgusted with the whole business, took his leave of her and went back to Spain.

The Queen took out her embarrassment and disappointment on the Protestants, whom she regarded as heretics, and her persecution of them was savage. Many were hanged and their bodies left to rot in public. At least 300 were burned at the stake. In all this Mary felt justified by her religion. A number of other false pregnancies followed but she was never genuinely pregnant. She was hated by the people and, soon after she died, everything she had done in the name of religion was undone.

Another case was that of a woman of 30 who had been married for three years to a very old and rich man, but had had no children. The man made a will which stipulated that she would inherit little unless she had a child by him. In that event, the whole estate would come to her. Two months before he died his wife's periods stopped. She had been anaemic but now her appetite improved, she gained weight rapidly and her abdomen became protuberant. Her breasts swelled and eventually she felt the movements of the baby. At the eighth month she was examined by a physician who stated that she was not pregnant. Another doctor was called and he confirmed the opinion of his colleague. At the tenth month she was enormous and still insisted that she was pregnant. The woman seems to have been unaware of the normal human gestation period, or perhaps she just lost count. During the twelfth month her periods started again and she was convinced that this was the beginning of labour. Eventually, she was persuaded that she was not pregnant. From that moment the excess weight began to melt away and in the course of a few weeks she lost 50 pounds.

Another woman who already had several children and who had had a very bad time in her previous pregnancies, missed a period and began to have morning sickness. She was seriously upset by this. According to the report: 'She made some wild efforts to end her supposed pregnancy, and, failing, acquiesced in her fate.' For eight months she had severe vomiting and was able to eat very little. Nevertheless, she took on so much fat on her breasts and abdomen as 'to excite unusual attention.' She was not seen by a doctor until the supposed labour began, at which point the truth became apparent. The woman was deeply relieved. As soon as she was convinced that she was not pregnant the fat disappeared and in two months she was back to her normal appearance. In this case it seems distinctly possible that the 'wild efforts' included the attempt to procure an abortion, which had succeeded. The record shows that she did have some scanty vaginal bleeding after the first missed period. This case is particularly interesting, however, as demonstrating that the desire for a child is not the only cause of pseudocyesis.

Phantom pregnancy is a most striking example of the power an extraordinary state of mind can have over the body. This is psychosomatism writ large. Powerful and sustained emotional states – whether prompted by the desire for, or by the fear of, pregnancy – will always have, as their physiological concomitant, a sustained production of hormones, especially cortisol and adrenaline. In the present state of our understanding of these things, it seems likely that the bodily changes occurring in pseudocyesis are mediated by hormones. There may, however, be other mechanisms of which we know nothing. There are certainly more things in heaven and earth than are dreamt of in our current psychology.

A mind possessed: demonic possession

Long before any written records were made, people have believed that various kinds of eccentric behaviour or other indications of disturbance of the mind are caused by 'possession by demons'. This belief was so strong that, for centuries, it was common to restrain these unfortunate people by force and to drill holes in their skulls, so as to let the evil spirit out. There is plenty of evidence of the number of times this operation was performed: numerous human skulls, dating from pre-history, and bearing neatly drilled holes have been found.

This practice is called trephining or trepanning. It is interesting to speculate on whether trephining of the skull implies that ancient people had more sense then their successors in believing that the brain, rather than the heart, was the root of the problem. It is also interesting that they should have thought it necessary to make a physical hole to allow the emergence of something that was obviously non-physical. It seems a little odd that an evil spirit should possess all kinds of abilities but not, apparently, the ability to find a natural exit-route.

The belief in 'possession' was not, apparently, shaken by the failure to observe the evil spirits either entering or leaving the body of the victim. There was, however, plenty of evidence that something was in there causing serious trouble. The personality of the possessed individual changed; sometimes he or she uttered strange and incomprehensible speech; there may have been seizures, groans, shrieks and cries of anguish. It was obvious that the person was being controlled by some supernatural agency. There is a hangover of the idea of possession to this very day in the prevalent custom of saying 'Bless you' when a person sneezes. It was once believed that a sneeze briefly drove the soul from the body. This provided an opportunity for an evil spirit to enter, but this could be prevented if someone said 'God bless you' quickly enough.

There was, equally obviously, a close link between spiritual possession and religion and it was clear that the new inhabitant was always strongly antagonistic to religion. Often an exceptionally pious person, especially one dedicated to a life of religious asceticism, would begin to utter blasphemies, find it impossible to pray, even exhibit terror before a Christian cross or other sacred objects. What could provide clearer evidence than this of the presence of a malignant spirit or demon that had taken possession of the normally holy person?

To thinking and imaginative churchmen, such a hypothesis was certainly preferable to the perhaps more probable one that nature was asserting herself and was producing in the victim a revulsion against deliberate repression of all fleshly appetites, including sex. One of the most detailed and scholarly examinations of this phenomenon is to be found in Aldous Huxley's book *The Devils of Loudun*. Huxley's account of the horrifying and tragic events occurring at Loudun formed the basis of a play by John Whiting, called *The Devils*, and a remarkable and deeply impressive film of the same title, directed by Ken Russell.

Looked at from our better informed point of view, we can see that sexual repression was not, of course, the sole, or even the principal cause of cases of 'demonic possession' in the past. Many cases were probably caused by epilepsy of the *grand mal* type. Others were what we now call schizophrenia. Some were plain hysteria; and some were depression or mania. Remarkably, this crudely superstitious belief in the existence of devils survives in the Christian and Judaic Churches and in some other religions to this very day. Some branches of the Christian Church include in their dogma the possibility of demonic possession and have evolved rituals of exorcism to deal with them. These rituals are centred on a solemn command, or adjuration, addressed to demons to require them to leave a person, place or object. Such processes seem to be dignified by their language, symbolic acts and dress, and thereby acquire some semblance of verisimilitude. But their survival seems, to me at least, to be superstitious nonsense that does no credit to the Church. Strangely enough, when much the same function is performed by common people as a folk tradition to ward off evil spirits, the practices are regarded with disapproval by churchmen who characterize them as witchcraft.

The Christian tradition of exorcism originates with the acts of Jesus and his followers in expelling demons. Around AD 250, certain members of the clergy were set aside to exercise the function of exorcism and this special capacity was said to be vouchsafed to them. The exorcism of people possessed by demons is regulated by Roman Catholic canon law, and the elaborate ritual involved is prescribed in detail. Superstitious beliefs of this kind are, today, more likely to be fostered in the minds of the gullible by writers of popular novels and cinema and television film scripts, who find in this subject a fruitful fillip for tired authorial imagination. But the official recognition of the subject by the Church confers on it a dubious respectability that can only encourage lay belief in its validity.

Demonic possession is intimately tied up with the subject of witchcraft, which, of course, dates from long before biblical times. The peak of interest in, and activity against, witches occurred, however, in the Middle Ages. The Benedictine abbot and scholar Johannes Trithemius, renowned for his piety and humane goodness, stated in his book *Antipalus Maleficiorum*,

> Witches can injure any part of the body. They make you possessed of devils so that you are tortured mercilessly. They even have carnal relations with devils. Witches are everywhere. No province is too small to contain them. Yet the Inquisitors who could avenge these offences against God are few and far between. Man and beast die as a result of the evil action of these women.

The principal action against supposed witches was taken by

two fanatical Dominican Brothers, the Professors of Theology and Inquisitors of heresy, Johann Sprenger and Heinrich Kraemer. Their book, the notorious *Malleus Maleficarum* (Hammer of the witches), was written with the express approval of Pope Innocent VIII and was finished in 1487. The Pope, in his bull, *Summis desiderantes affectibus*, commended the zeal of the pair and wrote:

> It has indeed lately come to Our ears ... that many persons of both sexes, unmindful of their own salvation and straying from the Catholic faith, have abandoned themselves to devils, incubi and succubi, and by their incantations, spells, conjurations, and other accursed charms and crafts, enormities and horrid offences, have slain infants yet in the mother's womb ... tormented men and women with terrible and piteous pains and sore diseases ... they have hindered men from performing the sexual act and women from conceiving ... they blasphemously renounce that Faith which is theirs by the Sacrament of Baptism, and at the instigation of the Enemy of Mankind they do not shrink from committing and perpetrating the foulest abominations and filthiest excesses to the deadly peril of their own souls.

The Pope went on to authorize Sprenger and Kraemer to 'proceed to the just correction, imprisonment and punishment of any persons, without let or hindrance.' They were to proceed:

> ... according to the regulations of the Inquisition, against any persons of whatsoever rank and high estate, correcting, mulcting, imprisoning, punishing as their crimes merit, the penalty being adapted to the offence. By Our supreme authority We grant them anew full and complete faculties.

He then stated that anyone, of whatever rank, estate, position, pre-eminence or dignity who molested or hindered the pair, should suffer excommunication and yet more terrible penalties without any right of appeal.

It is hardly to be wondered at that so much power in the hands of men like Sprenger and Kraemer should prove corrupting. The *Malleus Maleficarum* was just about the most horrible document ever written and its influence was enormous. The authors, determined to wring the last ounce of power out of their often reluctant peers, submitted the manuscript for approval to the Faculty of Theology at the University of Cologne. The Dean and four out of seven professors signed their approval. This did not satisfy Sprenger and Kraemer. Relying on the Pope's bull and a letter of approval from Maximilian, King of Rome, they wrote a stronger letter and re-submitted the book. This time, everyone endorsed it.

This book would doubtless have had less impact had it been written in the days when the only way of producing multiple copies of a book was by laborious hand-copying. However, movable type had just been invented by Johann Gutenberg, and was at once applied to printing the *Malleus Maleficarum*. Between 1487 and 1760 no less than 19 editions of this pernicious work appeared.

It is interesting to look into the state of the minds of these two men who, between them, were responsible for the torture and burning of hundreds of thousands of harmless women on the ultimate authority of the single statement in the Bible: 'Thou shalt not suffer a witch to live.' The tone of their book, far from being cold and legalistic, is argumentative, angry, deeply censorious and threatening. It is hard to believe that a book of this kind is motivated by a disinterested wish to serve God. These men, whatever their ostensible motives, must have been monsters of depravity and sadistic cruelty. No doubt they would have answered such an accusation by pointing out that nothing that happens during life compares in importance to the immortal soul. But it beggars the imagination to discern how priests who profess to be followers of Jesus Christ could have deliberately, and with all indications of satisfaction, set in motion a movement with such appalling consequences.

Their book is divided into three parts. The first part sets out to prove by argument that anyone who refuses to believe in witchcraft and witches is guilty of heresy. The second part is concerned with the methods of examining women so as to detect witchcraft, and the third with the legal technicalities for delivering witches to the secular arm of justice for execution, usually by burning alive.

Examination involved cruel and ingenious torture. Methods included the 'strappado', in which the wrists were tied together behind the back with a rope which was then passed over a pulley and by means of which the victim was hoisted into the air. The unfortunate subject would be allowed to fall suddenly, but not as far as the ground. This caused agonizing dislocation of the shoulders. Sometimes heavy weights were tied to the legs. Leg vices, thumb-screws, whipping stocks with spikes, lime baths, stretching racks – all the fiendish apparatus of medieval torture – was prescribed by these horrible men.

Often it was sufficient merely to threaten these methods to elicit a 'confession' and to obtain accusations of others. Tests for witches were given in great detail in the book. A suspected witch might be tied hand and foot and dropped into deep water. If she floated, the water was supposedly rejecting her, and so she was deemed guilty; if she sank, she was innocent. One of the classic no-win situations of all time. Witches were said to have areas of insensitivity to pain on their bodies. Pricking all over with a sharp awl was often used to find these areas. However emotionally and physically exhausted they were, victims who failed to respond to every prick of the awl would be condemned.

Women who had, inevitably, confessed to witchcraft were stripped naked; their head hair, body hair and eyebrows were shaved off, so that devils had nowhere to hide, sometimes their fingernails and toenails were torn off for the same reason, and they were then led into a public court for sentencing.

Among other atrocities, the *Malleus* eliminates the possibility that any accused witches could be excused on the grounds that they were suffering from mental disorders such as delusions or hallucinations. It admits that witches might, incidentally, be deluded – that they might wrongly believe, for instance, that they had been transported from place to place on a broomstick. But this was irrelevant. Whether they were transported (as, they claimed, many were) or not, they were still riding with the devil. They had voluntarily complied with the wishes of the Evil One, as their confessions under torture had shown. It was, it was argued, an act of extreme mercy that their souls, held in such sinful captivity, should be set free. The soul must be delivered and this could only be achieved by burning the body alive.

Sprenger and Kraemer had a passionate and sadistic hatred of women. Of the six ways in which devils could injure people, one was to promote illicit sex and one was to interfere with the 'genital act' or to induce abortion. There is a great deal of sexual detail in the *Malleus*, with lengthy particulars as to sexual 'perversions'. Much of this consists of accounts derived from the two inquisitors' prior witch-hunting work. Some chapters amount to a complete treatise on sexual anomalies and there are many stories with a sexual basis, included to 'prove' the points the authors were trying to make. No doubt this contributed to the popular success of the book at a time when such literature was almost non-existent. It was, of course, a meritorious act to read a book of this kind, which was sanctioned by no less an authority than the Pope himself, so the sales were enormous.

It will suffice to include one of the 'case histories' from the *Malleus*, selected for its literary merit rather than for its prurient interest. A certain nobleman of the Diocese of Strasbourg married a lady of high birth. But for three years from the time of the marriage, carnal knowledge of the lady was denied him because of his inexplicable impotence. In desperation, he prayed to the saints for relief, but to no avail. One day, while on business in Metz, he met a woman who had formerly been his mistress. Remembering their old friendship, he addressed her kindly and enquired how she had fared since last they had met. Moved by his concern she, in turn, asked in detail about his well-being. When he replied that he was prospering in everything and that all was well with him, she was strangely silent and seemed astonished. The nobleman again spoke kindly to her and she then enquired about his wife. He answered her that she, too, was well in all respects. The woman then asked if he had had children and he replied, mendaciously, that he now had three sons, one having been born each year.

The woman was even more astonished and said, 'I am happy over your good fortune, but I curse that old woman who promised to bewitch your body so that you could not have carnal knowledge of your wife.' In proof of this, she went on, 'there is, at the bottom of the well in your garden, a pot containing certain magical charms. The old woman swore to me that as long as the contents of the pot remained there, so long would you be incapable. But now I am glad that she was a liar and that all is well with you.'

The nobleman returned home and had the well drained. There, at the bottom, was a pot full of charms, just as the woman had said. All was burned and instantly, the nobleman recovered his sexual power. At that, his wife invited all the nobility to a new wedding celebration saying that she was now wife indeed after remaining for so long a virgin. This is a charming story, but it is to be hoped that Sprenger and Kraemer did not force the mistress to divulge the identity of the 'witch'.

Most of the text of the *Malleus* is greatly more sinister and horrifying than this simple tale. Many of its passages describe what can now readily be recognized as psychiatric disorders — for which many thousands of women were considered to deserve to be burned alive at the stake. It would be ridiculous to suggest that Sprenger and Kraemer were the principal cause of all this suffering, but they were important agents of it. The real cause was the almost universal ignorance and simplicity of mind that could encompass such superstitious beliefs.

The only remedy against this is the propagation of knowledge that can be shown to be true, and the use of it to oppose the products of ignorance and childish superstition. Human nature has not changed in the short time since we stopped burning witches. That is why science is so important and why we should not view with complacency contemporary indications of unreason and superstitious belief, however harmless they may seem.

The mind of Sigmund Freud:
pseudoscience

One of the most imaginative contributors to speculative human thought – and, I contend, one of the most astonishingly wrong-headed – was the Austrian doctor, neurologist and founder of psychoanalysis, Sigmund Freud (1856–1939). Freud's influence on twentieth-century culture is incalculable. No educated person can escape it. We are all profoundly affected by his ideas. But it is important to regard Freud in his correct context. In spite of his claims to scientific status, and in spite of the insistence of his followers in regarding him as a scientific figure, it has to be said that Freud was not in any sense a scientist. He was, in fact, a literary man, and a very distinguished and creative one at that. Throughout the whole of his long life he was directed and motivated, not by scientific principles, but by literary influences, and throughout his life he was impelled into literary creativity.

Freud was an exceptionally brilliant schoolboy who read Shakespeare with enjoyment at the age of eight and who topped all other students for results in six consecutive years. By his teenage years he had a command of many languages and the best of their literature. In addition to his native German and Hebrew, he left school a master of Latin, Greek, English, French, Italian and Spanish. Early influences are always the most powerful in determining personality and it is impossible that Freud should not have been profoundly affected by this kind of background.

Freud's early medical studies into neurology brought him into contact with the famous neurologist Jean Martin Charcot in Paris, who had clearly recognized the influence of the mind on physical symptoms and whose studies and demonstrations of hysteria profoundly influenced

Freud. Although many people assume that Freud 'discovered' the unconscious mind, this had long been recognized by numerous thinkers. At least as early as the end of the twelfth century, in the course of defining the soul, Isaac the Abbot of Stella wrote '*Nec versatur semper in intuitu scientis omne quod scitur.*' ('Not everything known is always present, nor is it always directly accessible to the mind's eye').

Freud's 'talking cure' was adopted from Sir Francis Galton's method of free association and, in the repressive times in which he lived, he inevitably found a strong sexual content in the half-concealed thoughts of his patients. This so impressed him that he became convinced that sex was at the basis of everything, and gradually evolved an empirical system of thought, based largely on the stories his patients told him and the dreams they recounted.

Consider some of the ideas that are central to Freud's schema and it will become plain that they are essentially of the nature of imaginative literature. Take the Oedipus complex. Freud got this idea from the legend in Homer, and later in Sophocles' drama, about the Theban hero, Oedipus (meaning 'swollen feet'). The story goes that Laius, King of Thebes, was tipped off by an oracle that his newborn son would try to usurp him as soon as he was big enough. So Laius handed over the child to a herdsman with orders to kill him. This man, however, was too full of the milk of human kindness, and, instead, tied up the child by his feet to the branch of a tree and left him hanging. The child was found, adopted, and named after the state of his feet. Years later Oedipus, driving along a narrow road in his chariot, met another chariot. Both refused to back up, and in the resultant episode of 'road rage', the driver of the other chariot killed one of Oedipus's horses. Oedipus responded by attacking and killing both the driver and his passenger, who just happened to be his father, Laius.

Oedipus then proceeded to Thebes, where he was waylaid by the Sphinx — a woman-breasted, winged lion who killed everyone who could not answer her riddle. The Sphinx had decimated the population of Thebes because none of the inhabitants had been able to find the right answer. 'Tell me,' said the Sphinx to Oedipus, 'what goes on four feet in the morning, on two at noon and on three in the evening?' 'That's easy,' said Oedipus, 'it's a man. He crawls as a child, walks upright as an adult and uses a stick in old age.'

At this, the Sphinx, overcome with chagrin, took a dive off her high rock and was killed. The grateful populace made Oedipus the new king; with the job, of course, went the widowed Queen Jocasta, whom Oedipus duly married. Later, when famine and pestilence fell on the land, it then came to light that Oedipus had killed his father and married his mother. Jocasta hanged herself, and Oedipus went mad and put out his own eyes.

Now this is a good story and it obviously deeply impressed Freud at an early stage in his life. When he came to think about the young child's relationship to its parents, this story naturally came to mind and must have modulated his thoughts. He even refers to the child's unspoken question: 'Where do babies come from?' as 'the riddle of the Sphinx.' In his book *The Interpretation of Dreams* (1899), he asserted that every young male child between the ages of about three and five years wants to kill his father and have sexual intercourse with his mother. If the parents behave well towards the child and are neither too bossy nor too affectionate, the stage, he claimed, will usually end when the child is mature enough to identify with the parent of the same sex and to repress its sexual instincts. But if anything goes wrong, the child will develop a neurosis that will poison the whole of the rest of its life.

Freud insisted that the reactions to overcome this complex brought about the most important social achievements of the human mind. The Oedipus complex could easily be made to 'explain' so many things that Freud came to regard it as the central element in his psychoanalytic theory. He wrote:

It has justly been said that the Oedipus complex is the nuclear complex of the neuroses ... Every new arrival on this planet is faced by the task of mastering the Oedipus complex; anyone who fails to do so falls a victim to neurosis. With the progress of psychoanalytic studies the importance of the Oedipus complex has become more and more clearly evident; its recognition has become the shibboleth that distinguishes the adherents of psychoanalysis from its opponents.

Freud also evolved a corresponding complex for little girls, called the Electra complex, again deriving the title from classical literature. Electra was the daughter of Agamemnon and Clytemnestra, who persuaded her brother Orestes to avenge their father by killing his murderess (Clytemnestra) and her lover, Aegisthus. Girls with the Electra complex supposedly want to kill their mothers and sleep with their fathers.

The 'castration complex' is, according to Freud, the fear associated with loss of the genitals in the male and, in females, the guilt experienced because they do not have a penis. This sense of deprivation forces women to prove that they possess an adequate symbolic substitute in some other organ, such as the vagina. Freud was convinced, wrongly, that girls had no vaginal sensation until puberty and that they interpret this as evidence that they lack a penis. This kind of proposition, strong on imagination but almost devoid of real basis, was not supported by any proof or experimental verification. Incidentally, in this matter, Freud betrayed the deep-rooted sense of male supremacy that was common to almost all men at the time. Since his day, the female castration complex has been so severely criticized that it is no longer taken seriously, even by psychoanalysts.

Another literary conceit of Freud's was the elegant notion of the id, the ego and the superego. *Ego* is the Latin word for 'I' and is generally taken to mean a person's consciousness of self. The word was in use, in English, long before Freud's time, but it was he who made the concept famous by describing the ego as a kind of rational internal person constantly being pushed into temptation by the id with its instinctual, wicked (and mainly sexual) drives, but sometimes saved from disaster by the virtuous superego. Freud changed his definition of the ego several times. This neat division of the mind into three has no existence in real life, but the concept has been used so widely and so impressively by the psychoanalytically oriented that many people believe it is real.

Freud's literary orientation also showed itself in his preoccupation with dreams. This was, for him, another prolific source of stories of which he was the arch-interpreter. Because the explicit content of the dreams was seldom sufficiently interesting or significant in itself, Freud conceived the idea that the real content of dreams was expressed in symbolic form. So he soon became deeply preoccupied with the role of sexual symbolism in dreams, and came to regard every elongated object as symbolic of the penis and every receptacle as symbolizing the vagina. He believed, rightly, that early experiences have a profound effect on later behaviour and personality and that these experiences became repressed and lay hidden under layers of subsequent mental accretion, but could be uncovered by analysis. He asserted, without proof, that the uncovering of these early experiences would disperse the psychopathology which he claimed they had caused. As a result, millions of people have devoted a substantial proportion of their time (and money) to the psychoanalytic process, mostly with no discernible effect. Few, if any, psychiatrists, even those steeped in the psychoanalytic tradition, can now believe that any case of psychosis or even of neurosis has ever been cured by psychoanalysis.

Another interesting window into the mind of Sigmund Freud is provided by one of his professional papers that he always regarded as a favourite work. This was an essay entitled 'Leonardo da Vinci and a memory of his childhood', and Freud considered it an important step in the application of psychoanalysis to biography and to cultural matters generally. Although Freud greatly admired Leonardo and thought him one of the greatest men of all time, he was not averse to drawing attention to aspects of his personality that must have seemed disgraceful at the time he was writing. 'There is no one so great,' he wrote, 'as to be disgraced by being subject to the laws which govern both normal and pathological activity with equal force.'

In this long, discursive but interesting biographical essay on

Leonardo, Freud, as is characteristic of his literary process, draws remarkable conclusions from a single brief reference of Leonardo's in one of his scientific notebooks. While writing about vultures, Leonardo breaks off to recount one of his earliest memories. He was in his cradle and a vulture landed near him, forced open his mouth with its tail and struck its tail repeatedly against his lips. Always on the lookout for grist to his 'scientific' mill, Freud was fascinated by this story, and immediately rejected the suggestion that it was a fantasy of Leonardo's. He then proceeded to interpret it. A tail is, of course, a symbol of the penis. Opening the child's mouth and beating about inside it implies oral sex (fellatio). The passivity of the fantasy is significant. It resembles, according to Freud, the passivity 'found in dreams and fantasies of women and passive homosexuals who play the part of the woman in sexual intercourse'. Freud was now at his most remarkably realistic and shocking. He points out that it was very common for women to take an erect penis into their mouths and suck at it – a practice considered to be a loathsome perversion in respectable society. Love, he said, removed the repulsion. So far so good. Freud then went on to suggest that Leonardo's memory was actually a symbol of his being suckled by his mother. The substitution of the vulture indicated that the child was aware that his father was absent and that he was alone with his mother. Leonardo was illegitimate and his father married another woman in the year he was born. So the baby Leonardo spent a long time alone with his natural mother, during which he was tormented by the great question of where babies come from and what the father had to do with it. Freud then explains the paradox implicit in the above by asserting that the penis is so important to little boys that they initially assume that everyone – both boys and girls – has one. When they later observe that girls do not, they assume that is has been cut off, leaving a wound. The baby Leonardo had not, however, reached that stage and was still assuming that his mother had a penis. All is now clear. Too much maternal love. Fellatio with his mother. Repression of a shameful memory. Homosexuality. QED. The mind boggles.

There was no scientific basis to Freud's theories. Scientists do not simply elaborate complex assertions without reasonable basis; rather, they propose the simplest possible hypothesis to account for an observed phenomenon and then proceed to carry out experiments to see whether that hypothesis stands up. None of Freud's 'explanations' were tested by experiment, mainly because they were not of a nature to be susceptible to experiment. In fact, being literary rather than scientific in nature, they were inherently incapable of being disproved. This, according to Popper, is a principal characteristic of a pseudo-science. Pseudosciences are not discovered; they are invented. Unfortunately, major pseudosciences such as psychoanalysis or communism have an unhappy tendency rapidly to convert to religions. They attract thousands of acolytes who see in them the answer to all their problems; they have their canons of rigid dogma, their priestly hierarchies, their saints and martyrs; they are 'by schisms rent asunder, by heresies distressed'; and they invariably end up by doing a great deal more harm than good.

Despite these criticisms, it has to be said that the remarkable mind of Sigmund Freud has had an enormous influence on twentieth-century thought and attitude – certainly comparable to that of Karl Marx. Whether that influence was wholly beneficial is an entirely different matter.

Of superstition:
credulity, crassness or culture?

The word 'superstition' will usually evoke ideas about the remote past or about walking under ladders, black cats, four-leaf clover and rabbits' feet. If that were all there were to it, the subject would hardly merit inclusion in a book about extraordinary states of mind. But superstition is far more pervasive, and has a far wider effect, than most people realize. The subject is far from trivial because superstition has had an enormously damaging effect on human history, and continues to have such an effect today. One need only mention the burning of witches and religious 'heretics' (see **A mind possessed**), the horrors of the Crusades against the 'infidels'; the terrors perpetrated in the name of fundamental religion; the tortures of the Spanish Inquisition; the enslavement of coloured races; and the perennial persecution of the Jews (see **The prejudiced mind**). The basis or justification for all these shameful chapters of history is superstitious belief.

A superstition is an irrational belief concerning the unknown, usually based on ignorance or fear. The definition is commonly extended to include any irrational belief that tends to give rise to acts or rituals, respect for omens, and the use of charms. The extraordinary thing about it is that millions of people today, who would insist that they are rational, sensible beings, are, in fact, deeply influenced by superstitious beliefs and are regularly engaged in superstitious practices. I am not referring to harmless amusements, such as reading one's horoscope, but to far more important matters, as we shall see.

Humans have an insatiable need for explanations of phenomena but, remarkably, are very easily satisfied with easy explanations.

Proposed explanations need not be in the least rational and, once accepted, tend to be retained even after they are seen to be nonsensical. A child asks: 'What makes thunder?' and is told: 'Clouds banging together.' An old woman asks: 'Why do I have this pain?' The doctor replies: 'My dear, you have a gastric stomach.' The child and the old woman go off, respectively satisfied with their 'explanations'. The fact that clouds are made of intangible water vapour and that a 'gastric stomach' means 'a stomach-type stomach' are really irrelevant. For most people it is the provision of an explanation that matters.

Superstition certainly has a long history. In pre-scientific times there were, of course, few or no rational explanations of most natural phenomena but this did not in any way diminish the human need for answers to the questions why, what and how? Certain humans, perhaps more imaginative than most, saw in this situation a source of profit and status for themselves and set up as experts. The fact that they were self-styled experts did not matter in the least. They were sources of explanation and, since most people were entirely uncritical of what they were told, these clever men and women were valued by others. People would crowd around these shamans, or gurus or witchdoctors or priests, taking it all in, and the experts were quick to exploit, and were not necessarily above abusing, the situation.

The early proffered explanations of inexplicable phenomena usually involved magic (occult forces) and animism (active spirits), but were, of course, limited by the human experience of the experts. In those days, their explanation for the phenomenon of thunder was that it was the noise made by the gods when they were angry. These gods were powerful (could they not split oak trees in two with their lightning strikes?); the 'experts', needless to say, set themselves up as intermediaries who could (for a fee) 'talk' to the gods and and placate them.

Today such explanations seem simplistic to us. But, apart from a few educational advantages, humans have not changed significantly in the past 10,000 years. They are still perfectly capable of accepting, and living by, most of the superstitions extant during that period. In matters not susceptible to scientific experiment and demonstration, authoritative pronouncements by self-styled gurus or experts are all we have to go on.

Today, superstition is alive and well. Millions of people believe in astrology, table-rapping, flying saucers (see **Alien abduction**), the Bermuda triangle, iridology, tea-leaf fortune-telling, palm reading, spiritualist seances (see **The mind of the medium**), ghosts, poltergeists, haunted houses, etc., and such subjects are promoted by current popular culture, whether with credulity or with cynical indifference. At the time of writing, an extremely popular television series presents, as apparent fact, a succession of paranormal mysteries. Millions of people, watching this absurd, if highly entertaining, drivel, are led to believe that 'there must be something in it'. There is never any mention that the material presented is based on other than plain truth.

A substantial proportion of the American population believe in the validity and moral rightness of what is called 'creation science'. This is a body of rationalization purporting to prove scientifically that the statements made in the first chapter of the first book of the Old Testament (Genesis) are literally true. Neglecting the fact that this version of the truth sets aside the entire corpus of geological science which applies principles of reason on which we must all trust our lives every day, it asserts that the universe was made, some six thousand years ago, in six days (see **Of faith and fossils**). The basis of this is the belief that everything in the Bible, however intrinsically contradictory, is literally true. It is an extraordinary tribute to the power of confident and authoritative assertion over the minds of humans that millions fail to see that two statements, one of which categorically denies the other, cannot both be true. The Bible, being an elaborate collection of many different writings by many different people with different ideas, inevitably contains many such pairs of contradictory statements.

Although human brains, and their characteristics, have not changed, a few millennia of experience, observation and thought, have led to us evolving some practical and well-tried systems of reasoning that can help us avoid succumbing to superstitious beliefs. Throughout enlightened times, the best minds have applied themselves to the question and there is available, today, a body of writing, by philosophers, logicians, scientists and commentators, that is more than sufficient to provide good grounds to set aside much of contemporary superstition. Plato and Aristotle were among the first to formalize rational thought and to provide humans with rules for the avoidance of logical error.

Aristotle (384–322 BC), in particular, one of the most influential figures in the history of Western thought, taught extensively on many subjects, including formal logic. His ideas, collected and recorded by his pupils, inspired and influenced the whole of medieval and Islamic philosophy. Aristotle invented the syllogism, an example of which is: 'Caius is a man. All men are mortal. Therefore Caius is mortal.' He went on to analyse the various forms of the syllogism and to point out common errors, such as the fallacy: 'Caius is mortal. All men are mortal. Therefore Caius is a man.' Aristotle described how truth may be determined, either by induction (working from many observations to a principle) or by deduction (deriving conclusions that cannot be false if the premises are true). He demonstrated the shortcomings of inductive reasoning (the sighting of one black swan destroys the inductive conclusion that all swans are white) and devoted most of his logical thought to working out the theory of deduction and presenting it in a way that would be easily remembered and used. His logical system, known as the *Organon* (instrument), served, from then on, as a guide to rational thought.

In the context of superstition and religion, the English philosopher and essayist Francis Bacon (1561–1626) had some surprising things to say:

It were better to have no opinion of God at all, than such an opinion as is unworthy of him: for the one is unbelief, the other is insulting: and certainly superstition is the reproach of the Deity... Atheism leaves a man to sense, to philosophy, to natural piety, to laws, to reputation; all which may be guides to an outward moral virtue, though religion were not: but superstition mounts all these, and erecteth an absolute monarch in the minds of men. Therefore atheism never did perturb states; for it makes men wary of themselves, as looking no farther: and we see the times inclined to atheism, as the time of Augustus Caesar, were civil times. But superstition hath been the confusion of many states... The master of superstition is the people; and in all superstition wise men follow fools; and arguments are fitted to practice in a reverse order. The causes of superstition are: pleasing and sensual rites and ceremonies; excess of outwards and pharisaical holiness; over-great reverence of traditions; the stratagems of prelates for their own ambition and lucre.

The Scottish philosopher and historian David Hume (1711–76) also had some cogent things to say about superstition. Here are some extracts from his essay *Of superstition and enthusiasm* (note that, in Hume's day, the word 'enthusiasm' meant 'extravagant or unbalanced religious fervour'):

The mind of man is subject to certain unaccountable terrors and apprehensions, proceeding either from the unhappy situation of private or public affairs, from ill health, from a gloomy and melancholy disposition, or from the concurrence of all these circumstances. In such a state of mind, infinite unknown evils are dreaded from unknown agents; and where real objects of terror are wanting, the soul, active to its own prejudice, finds imaginary ones, to whose power and malevolence it sets no limits.

As these enemies are entirely invisible and unknown, the methods taken to appease them are equally unaccountable, and consist in ceremonies, observances, mortifications, sacrifices, presents, or in any practice, however absurd or frivolous, which either folly or knavery recommends to a blind and terrified credulity. Weakness, fear, melancholy, together with ignorance are, therefore, the true sources of superstition.

Superstition is favourable to priestly power... it represents the man to himself in such despicable colours, that he appears unworthy, in his own eyes, of approaching the Divine presence, and naturally has recourse to any other person whose sanctity of life, or perhaps impudence and cunning, have made him to be supposed to be more favoured by the Divinity. Hence the origin of priests... Superstition is an enemy to civil liberty. As superstition groans under the dominion of priests...it renders men tame and abject, and fits them for slavery.

In his celebrated essay on miracles, Hume provides valuable guidance for a determined assault on superstition. He points out that what we call the laws of nature are established by 'firm and unalterable experience' – by an enormous amount of observation. We know, without question, that men must die, that a heavy weight cannot, of itself, remain suspended in the air, that water can extinguish fire, and so on. A miracle is a suspension of laws of this kind. Since we hold these laws by having observed them in action so often, we require very strong proof to accept that they can be violated. That a dead man should come to life is a miracle because that has never been observed in any age or country. If someone testifies that he has seen a dead man come to life we should immediately consider which is more likely – that a dead man has truly come to life; or that the man who says so is a liar or has been deceived? Which would be the greater miracle? Hume recommends us to weigh matters in this manner and always to reject the greater miracle. As he puts it: 'No testimony is sufficient to establish a miracle, unless the testimony be of such kind, that its falsehood would be more miraculous than the fact which it endeavours to establish.'

Nearly all modern superstitious beliefs – things like little green men coming out of flying saucers, or corn circles caused by extraterrestrial forces – are held simply on the basis of testimony. 'Someone told my aunt that they knew a man whose sister saw it happening.' If we apply Hume's principle to the endless succession of stories in the flying saucer or poltergeist class, we will see how credible they sound. Unfortunately, the great majority of ordinary people are not really interested in the demonstrable truth or the debunking of alleged miracles. They have an insatiable appetite for wonders, marvels, pseudoscience and general baloney and will always go for these things rather than boring old fact. This appetite can be profitably exploited, and the media know very well what sells. Thirty American publishers rejected an excellently written book by David Marks and Richard Kamman which disproved most current popular superstitions. The same publishers were feverishly searching for books that promoted psychic phenomena and the like.

So, as always, Mammon will prevail over truth, honour, propriety and standards of behaviour. This is a sad commentary on human frailty but it is far from being the worst aspect of superstition. Today, we do not burn witches, but we do persecute all kinds of people because of the superstitious belief that they differ from us. Given a loosening of the restraints of civilization or law, or even democratic government, we could quickly return to the dark ages. This happened in Europe as recently as the first half of the twentieth century when a whole nation was seduced by a demagogue into a superstitious belief in the entirely imaginary concept of Aryan superiority.

The mind of the musician: nature or nurture?

The mind of the musician is capable of synthesizing internal music that is heard almost exactly as performed music is heard. It is capable of responding emotionally to musical experience in a manner shared by other musicians. All musicians agree that major keys are bright and minor keys sombre. All respond emotionally in much the same way to pentatonic modes (music using only the black keys on a keyboard). Many keyboard musicians share subtle emotional responses in common to different keys, although equal temperament tuning is supposed to make the intervals between all semitones the same. The latter capacity also seems to have survived several changes in the frequency of the standard pitch for music (see also **The chromatic mind**). Many musicians have 'perfect pitch' – the ability to name with complete accuracy any note played. Musical physiologists believe that this capacity is possible because such people have an internal standard of pitch – a reliable memory of a single note, such as A (440 hertz) – to which other notes are related.

Musicians can not only perform known music internally, creating ideal performances that they might not be able to match on the concert platform, they can also perform new imagined music, both as an almost unwilled improvization and in a controlled and carefully structured manner. The ability to convert printed music to internally heard sound is remarkable. A musician will pick up a score of a string quartet and will at once 'hear' the music. In the same way, the creative musician can translate what he or she hears in the mind into a complex score. Many composers do not compose on an instrument, but in their head, writing their composition down without having to play it first.

Musical memory is another extraordinary feature of the mind of the musician. It is a commonplace of musical biography to read of pianists learning a new piece from the music while travelling in a train and giving a creditable public performance without the music, on arrival. The German conductor von Bulow even memorized the whole score of a symphony by Stanford in the course of a train journey and was then able to conduct the work without score. Menuhin reports a remarkable instance of musical memory by the Romanian violinist and composer Georges Enesco (1881–1955). Enesco and Ravel were trying out a new violin sonata that Ravel had just written. After going through it once, Enesco suggested that they play it again just to be sure that everything was right. To Ravel's amazement, Enesco closed the violin part and played the whole work entirely from memory. Liszt's favourite pupil, Karl Tausig (1841–71) is said, by the age of 29, to have memorized every important work in the whole pianoforte and harpsichord literature as it then existed.

The question of musical taste is a difficult one. In general, taste is related to the overall standard of musicality and grows with musical education and experience. It is, of course, variable. Some executive musicians of extraordinary skills are capable of displaying lapses of taste that horrify the discriminating. On the other hand, taste – which includes originality and unpredictability – is generally deemed to be the most important element in determining artistic quality both in performance and in composition. Today, a very high standard of technical performance is expected of all professional musicians and, to a large extent, the factors that distinguish the great from the merely competent are those indefinable elements we mean when we talk of taste.

The kind of music for which a musician is best known does not necessarily correspond to his or her ideal of taste. Economic factors may determine the direction of a musical career. There are even cases on record in which a high level of taste can be inhibitory. Musicality, as we shall see, runs in families. When one highly musical family was studied it was found that there was one member who, in the opinion of the others, was quite devoid of musical talent. On investigation, however, this man was found to have all the elements of musical ability present to an unparalleled degree — significantly greater than those of his very famous brother. It turned out that he was intensely musical but that the level of his taste was so high that nearly all the music he heard sounded banal and boring to him and he could not bear either to perform or to hear it.

Musicians live in a world of emotion and artistry, rather than in a world of reason. It does not seem to be necessary to be particularly intelligent in order to be a capable musician; indeed, some mentally retarded people show high musical sensitivity and even talent. For these reasons it has occasionally been suggested that musicians are commonly short on intelligence. This is a typical case of arguing from the particular to the general and it is as wrong as such arguments usually are. There is no evidence that musicians, as a class, are any less bright — or more bright, for that matter — than a comparable group of non-musicians. The distribution of intelligence seems to be the same in musical populations as in general populations. It has to be said, however, that musicians in the highest class are commonly supremely intelligent people. Professional distinction in music demand the same high levels of intelligence as distinction in any other profession.

It seems possible that obsessive–compulsive neurosis (or perhaps just plain superstition) is commoner in performing musicians than in the generality of mankind. There are numerous tales of the eccentric antics of instrumental players, singers and conductors arising from this particular idiosyncrasy. The pianist Vladimir Pachmann could never get his piano stool at the right height. It is on record that he asked whether anyone in the audience had a train ticket he could borrow. Other pianists will sit staring at the audience until the silence is absolute and no one dare breathe. Shura Cherkassky must always step on to the stage with his right foot first, and his practice time is measured exactly to the second. Luciano Pavarotti has to find a bent nail in the floorboards before beginning a concert. The conductor

Artur Rodzinski always had a loaded gun in his pocket when at work on the rostrum.

Professional musical performers differ from ordinary mortals in more ways than the purely psychological. If they are to be successful they require certain innate physical abilities some of which are rare outside the world of music. Carl Seashore, the doyen of musical psychology and physiology, once put together a battery of tests called the 'Seashore Measures of Musical Talent'. These include such things as the ability accurately to discriminate pitch and interval, to maintain strict tempo, to analyse rhythmical patterns, to appreciate subtle differences in loudness, to distinguish differences in timbre (such as the difference between the same note played on a clarinet and on an oboe), and to understand phrasing in a succession of notes. What may surprise many people is that one of the important standard measurements of musical capacity is the ability to move the fingers very quickly. People with a naturally slow tapping rate – less than about seven taps per second, averaged over a 5 second period – can improve to some extent with practice, but will never become virtuoso performers. Seashore says that the tapping rate, in association with steadiness, precision and endurance, deserves to be rated highly in the selection of young musicians for training. Few people can achieve more than 12 taps per second.

One aspect of the musical mind that seems incomprehensible to non-musicians is the ability to dissociate musical activity from everyday thought and to engage in both simultaneously. A competent sight-reader can give an adequate performance while thinking about something quite different. This is not to suggest that a brilliant performance is possible if the leader of a string quartet is having fantasies about the beautiful girl in the front row. But that it should be possible to do this at all is remarkable and tells us something about the nature of musical execution and how it differs from other mental activity. Edvard Grieg showed the manuscript of his piano concerto to Franz Liszt for the first time. Many guests were present and Liszt asked Grieg to play it. Grieg demurred, though, saying he had never practised it. Liszt went to the piano and read off the work at sight, giving a remarkable performance. Astonishingly, in the course of this, at a time when his interpretation was at its finest, he started to talk to the guests about the work, indicating to one or to the other which parts he especially liked.

So how does the mind of the musician come about? There have been great arguments about whether musical capacity is inherited or the result of environmental influences, and these arguments still go on. Unfortunately, the same evidence can be used by both sides. There are numerous historical examples of musical families in which the talent appears in generation after generation. But a musical family necessarily provides an intensely musical environment to which new children are exposed. So the process could operate in either way or both.

There is, however, a good deal of evidence to show that genetics is important in determining musicality. Take, for instance, the case of Mozart, who is regarded by many as the greatest musician of all time. Mozart certainly came from a musical family, but his talents were apparent at such an early age that they could hardly have been wholly the result of this environment. It must be remembered that the full expression of musical ability cannot occur before the neurological development of the individual allows it or before considerable musical education has occurred, so the very early years may show little of the potential. We have unique information in this context in the case of Mozart because, when he was eight years old, his musical powers were formally studied in London by the lawyer, antiquary and amateur scientist the Honourable Daines Barrington (1727–1800). This careful man sent a report to the Royal Society entitled 'An account of a very remarkable musician'. By the time Barrington studied Mozart the musician was already performing regularly in public, and it was in the course of one of the overseas tours in which his talents were being exploited by his father, Leopold Mozart, that Barrington met him. Barrington's report contains documentary evidence of Mozart's age, and records the boy's prowess at playing at sight from a previously unseen five-part score. It seems that the boy was a better sight-reader than his experienced father. The report also records Mozart's skills at improvization in various styles. There is a remarkable insight into the mind of the true musician, in that on being asked to improvise an angry piece, Mozart became so emotionally involved that, in the course of the performance, he was worked up to a frenzy, rose to his feet and beat the harpsichord like a mad person. Although his little fingers could only stretch to a fifth, he played with amazing skill and musical understanding, especially in his own compositions. In particular, he was able to modulate freely from one key to another – an indication of remarkable musical maturity in one so young. From other evidence we know that Mozart was playing and composing at the age of four and that his musical memory was phenomenal. After hearing Allegri's *Miserere* in the Sistine Chapel, Mozart went home and wrote out the entire score from memory. This was a major work in nine parts scored for two choirs.

It is inconceivable that Mozart's musical abilities could have arisen – and at such an early age – from purely environmental influences. Most of the qualities that enabled him to become a musician of such stature and to develop into such a great composer must have been innate and hence of genetic origin. It is apparent, however, that musical capacity is a complex entity: there can be no question of a single gene for musicality. This is an example of what geneticists call multifactorial inheritance, involving a number of different genes.

In Mozart's case, and in that of many other great musicians, we are dealing with an exceptionally rare combination of genetic factors that laid down the potential for high musicality. It is possible that, in the absence of a musical environment, explicit musical capacity might not have developed. But it seems likely that it does not require a highly musical environment to stimulate the musical interests and ambitions of people genetically endowed to this degree. If the underlying set of abilities is present, almost any exposure to music would prompt in the person concerned a powerful desire to hear and to make music. The greatest value of a musical environment is in its educational effect.

Much music will be heard, taste will be formed, and familiarity with the current stage of musical evolution quickly achieved. At this point, the way will be open for new and original creativity. This process can readily be followed in the careers of the great composers.

Child sexual abuse:
the mind of the paedophile

There is a passage in Captain Cook's journals of his voyage around the world in which he describes a public act of sexual intercourse – he calls it 'the rite of Venus' – between an 11-year-old girl and a South Pacific islander. Because Cook was, as he would regard it, among savages, he presumably felt he was absolved from the necessity to express the sentiments appropriate to a London drawing room. In the event, he contented himself with the remark that the girl 'did not seem to stand much in need' of the attention. The psychotherapist Roy Eskapa, in his scholarly book *Bizarre Sex*, recounts how, in a minority of primitive cultures, this kind of thing, as well as regular masturbation of children by their parents, is considered normal and entirely acceptable.

For most people, however, the mind of the paedophile is hard to envisage. There is a debate as to whether child sexual molestation should be regarded as a disease or simply as a criminal tendency. Psychologists tend to call it a 'psychosexual disorder', thereby seeming to provide grounds for some kind of defence, but the law is not so generous and choses to consider this a matter of considerable gravity that attracts severe penalties.

The great majority of ordinary citizens would agree with this view. A person who obtains sexual arousal and gratification by sexual contact with prepubescent children is deemed by almost all to be beyond the pale. There are two main reasons for the strength of the emotional response against the paedophile. First, because the child is incapable of consenting to sexual activity as a mature adult can, its freedom is seen to be grossly violated. Secondly, there is a general view that such activity causes long-term damage of various kinds to the child. There is considerable evidence that this view is correct. So it is considered outrageous by most of us that there are those who actively promote paedophilic activities and assert that paedophiles have rights in the matter.

A good deal is now known about the characteristics of paedophiles. Most of them are men: sexual molestation of children does occasionally occur in women but is extremely rare. The typical paedophile is socially inept and is incapable of promoting a mature adult sexual relationship. He often has a low level of self-esteem. He uses children sexually because he sees this as less threatening than sex with an adult. Perhaps for this reason, paedophiles tend to be older than other sex offenders – the average age is about 35. Girls are the victims more often than boys. The fact that a boy may be selected as a victim does not necessarily imply that the paedophile is homosexual.

The paedophile is frequently a person thought to be of high moral character. Remarkably he commonly holds strong religious views, or displays – and often voices – rigidly puritanical views on sex. He will commonly believe that sexual promiscuity in women is to be more severely condemned than promiscuity in men. These expressions of morality may be an attempt to assuage the feelings of guilt but there is often a long-term conflict between religious beliefs and the paedophilia, which is regarded as sin. Many such people pray regularly to be relieved of their temptations.

Actual physical violence is uncommon in paedophilia, and occurs in no more than 3 per cent of cases. Aggressive paedophiles are rare. They derive sexual arousal from hurting the child. Even coercion and threats are the exception rather than the rule and occur in about 15 per cent of cases. Contrary to common belief, many paedophiles do not engage in penetrative sexual intercourse. Most content themselves with sexual fondling and display of the genitals to the child. Also contrary to general belief, the great majority of paedophiles are not strangers, but are well known to the child and are either family members, relatives or neighbours. More than half of the men arrested for paedophilia are relatives or acquaintances of the child. Incestuous paedophilia is common. The offences usually occur in the child's own home or when he or she is on a visit to a relative or friend.

The tendency is far commoner than most people appreciate. Of all those convicted of sex offences, about one third are for paedophilia. According to Kinsey's investigations, between a quarter and a third of all adults will admit that they were approached sexually by an adult when they were children. In a great many cases the matter is hushed up for various reasons. Even allowing for mistakes and misinterpretation of innocent play, this still leaves a horrifying statistic. It also suggests, however, that not all genuine paedophilic experience causes permanent harm to the victim. In Kinsey's statistics, the majority of sexually abused children, interviewed as adults, had not, apparently, been emotionally harmed by the experience although they said they had been distressed at the time.

Children react to paedophilic experience in different ways, depending especially on the kind of behaviour of the paedophile. Violence and force will, of course, cause fright, but in other cases the reaction is mainly one of initial bewilderment followed by boredom and disgust. Some children accept the situation passively and may even occasionally enjoy it. Some are more seriously upset by paedophilia because their parents have warned them so determinedly against an activity they cannot really understand. The most serious effects occur when children have been subjected to sexual encounters associated with violence or pain. There is no doubt that many children who have been the victims of paedophiles become psychologically disturbed adults. Boys who are sexually abused are more likely to become adult sex offenders than those who have not. In the case of sexually abused girls a higher proportion than usual become prostitutes or resort to drug abuse.

Paedophilia rightly attracts more severe legal penalties than other sexual offences. Penalties tend to be higher the younger the child and the greater the difference in age between participants. The most severe penalties are usually awarded to male paedophiles guilty of anal intercourse. Paedophiles in prison commonly attract hostility and violence from other prisoners.

Unacceptable body image: self-mutilation

Most people would assume that people who cut off parts of their own bodies — particularly their genitals — must be suffering from a severe mental disorder. However, this is not necessarily true. Self-mutilation is surprisingly common and, although most of those who do this (they are usually men) are clearly suffering from a psychotic disorder, a substantial minority of them are not. In the case of genital excision, the members of this minority have reasons which seem to them entirely reasonable and good, as we shall see.

There is a considerable literature on the subject of self-mutilation. The most popular form of this activity — gouging out one's own eyes — recurs repeatedly in written records throughout the ages. There is no reason to suppose that, simply because the account is in Homer, it was Oedipus who started this fashion. Cutting off an ear is not uncommon either, the most celebrated instance being that of the painter Vincent van Gogh who, on Christmas Eve 1888, in the course of a psychiatric breakdown, cut off part of his left ear and sent it to a girlfriend. It is not too easy to amputate the limbs but there are records of people who have tried and, in a few cases, succeeded. There is even an account of a woman who tried to cut off her own head and who succeeded in severing, from behind, the skin, muscles, ligaments and bone as far forward as the spinal cord.

Ocular and genital self-mutilation are much easier and numerous cases have been reported. It is unnecessary to go into details of these, but one bizarre case might be mentioned. It is taken from an account in a Russian medical journal of 1883. A 29-year-old peasant was sitting on a bank, reading his favourite book. Suddenly, without a word, and in one movement, he tore away his scrotum and testicles.

He then got up and quietly handed the avulsed parts to his mother who was sitting nearby. 'Take that,' he said, 'I don't want it any more.' Questioning failed to elicit any reason for this extraordinary act.

So far as the motivation for genital self-mutilation is concerned, this can be divided into two rough groups – the mad and the sane. In the first category come such reasons as the following, all taken from medical records: guilt over masturbation; desire to be circumcised; acquisition of a venereal disease; delusory conviction that enemies wanted to steal the genitals; desire for castration; delirium tremens; guilt over nocturnal emission ('wet dreams'); remorse over consort with a prostitute; guilt over homosexuality; guilt over incest; religious desire for 'purification'; desire to resist sexual temptation; obedience to hallucinatory commands; exorcism of demons; revenge against women; punishment of failure of masculinity; prevention of transmission of real or imagined genetic defect; attempted suicide; and desire to lead a 'holy life'. Alcohol or drug intoxication is a factor, often an important factor, in about half the cases.

The second category – the sane motives – accounts for about 13 per cent of cases and is more interesting. This group consists almost exclusively of people who have gender identity problems – specifically, men who passionately desire to have bodies that conform to their true psychological sex, i.e. that of a woman. Such people are said to suffer from trans-sexualism. Men in this situation always think of themselves as women and consider their genitals disgusting. Often they will seek sex-reassignment surgery, but this is not easy to achieve because doctors are very chary of people who ask for it, many of whom do not have real gender identity problems (see also **The mind in the wrong body**). Proper medical care can probably eliminate those sad cases in which victims of this situation feel they have to resort to the desperate expedient of genital self-mutilation.

Of sexual jealousy: Othello syndrome

Shakespeare's *Othello* is an unparalleled account of the state of mind of an acutely jealous man. Othello was no match for the villainous Iago who was capable, while engineering every possible circumstance to inflame the Moor's jealousy, of saying to him:

> O! beware, my lord, of jealousy;
> It is the green-eyed monster which doth mock
> The meat it feeds on. That cuckold lives in bliss
> Who, certain of his fate, loves not his wronger;
> But, O, what damned minutes tells he o'er
> Who dotes, yet doubts, suspects, yet strongly loves!

As Dr Johnson puts it:

> the cool malignity of Iago, silent in his resentment, subtle in his designs, and studious at once of his interest and his vengeance ... are such proofs of Shakespeare's skill in human nature, as, I suppose, it is vain to seek in any modern writer. The gradual progress which Iago makes in the Moor's conviction, and the circumstances which he employs to inflame him, are so artfully natural, that, though it will perhaps not be said of him as he says of himself, that he is *a man not easily jealous*, yet we cannot but pity him when at last we find him *perplexed in the extreme*.

Othello was not Shakespeare's only essay into the subject of jealousy. He also dealt with the matter in *A Winter's Tale*, and there are, of course, many references in his other works.

Although Othello's case is probably the best-known example of extreme jealousy in imaginative literature, it is far from unique. Greek mythology is full of sexual jealousy. Leto, a Titan, and mother of the god Apollo and the goddess Artemis, was a victim of jealousy. When Zeus had got her pregnant with Apollo and Artemis, she had to go wandering to find a place of refuge to be delivered and finally settled on the barren isle of Delos. The reason she could not have the babies at home was that Zeus's wife, Hera, was bitterly jealous of her for bearing his children. Later, Daphne, the beautiful daughter of a river god, was lusted after by Apollo but she was too virtuous for him and he got nowhere with her. In spite of this, Apollo had no time for rivals, and Leucippus, who also loved her, was killed because of Apollo's jealousy. The unfortunate Daphne ended up as a laurel tree.

Orion, too, had a bad time. He was born out of the earth and emerged from a buried bull hide on which three gods had urinated. He was blinded by the king of Chios whose daughter Merope he fancied. Later he went to Crete to live with Artemis for the hunting. Some legends say that Artemis killed him out of jealousy; others blame Apollo who was said to be jealous over his sister Artemis's love of Orion. It seems that Apollo, for all his beauty, was much given to jealousy. Maybe he was jealous of Orion's beauty, which was said to be remarkable.

Coming to more modern times, it is worth mentioning at least one literary man who was responsible for arousing a good deal of jealousy. Johann Wolfgang von Goethe (1749–1832) was a great ladies' man and had many close relationships with women. Perhaps the most notable case was that of Maximiliane Brentano and her daughter, Bettina von Arnim. Maximiliane and Goethe had been close friends before her marriage but this association was abruptly terminated when her husband became jealous of the great man. Thirty-five years later, the daughter took her mother's place as a close friend of the now 57-year-old writer and polymath. Inevitably, Bettina formed a close attachment to the most fascinating man of the time and this friendship lasted for about five years, until 1811. Bettina was a remarkable lady in her own right and a talented writer. The friendship matured, however, to the point at which Goethe's wife allowed her jealousy to flare up into a public row with Bettina. This caused Goethe to break off relations with her. Later, Bettina published an account of her correspondence with Goethe under the title *Goethes Briefwechsel mit einem Kinde* (Letters between Goethe and a child), which appeared in 1835.

There are plenty of literary examples of sexual jealousy from which to chose. Tolstoy's novella, *The Kreutzer Sonata*, a fine study of the subject, need only be mentioned in passing. Less well-known is Robbe-Grillet's novel of the punning title *La Jalousie* (1957). In the latter, the narrator's obsessive suspicion of his wife's infidelity is increased in interest because it is neither confirmed nor denied, although he watches her and her suspected lover through a louvre shutter, or *jalousie*. The Belgian playwright Fernand Crommelynck (1885–1970) specialized in revealing the weaknesses of us all by magnifying them into obsessions. His plays have titles such as *We'll Go No More to the Woods* and *The Magnificent Cuckold*. The latter, in particular, although described as a farce, is a penetrating study of sexual jealousy. The husband's inability to control his suspicion of his wife ends by driving her into infidelity, thereby, ironically, resolving his doubts. Guy de Maupassant's story *Pierre et Jean* (1888) also illustrates powerfully the terrible effects of jealousy.

The most important work of the Brazilian poet, novelist, and short-story writer, Joaquim Maria Machado de Assis (1839–1908), an outstanding nineteenth-century exponent of classical Brazilian literature, was *Dom Casmurro* (1899). This was published in English translation in 1953 and has been described as 'a haunting and terrible journey into a mind warped by jealousy'.

The Polish novelist and playwright Michal Choromanski (1904–72) had his first literary success with the novel *Zazdość i medycyna* (Jealousy and medicine), published in 1932. This work is remarkable for its analysis of jealousy and eroticism in the context of a love triangle. Choromanski also produced excellent psychological studies of various extraordinary states of mind, again with a strong sexual and pathological emphasis, in his collection of essays and short stories entitled *Kobieta i mezczyzna* (Female and male), published in 1959.

Popular ballads also contain many references to sexual jealousy. The eponymous Lord Randal is poisoned by his sweetheart; Little Musgrave is found in bed with Lady Barnard and is summarily despatched by the noble Lord, her husband; and, of course, Johnny (who 'done her wrong') is duly knocked off by Frankie.

So what is the nature of this common state of mind known as jealousy? As Descartes puts it in his work *The Passions of the Soul*,

Jealousy is a kind of fear relating to our desire to retain possession of something; and it proceeds less from the strength of our reasons for thinking we might lose it, than from the high estimation in which we hold it. Jealousy causes us to examine even the tiniest grounds for suspicion that we might lose the thing and makes us consider them strong reasons for anxiety. The passion of jealousy is right to the extent that we should value good possessions. But it is blameworthy when the possession is guarded with more care than it warrants. We scorn a miser when he is jealous of, and gloats over, his treasure and will never be away from it in case he is robbed. And we despise a man who is jealous of his wife, because it shows that he does not love her in the right way, and that he has a bad opinion of himself or of her. If he had a true love for her, he would have no inclination to distrust her. In the case of a jealous husband, it is not truly she whom he loves, but just the good which he conceives as consisting in having sole possession of her. And he would not fear to lose this good did he not judge himself to be unworthy of it, or else conceive that his wife is unfaithful. For the rest, this passion only relates to suspicion and distrust, since it is not, properly speaking, being jealous to try to avoid some evil when we have just cause to fear it.

Descartes' definition and explanation have repeatedly been borne out in everyday life and shown to be just. More recently, developments in psychiatry have added a further dimension to the subject. Sexual jealousy arising from a delusion that the spouse or partner is being unfaithful is known as the Othello syndrome. This is a bit hard on Othello and suggests the possibility that those who named the condition might have been unfamiliar with the details of Shakespeare's play. By definition, a delusion is a fixed belief held in spite of evidence to the contrary – one that is resistant to all reason. The unfortunate Othello, as a result of the machinations of Iago, had every reason to believe that Desdemona was being unfaithful to him with Cassio. So he was not suffering from a delusion. It may be argued that to kill a woman like Desdemona out of jealousy supported only by circumstantial evidence suggests a pathological state – that Othello was driven mad by jealousy. But this is a weak argument. The play was set in a time when husbands assumed, as of right, extreme proprietary claims over their wives, and when the double standard operated without question. Othello was certainly driven mad with jealousy, but only in the metaphorical sense.

True cases of the Othello syndrome are different and are characterized by the absence of real grounds for the jealousy. It is, for instance, usual, for the affected person to be unable to name or even identify the person suspected of conducting an affair with the spouse or partner. The conviction that such an affair is going on is purely delusory. The Othello syndrome is common and may be the only indication of mental abnormality or it may be part of an established psychotic condition. When it is, it tends to be the most prominent feature of the condition.

The clinical features of the syndrome have been well described in the medical literature. Affected people are often naturally jealous and will have given indications of this from the earliest stage of the association. They are also often socially less adept than the spouse and may be of a significantly lower educational level. They are usually quiet, reserved, less gregarious and with a narrower range of interests than the spouse. Their sexual life is usually important to them and it is notable that, as the syndrome develops, their sexual demands will often increase.

The onset of the syndrome will often appear to be sudden, but this may only be because the affected person has been secretly harbouring suspicions for months. What is usually sudden is the accusation of infidelity. This will commonly take the spouse or partner completely by surprise, but the reaction will do nothing to allay suspicion. There now starts a very bad time for the innocent partner whose behaviour and demeanour will be subjected to a detailed scrutiny. Clothing is regularly inspected for incriminating stains, foreign hairs or other 'evidence'. Underclothing is checked for semen stains or tears; shirts for lipstick marks. The movements are closely monitored; a spouse may be shadowed to establish where he or she is going. The most innocent remarks or circumstances are elaborately misinterpreted, and complex theories are developed, to provide unequivocal 'proof' of guilt.

The situation of the innocent party is indeed pitiable. Nothing that he or she can say or do will persuade the affected person that there is no foundation for the allegations. The association of determined accusations of infidelity together with the increased demand for sex may be particularly distressing, especially to a woman who believed that sex should be a manifestation of affection and trust rather than simply a source of erotic pleasure. There is constant interrogation, constant lengthy arguments on the same tedious subject, often furious quarrels and sometimes violence. The condition has, in many cases, led to violent crime, including killing. Short of that, the situation commonly leads to separation or divorce.

There is a strange irony in many cases of the Othello syndrome in that the affected person will often seem to have an underlying awareness that his or her accusations are false. This leads the accuser to avoid following up obvious lines of enquiry which would demonstrate that the allegations are untrue. An affected man might accuse his wife of having made a booking at a hotel to spend a weekend with her alleged lover. If the wife insists that they go to the hotel to confirm that this is not so, the husband will immediately change the subject, usually to take up another line of accusation.

This feature of the condition, taken in conjunction with Descartes' definition, throws light on its origins. It seems from psychiatric studies of cases that the essential feature of people with this disorder is an underlying, only partly conscious, awareness of inferiority or inadequacy – a feeling invariably associated with hypersensitivity, insecurity and anxiety. As usual, this state of affairs is largely repressed and manifests itself by behaviour that suggests egocentric superiority. There are all sorts of reasons for the underlying sense of inadequacy, the commonest being actual inadequacy in relation to the current social or marital context. We are all of us, of course, inadequate in relation to something or somebody; those of us who are fortunate enough to find a context in which we are just a little more than averagely adequate will be spared the unhappy consequences.

This is not to suggest, of course, that the Othello syndrome is the inevitable outcome of awareness of inadequacy; it occurs, or may occur, when the inadequacy, or sense of it, is specifically in relation to a spouse or partner and has some kind of sexual, social or relational basis. Often the problem arises from a previous history of sexual infidelity on the part of the person with the Othello syndrome. Sometimes there is a barely acknowledged or repressed homosexuality or a conviction of inadequacy in the sexual performance. Above all, the feeling of inadequacy may stem from a repressed failure of love for the spouse or partner. As Descartes said,

> If he had a true love for her, he would have no inclination to distrust her... and he would not fear to lose this good did he not judge himself to be unworthy of it.

Universal self-delusion: defence mechanisms

The exhortation, 'Know thyself!' goes back a long way. Diogenes Laërtius attributes it to Thales (c.624–545 BC), one of the seven wise men of Greece. Antisthenes, in his *Succession of the Philosophers*, says it was first spoken by Phemonoë. Others attribute it to Chilon or Solon (638–559 BC). Certainly it was the first of the three maxims inscribed on the wall of the Temple of Apollo at Delphi. Since then, many other philosophers and poets have, through the ages, emphasized the importance of self-knowledge. As usual, Pope put it rather well:

> Know then thyself, presume not God to scan;
> The proper study of mankind is man.

Exhortations are all very well but they are not always easy to comply with. One reason for the difficulty in taking the advice of Thales (or whoever) is the existence of defence mechanisms. These are the many mental ploys by which we are enabled to live reasonably comfortably with our own inadequacies, dishonesties, stupidities and other short-comings. They are also used as techniques for coping with the stress and anxiety caused by the conflict between our spontaneous desires and socially approved behaviour and beliefs. Some are consciously applied; most just swing into action without our realizing it.

An awareness of defence mechanisms, whether as formal entities or not, may or may not allow us to better ourselves. But they will certainly help us to win friends and influence people by recognizing – and, when appropriate, respecting – their defence mechanisms. Many successful people who have never heard of defence mechanisms are clearly aware of these psychological processes and act accordingly.

Failure to recognize them can lead people to destroy relationships by attacking the defence mechanisms of their associates.

Nowadays, American psychologists sometimes call these 'coping strategies' and it is hard to decide which is the better title. Each reflects one aspect of the matter. What is beyond doubt is that they are important and should be as widely understood as possible, by writers as well as by everyone else. The justification for including an account of them in this book is that even a cursory glance at them will show us that extraordinary states of mind are far commoner than most of us appreciate. These mechanisms vary from person to person but some of them are present in all of us. To some extent they determine our characters and tend to become a fixed feature of our personality.

Although we all employ defence mechanisms and enjoy, thereby, the ability to live more comfortably with ourselves, it would never do to imply that they should all be cultivated or encouraged. One must be discriminating. Some are valuable; most are undesirable, although useful to recognize in others. Robbie Burns was, in a way, restating the exhortation of Thales (or whoever) when he said, in *To a Louse* (1786),

> Oh wad some Pow'r the giftie gie us
> To see oursels as ithers see us!

Unfortunately, the functioning of the self-protective defence mechanisms make this almost impossible, and this is a pity. But all is not lost. The ability to *recognize* defence mechanisms can, at least in theory, help us to do this. It is not easy, but one thing is certain: it will be a lot harder if we do not even begin to know what the defence mechanisms are. So here is a gleam of insight into a very important matter. With a bit of luck it may throw a little light into some of the darker recesses of your mind and mine, and perhaps even enable us to dispense with some of these less desirable reactions. Perhaps it may, to that extent, make us, if not better people, at least nicer to know. This is a complex subject, really calling for a book in its own right, and only the general outlines can be sketched in here. Readers who object to being attacked in this way need read no further in this short chapter.

The states of mind of people heavily protected by a repertoire of defence mechanisms manifest a variety of absurdities. These affect their behaviour in such a way as often to provoke a pejorative reaction in others. Such people may, for instance, believe themselves to be honourable, pure in their motives, kind, considerate, generous and broad-minded, when everyone who knows them is aware that they are deceitful, selfish, grasping and prejudiced. They may see themselves as highly logical and rational when, in fact, most of their friends are astounded by the irrationality of their beliefs and opinions. They may genuinely believe themselves to be inferior in some respect, while actually outperforming all the competition. They may be unaware of faults in themselves for which they are constantly, and often unjustly, criticizing others. Most of us will recognize some of these patterns in people we know, but by the operation of our own defence mechanisms will probably be unaware of any of them in ourselves.

The list of mechanisms is long and the terminology sometimes variable, but usually includes such categories as *repression* (unconscious exclusion from consciousness of threatening desires and feelings); *suppression* (conscious and deliberate attempts to forget something painful); *denial* (refusal to recognize the existence of emotionally threatening external factors); *identification* (strong tendency to mirror the opinions, habits and general behaviour of the group); *fantasy* (constant indulgence in wish-fulfilment day-dreaming); *displacement* (redirection of emotional energy, especially hostility, from one person, situation or object to another deemed to be a safer target); *compensation* (making exceptional efforts to achieve success in an area of real or imagined inferiority); *sublimation* (rechannelling of sexual energy into an important non-sexual and socially acceptable activity); *rationalization* (explaining away motives for unacceptable personal actions as being logically justified or the result of external circumstances); *intellectualization* (repressing the emotional content of a situation and restating it as a coldly abstract analysis); *projection* (transferring one's own unacceptable qualities and desires to others); *displacement* (transfer, to a second person, of unacceptable feelings about a first); and *reaction* (exaggerating tendencies and impulses which oppose those perceived within oneself).

Displacement is a particularly dangerous defence mechanism. It can take various forms, depending on the impulse concerned. If this is a feeling of aggression or hostility, displacement is called scape-goating. A critical, unreasonable and job-threatening boss makes an employee very angry but, since it would be disastrous to take this out on him or even to allow this to show, the worker goes to a sports club and takes out his anger on a squash ball. More seriously, he might go home and take it out on his wife or children.

Worse still is the kind of systematized or organized displacement that results in anger being vented on minority groups. To a liberal person, southern American, pcor-white, economic hatreds that are displaced into lynching of black people, or the anger of unsuccessful small business people that is displaced into antisemitism, seem to manifest a truly extraordinary state of mind. But this is the way people are. Such aggressive emotion must be displaced or it will turn inwards and cause depression or psychosomatic illness. It is a moot point whether it is likely to be easier to eradicate this kind of defence mechanism or to eradicate the causes of the aggression. Education, which can attack both, would seem to be the only plausible solution.

Although defence mechanisms, in others, often seem illogical, immature, ridiculous and damaging, their importance to the individual should be remembered and recognized. Much marital and other interpersonal strife arises from unwise attempts to point out and demolish each other's protective defence mechanisms. In this, one must go very gently. At the same time the quest for maturity and equality in a relationship demands that there should be insight on both sides. One strategy may be to identify, with preternatural honesty, a harmful defence mechanism in oneself; bring this out into the open, express and explain it to the other person; and wait, hopefully, for the penny to drop.

The now well-informed gentle reader is invited to identify the defence mechanisms currently being employed by the author.

The mind of a twin: mental identity

There are two kinds of twins. The commonest type (dizygotic or fraternal twins) occurs when two different eggs are fertilized by two different sperms. The only unusual thing that twins of this kind have in common is that they are born at about the same time. They can, of course, be of different sex or of the same sex, and, biologically, they are no more like each other than any pair of siblings.

The kind of twins we are interested in here is the less common type, identical twins. These occur when one egg is fertilized by one sperm and then starts to divide in the usual way. But after the first division, the two resulting cells, instead of sticking together, move apart and then continue to divide to form two different embryos. Normally, when these cells divide, they remain in contact and soon form a mass, from which the early embryo develops. In this case, two such masses are formed and each develops into its own embryo, then fetus, then baby.

The fascinating thing about these monovular, or monozygotic, twins is that, biologically, they start out identical in every way. They have exactly the same genes. Because of this, identical twins are of the greatest interest to medical and genetic researchers interested in discovering the relative importance of heredity (nature) and environment (nurture) in determining human characteristics. Perhaps most interesting of all are those pairs of identical twins who have been separated at or soon after birth so that they have had different environmental influences acting on them. The study of identical twins has made a great contribution to the 'nature or nurture' debate and we now have excellent grounds for the current views on this perennial argument.

Studies have been made of children from deprived families who were adopted by well-to-do families soon after birth. When the adopted children were compared with their siblings who had not been adopted, they showed consistently higher IQ scores. The adopted children had an average IQ of 111; their non-adopted siblings an average of 95. This is an example of nurture winning over nature. It is recognized that variations of this kind might be due to factors such as differences in nutrition, rather than simply to educational differences, because we know that young children who are severely nutritionally deprived often suffer permanent loss of intellectual ability. The surprising thing about the result of these studies, however, is the extent to which nature prevails over nurture.

It is hardly necessary to refer to the physical similarity of identical twins. They look alike, are the same sex and size, have the same colouring of hair and skin, weigh the same, speak in similar accents and intonation, and are of equal strength. They will develop toothache at the same time and sometimes in the same tooth; they often develop the same diseases and may do so almost simultaneously. They will often die from the same diseases and commonly die at around the same time. This would not occasion much surprise in the case of infectious diseases, but twins will commonly develop degenerative or malignant conditions unconnected with bacteria or viruses. Darwin quotes a case of twin brothers, one living in Paris and one in Vienna. The Paris brother developed a recurring internal inflammatory eye disease now called uveitis but then known simply as 'ophthalmia'. He saw his doctor and said: 'My brother in Vienna will be having an ophthalmia like mine.' The doctor was sceptical but, a few days later, the patient produced a letter from his brother that said: 'My ophthalmia has recurred. You must be having yours.'

It is quite common for parents to have difficulty in distinguishing twins and occasionally one is punished for the other's misdeeds. There are instances of twins having been accidentally changed in the bath so that all certainty as to their nominal identity is lost. Twins will sometimes look in a full-length mirror and speak to the image they take to be the other twin. These problems lessen as the twins grow, become conscious of their identity and acquire minor distinguishing characteristics. Even so, there is a recorded case of a painter who was working on separate portraits of two twins and who, after a time, ceased to be able to tell to which child each portrait belonged.

Because of their genetic identity, it is to be expected that identical twins should have great mental similarities. This is borne out in experience. Numerous accounts exist of twins whose tastes, interests, beliefs and preoccupations were so similar as to suggest that they were, in a sense, one person. Twins will suffer the same mental and physical disorders with onset usually at the same time. Even if separated early, they will marry very similar partners, live in similar kinds of houses, share fundamental beliefs, wear the same kind of clothes, seek the same kind of work, play the same sports and join the same political party.

Twins will commonly both fall in love with the same person and this can cause problems. When identical twins marry identical twins the spouses are sometimes unable to make clear distinctions. Fortunately, identical twins are usually deeply devoted to one another and can usually resolve such problems amicably. Identical twins suffer, or even pine severely, if forcibly separated. This affinity is recognized by the British Army which will usually recruit identical twins into the same unit so that they can serve together, and will avoid, if possible, posting them apart.

Some of the accounts of the extraordinary mental similarities of identical twins are remarkable. In one instance a pair of identical male twins were separated at birth when both were adopted into separate American families. At school both hated spelling but were quite good at mathematics. They both joined the police and both reached the same rank, Deputy Sheriff. Both drove Chevrolet cars. Both had dogs which they called Toy. They both married women called Linda and were divorced. Both married again – to women who were both called Betty.

Identical twins seem to share thought processes. They will often make the same spontaneous remark simultaneously. One will start a sentence and the other will finish it. They will begin singing the same song together. There is a record of a twin who was in Scotland observing some fine champagne glasses, deciding that his twin brother would like them, and buying them. Meantime his brother, who was in England, came across the identical glasses there and bought them as a surprise for the other twin.

This similarity of temperament and personality extends also to mental disorders. There is a record of a case of twin brothers treated in a mental hospital. These men were morose and secretive and were kept completely apart. There was no communication between them. In spite of this, they had identical delusions of persecution by the same enemies who were determined to destroy them by the same means. Both brothers had auditory hallucinations. From time to time, at intervals of several months and with exact synchronicity, the two brothers would undergo a striking change in their mental state. They would rouse themselves, make the same complaints, demand to see the doctor and would insist on being released from confinement.

The only conclusion that can be drawn from all this evidence is that people with identical brains have minds that come close to being identical. The mind depends on brain function, and the structure of the brain is determined by the proteins it contains, which in turn is determined by the DNA. Identical twins have identical DNA. However, from the time of the development of the brain and the sense organs, the brain is also subject to input that is *not* determined by DNA. We know that this environmental input has a major effect on brain development and consequently on the development of the mind. But the evidence of identical twins shows us that even when they are exposed to what seem to be widely different environmental influences, they often retain remarkably similar minds. This may be partly because that initial similarity causes such twins to seek similar environments. It is even possible that their neurological similarity causes them to modulate or interpret incoming information in such a way as to make diverse inputs more similar. Whatever the reason for similar minds, it can have no basic cause other than similar DNA.

Of social isolation: autism

Autism is completely different from mental deficiency. It is a distressing state of mind in which the affected person is denied one of the most fundamental freedoms of human beings – the freedom to associate socially with others. It affects boys about four times as often as girls, and one of its principal features is the inability of the autistic person to form normal social relationships. As a result there appears to be a withdrawal from reality and often the development of a secret fantasy life. Autistic children do not communicate normally and have an intense resistance to environmental change. They have difficulty in expressing themselves in normal language and may repeat the same sequence of words endlessly. They appear to have severe difficulty in grasping the concept of human relationships and can form little or no idea of what is going on in other people's minds. This latter difficulty seems to be the essence of the problem.

Infantile autism can usually be recognized in the first year of life. The child wishes to be alone, will reject cuddling and will avoid eye contact. There are repetitive, ritual acts, abnormal attachment to familiar objects, and speech problems which may amount to total muteness. At best, the language will be strange and difficult to follow. Intellectual performance varies considerably but it is rarely possible to carry out reliable or meaningful intelligence tests. In most cases, full neurological examination fails to reveal any organic abnormality. Autism can, however, be a feature of several serious neurological disorders. Contrary to what was once believed, autism is now known to be a genetic disorder. There is evidence that it is connected with the X chromosome, one of the sex chromosomes.

The cause or causes of autism remain unknown. At one time it was believed that autism was caused by lack of the expression of parental affection. Coldness and aloofness by mother and father was blamed. There was no real evidence for this theory and it has now been abandoned. Most of the current ideas on causation relate to the knowledge that a number of genetic neurological disorders show at least some of the features of autism. However, the most detailed studies, by brain scanning, of autistic people have failed to show any visible abnormalities in brain structure. The experts believe that there is something wrong with the brain, but at a cellular level. Although agreeing that there is a genetic element in autism, they do not know much about the cause.

Autism is a life-long problem: it cannot be cured. Although children who show disturbed behaviour tend to improve spontaneously between the ages of 6 and 10, there may be some worsening of autism again in adolescence and early adult life. Most autistic people settle to a fairly reasonable state by middle age.

Autistic people of any age, whose intelligence is not affected, can, with proper treatment, learn to live an almost normal life. In some cases their achievement can be remarkable. One of the most extraordinary and inspiring cases of success in living in spite of autism is that of the American academic Dr Temple Grandin, who not only achieved a university degree but also took her Ph.D. at the University of Illinois in Urbana, and became a Professor of Animal Science at Colorado State University. Dr Grandin's account of her own experiences and difficulties form a uniquely valuable and important contribution to the understanding of the condition of high-functioning autism. Her description demonstrates the profound difficulty autistic people have in coping with abstract thought. Her family background is interesting, and it is clear that she has inherited genes both for high intelligence and for mechanical or visual skills. One grandfather was co-inventor of the autopilot for aircraft. Her brother has considerable mechanical skills and can build anything, but had problems with calculus when studying for a higher degree in engineering. He ended up as a successful banker. A younger sister is a sculptress and another sister is a brilliant house decorator.

For the autistic person, thinking has to be visual or acoustic, and every concept has to be represented in some form of concrete imagery or heard sound. To consider the idea of meeting and relating to a person, for instance, Dr Grandin has to use the symbolic image of the opening of a sliding glass door. There is a further symbolism in this, in that she knows that she must approach a potential relationship with care. A too-hasty approach might shatter the glass of the door.

Dr Grandin's visual thinking is of a high order and provides her with some compensatory advantages over most other people. She is able, for instance, to see at once how a piece of physical equipment can be put together and she can immediately recognize faults in the design of existing equipment. In any context in which a problem can be solved by visual thinking rather than by abstract thought, she will do well. She is particularly good at the practical design of steel and concrete animal stockyards and animal handling equipment – a subject in which she is an acknowledged expert.

Dr Grandin refers repeatedly to 'playing a video' as her alternative for abstract thinking. These 'videos' may take some time to 'record' but once this is done, she can play them back at will as required. By playing back a 'video' of a site in which equipment is to be installed, she can then produce a detailed drawing. She has developed many visualizing strategies for remembering concepts that are difficult for her. To remember that a dimension is in feet, for instance, she will visualize a row of shoes end to end. To remember a triangle, she visualized a three-cornered pennant carried by a rider on a horse.

To a person of Dr Grandin's academic status, reading is, of course, essential. She believed she would never have learned to read had it not been for her mother. There was no question of her memorizing large numbers of words – that would involve the use of abstractions that were not available to her. So she learned by a purely phonetic method. Once she was able to pronounce a printed or written word and hear the sound of it she could work out what it meant. She describes how her mother would read stories to her and then stop at an exciting point so as to encourage her to go on sounding the words of the next sentence on her own. Initially, she could only read by reading aloud. Even today she has to sound some words silently. Visualization of images evoked by recognized words is also an essential part of reading. She also still finds it helpful to express her thoughts aloud. This makes them more concrete for her.

Dr Grandin was lucky in the people who initially looked after her. As a small child she showed all the typical features of autism. At the time, little or nothing was known of the subject but, instead of being sent to an institution for the mentally retarded, her neurologist recommended speech therapy. This proved vital. She also had a governess from the age of three who ensured that she engaged in a structured schedule of physical activities. She was recognized as being gifted, but there were many problems to be overcome, especially during puberty and adolescence. Fortunately, she had a sensitive science teacher who recognized that her fixation on physical objects could be channelled into an interest in science.

Temple Grandin made the best use possible of her faculties and did so in an imaginative manner. Because she was intensely aware of her aversion to being held and hugged by a human being, but was equally aware that she longed for the stimulus of deep pressure and should fight this seemingly anti-human tendency, she invented a 'squeeze machine'. This was a device lined with foam rubber which could provide her with comforting pressure to large areas of her body. Her school psychologist wanted to deprive her of this, but her science teacher recognized its value and used the idea of the machine to encourage her to research the scientific journals. He suggested that she should try to find out why the machine had a calming effect on her and greatly reduced her aggressive tendencies. Squeeze machines are in now used in autism clinics. They can help to induce a measure of empathy with others and the ability to accept normal human contact.

Dr Grandin is anxious to share her experience with other autistic people so that they can benefit from it. She has much to tell them. Among many other things, she makes the important point that, although tests of her hearing acuity suggest that this is normal, she is unable to make normal discrimination between different incoming sounds. This prevents her from being able to select what she wants to hear – an important property of normal hearing. To her it is as if her ears were 'amplifiers turned up to full volume'. This phenomenon, which is common to a great many autistic people, has serious effects. She can either put up with a devastating volume of incoming sound or she can ignore it all and behave as if she were deaf. This is what she did as a child. She found that she could shut out the horrible noise by engaging in the typical rhythmical repetitive behaviour of the autistic child. Young children are, of course, incapable of describing their subjective experiences. They just suffer and do the best they can to ameliorate their situation. It must be understood that autistic children are not deaf but are trying to protect themselves against intolerable noise. This is one of the main reasons why they do not benefit from normal schooling.

It is thus of enormous value when a person like Temple Grandin is able to describe her experiences at an academic level. She has written books and hundreds of professional papers on the subject and has released into the Internet a great deal of information, which is available to any concerned person.

I have been here before: *déjà vu*

The extraordinary, if brief, state of mind known as *déjà vu* has been experienced by millions. Indeed, it seems to be almost universal. There is no reason to suppose, just because the title is French (for 'already seen') and the phenomenon is sometimes referred to as *fausse reconnaissance* ('false recognition'), that *déjà vu* is commoner in France than any other country. The explanation is that one of the first to investigate the matter thoroughly was the French psychologist and pupil of Charcot, Pierre Janet (1859–1947). Although it is not widely recognized, Janet was a distinguished thinker and scholar whose contribution to the establishment of psychology as a formal discipline ranks with those of William James and Wilhelm Wundt. Janet's work on *déjà vu* was only one tiny facet of his extensive labours in psychology and philosophy.

Another French connection is that of the novelist Marcel Proust, who used the idea as the basis, or starting point, for one of the longest and most reader-challenging novels ever written – *À la recherche du temps perdu* (The remembrance of things past). Perhaps unsurprisingly, writers in general have been fascinated by the *déjà vu* phenomenon, and there are references to it in many literary works, including those of Leo Tolstoy, Charles Dickens, Percy Bysshe Shelley and Nathaniel Hawthorne.

Déjà vu is the sudden powerful, but mistaken, conviction that something that had happened before is happening again. There is a compelling sense of familiarity, usually lasting for only a few seconds, and a persuasion, almost always disappointed, that one knows in detail what is round the next corner or what is going to happen in the next few seconds. The phenomenon is much commoner in young people than in old and may be related to periods of stress, tiredness or heightened awareness from any cause. *Déjà vu* may be purely visual, purely auditory or olfactory (pertaining to smell) or even, as in Proust's case, purely gustatory (pertaining to taste) (Proust's memories were evoked by the taste of a *madeleine*, a kind of cake) but more commonly it affects all aspects of experience including everything that the affected person is doing. In most cases, as experienced by healthy people, it passes off within a few seconds or minutes.

Proust's extended *déjà vu*, however justified as an effective literary device, does not occur in real life. (Indeed, *pace* the critics, the celebrated experience of the memory of the *madeleine* dipped in tea was not really a case of *déjà vu* since it actually *had* happened before). But in certain neurological disorders, such as some forms of epilepsy, *déjà vu* may continue for hours or days. In this extraordinary state, the victim necessarily has major problems in dealing with reality and it is not surprising if the behaviour gives rise to the assumption that he or she is suffering from some kind of delusional state. Contemplating such a case, one is compelled to ponder on the fragility of our experiential link with the physical world and to pose the question 'What is reality?'

Since, by definition, *déjà vu* does not relate to actual repeat experiences or memories, the interest lies in why the conviction of repetition occurs and why it is so strong. One possibility is that it is the recall of some repressed dream or fantasy. Few people who have experienced *déjà vu* are much impressed by this explanation. Neither was Pierre Janet. Janet saw at once that the essence of the problem of *déjà vu* was not 'affirmation of the past' but 'negation of the present'. The recall is so detailed and circumstantial, and the impossibility of the event actually having happened before so common, as to dismiss this as a non-starter. Even so, this 'explanation' has been widely accepted by the psychoanalytic school, anxious to find support for their now largely discredited theories. Psychoanalysts will point out that *déjà vu*, or something very like it, can be induced by hypnosis. A person in a hypnotic state is asked to study a photo of a particular, previously unknown scene and then is instructed to forget it. Later, on being shown the scene, or other pictures of it, *déjà vu* occurs with its characteristic sense of strong familiarity.

The occurrence of *déjà vu* in epilepsy has led some psychologists to suggest that it invariably implies some neurological abnormality and is in the nature of a hallucination. This view is presumably adhered to by psychologists who have never experienced *déjà vu* and opposed by those who have. Scientific opinion or bias is commonly based on no stronger grounds than that. A more physiological explanation is that the phenomenon results from a brief neurological short-circuit, with data from the current observation reaching the memory store before they reach consciousness. The conscious experience of such a memory would be very strong, as it is so recent. This suggestion is supported by the fact that *déjà vu* is a very common symptom of disorders resulting from brain damage, such as temporal lobe epilepsy.

Most modern cognitive psychologists agree that the process of remembering is not simply a matter of recall of a fixed, established previous event, but is a rapid reconstruction or synthesis, from stored memory components. Each successive recall of the event is merely the recall of the last reconstruction and this process necessarily involves elaborations, errors and omissions. The sense of recognition involves achieving a good match between the present experience and the latest version of our stored data. The better the match, the stronger will be the sense of familiarity. Also, the more often recollections have been recollected the greater will be the error content and the poorer the match between the current recollection and any new presentation of the original data. Most of us have had experience of how, over time, we falsify our memory of early experience.

If, now, we have some new experience which conforms closely, not to a previous experience, but to the totality of the errors or distortions caused by these memories of memories, the sense of familiarity will be very strong. If we know that we could not previously have had the experience, we will feel bewildered because of the logical anomaly. This experience may be what we mean when we refer to *déjà vu*. Cognitive psychology is currently the favoured branch of psychology and is widely supported by scientific psychologists. But this explanation, although highly plausible, is unlikely to put an end to the controversy. Psychologists are still arguing about *déjà vu* and will continue to do so until much more is known about the mechanisms of the brain.

A much rarer phenomenon which, at first sight, appears to be a variant of *déjà vu*, is the antithetical situation known as *jamais vu* ('never seen'). This features an equally strong but delusory sense of unfamiliarity with an event which has, in fact, been experienced before and should be perfectly familiar. It is not clear whether this is related in any way to *déjà vu*.

Compromising with unreason:
mass delusional insanity

There is much to be said for the absurd, in certain contexts. In literature it is often highly amusing and creative. Whole generations have been entertained and stimulated by the zany absurdities of the Marx brothers on film, the Goons on radio or 'Monty Python' on television. Surrealism, in any of the arts — with emphasis, as André Breton saw it, on 'tapping the unconscious as the wellspring of the imagination' — has produced powerful and moving works. Perception of absurdity can also be used to make effective points in logic by the powerful technique of *reductio ad absurdum* (see **The mind of the mathematician**).

But there are realms in which it is important to make a clear demarcation between absurdity and reason. This line has never been very clearly marked and it is ironical that, today, when we are better equipped than ever before to see where it should be drawn, the forces of unreason and superstition are as active as ever. In this era of alternative medicine and of claims to intellectual respectability by the proponents of the paranormal, some guidelines are badly needed as to the difference between an open mind and sheer gullibility. What is wanted is some indication of the limits of the absurd. When people claiming to be scientific suggest that there may be something in astrology; that one should not reject out of hand the propositions that saying certain things to plants can enhance their growth; or that tape recorders can pick up the voices of the dead; when the *Lancet* can announce a controlled trial of the treatment of cataract by faith; when the US Army Missile Research and Development Department spends many thousands of dollars researching into Kirlian photography of the human aura; when the US and French governments sponsor investigation into UFOs (see **Alien abduction**); when an anthropologist of the status of Margaret Mead can express belief in the occult; then it is clear that even the most intelligent of human minds can compromise with unreason.

The range of beliefs held today, when there is ready access to all the information necessary to demonstrate their absurdity, almost defies credibility. It includes, listed in no significant order, belief in: witches, ghosts and haunting; fortune-telling; bodily levitation; magic (both black and white); the prophecies of Nostradamus; Old Moore's Almanac; reflexology; psychokinesis; spoon bending without the application of physical force; extrasensory perception; diagnosing disease by examining the irides of the eyes (iridiology); Kirlian photography; the existence of the human aura; dreams as portents of the future; polarity theory; spiritualism; radionics; ectoplasm; water divining; the numerology of the Book of Revelations; the determination of personality by sign of the Zodiac; omens; palmistry; communication with the dead; the acupuncture meridians; amulets and other good-luck charms; evil spirits (see **A mind possessed**); aromatherapy; 'The X Files'; the determination of character from facial features; psychic healing; clairvoyance; diagnosis by pendulum; precognition; the Bermuda triangle; hypnotic regression to an earlier life; the arrival of flying saucers from other worlds (see **Alien abduction**); the extraterrestrial origin of corn circles; and there being a reasonable possibility of winning the jackpot in the National Lottery. This is merely a random selection. The list is huge.

Several attempts have been made to provide a demarcation of absurdity, and various sets of criteria for pseudoscience have been proposed. Unfortunately, none of these is quite satisfactory, not even Karl Popper's shrewd observation that a central feature of a pseudoscientific hypothesis is that it cannot be disproved, while a scientific one can. Two possible guidelines, however, are to consider the inherent plausibility of the suggestion in the light of what is known, and to consider the relevance of the status of the claimant.

To give an example: propositions, such as those which form the basis of homoeopathy, must be viewed in the context of known fact. For anyone who knows that the pharmacological effect of a drug decreases with decreasing dosage and that repeated dilution soon leads to the absence of a single molecule of the original drug, is not only entitled, it is logical to take a sternly sceptical attitude to homoeopathy (see **The celebrated Hahnemann delusion**), and such scepticism should not be in any way influenced by the wide popular approval of homoeopathy.

The status of the claimant is certainly important, but only to the extent that it is relevant to the proposition. If a noted and distinguished research pathologist makes an astonishing statement about a possibility of curing a certain form of cancer, we should pay close attention and give his or her statement due credibility. But if a noble member of the House of Lords with a background of Sanskrit studies claims to have proved that cancer can be cured by drinking one's own urine, we should not be influenced in our judgment of his proposition by the fact that he was the son of a Peer.

It is not too difficult to account for popular superstition. There is a deep longing in humans for intimations of something more emotionally and spiritually satisfying than the purely material. This is clearly shown by the remarkable success of books, however ridiculous, that purport to satisfy this longing. The sale of books that promise miracles of any kind or that claim to provide evidence of miracles, is many times greater than the sale of books that provide the cold, boring but demonstrable facts of science. The book *The Bermuda Triangle* sold five million copies. Books on the Shroud of Turin have attracted enormous public interest. A more recent book making the ridiculous claim that the Bible contains unique hidden messages, which can be revealed only by computer analysis, has also sold well.

Because of this longing for magic, logic is distorted. Phenomena that seem to support the supernatural or the paranormal (which is the same thing) are noted, recorded and remembered, while those that tend to disprove it are ignored, forgotten or actively rejected. The *post hoc, ergo propter hoc* fallacy (because B follows A, A must be the cause of B) reigns supreme, and provides satisfactory 'explanations' for many people, even for professional logicians.

A considerable percentage of people have had strange or 'mystical' experiences of one kind or another that they cannot explain in rational terms. Like nearly everyone else, these people are not particularly critical about the evidence for anything. They have been deeply impressed by what happened to them and they are already halfway to being persuaded of the truth of the paranormal. Plenty of help is available to them. Anecdotal evidence abounds – mostly derived from selective memory – but persuasive nevertheless. Coincidence also plays a large part in supporting claims for the paranormal. When such coincidences occur – things like a vivid dream followed by the occurrence of the event depicted in the dream – they are always remembered and reported. There is, of course, no interest in the endless number of occasions in which coincidence does not operate.

The enormous output of books purporting to provide evidence for the supernatural, and their preponderance over books that debunk the supernatural, is good enough for most people. The fact that there is no conclusive, or even strongly suggestive, evidence for the supernatural would surprise most people, but is true. People are also not particularly interested in the reason why so many books of this kind appear. The publishers of these often absurd books are no less honest than anyone else. Very few of them are driven by a desire to propagate paranormal belief, and many of them must be aware that a lot of the stuff they publish is almost certainly nonsensical. But what publishers are driven by is a realistic and far from disinterested desire to sell as many books as possible so as to make a profit. This means that they must publish books that a large number of people are likely to buy.

David Hume, the hard-headed Scottish philosopher and rational sceptic wrote more sound common sense than most (see **Of superstition**). Were he alive today, he would probably be even more vociferous in his condemnation of popular balderdash than he was of that of his own generation. We need more people like David Hume in this age when the forces of superstition are so strong that protesting writers are either ignored or intimidated. Those who care about the attack on Truth seem now to be in the minority.

Tarantella: the dancing mania

The name 'tarantula' is given to any one of the various large hairy spiders of the family Theraphosidae found mainly in tropical America. It is also used for a quite unrelated species, the large hairy spider *Lycosa tarentula*, found in Southern Europe. There is plenty of historical evidence to show that the bite of the tarantula formerly caused a disorder called tarantism or the dancing mania. To this day, we still have a furious dance, the tarantella, which is often said to represent the behaviour of a person poisoned by a bite from a tarantula spider. This is a common error. The tarantella was in fact developed as *treatment* for the bite of the tarantula. By engaging in this energetic dance, a person bitten by a tarantula could, it was believed, be saved from death. Down in the heel of Italy is the seaport of Taranto and in the rough country around Taranto plenty of tarantulas were to be found. This may well be where the disorder started.

Samuel Pepys, in his diary, records that a traveller told him that itinerant fiddlers in Italy were kept busy providing tarantella accompaniments for people bitten by spiders so as to ensure that they danced furiously enough. In the seventeenth century, epidemics of this terrible 'disease' were very common. Some of these involved large numbers of people. It was sad when old and sick people were bitten because these were often driven to exhaustion by the need to dance the tarantella. In many cases, such debilitated people were unable to dance energetically enough. Many of them died. The early epidemics were remarkable in that the condition, initially acquired by a person from a spider bite, appeared to be contagious to others. The disease became less common with the passage of time and the last cases were seen in the early part of the twentieth century.

The tarantella can, of course, be danced to a great variety of *presto* tunes, but some were more popular than others and thought to be more efficacious. In a book called *La Théologie des insectes*, the Italian melody *L'air turchesca* was especially recommended. The really remarkable thing about this 'disease' – and the justification for its inclusion in this book – is that the bite of the tarantula spider is completely harmless! This is an example of mass hysteria, and tarantism it is by no means the only form of dancing mania. It has been given various names, including epidemic chorea, St Guy's dance, orchestromania, St Anthony's dance, choromania, dance of St Modesti and *tanzplage*.

Reports of the 'dancing mania' go back a long way. Its first appearance, in epidemic form, is said to have been about 1374, but some authorities state that it was not new even then. The records show that men and women would assemble and, impelled by fear of death, would dance in a wild and abandoned manner until exhausted. Cemeteries were popular for the dances and these often became positively Bacchantic. The condition was not confined to Italy. Tarantism also occurred in France, Germany, Holland and England. Similar epidemics occurred in Abyssinia (now Ethiopia) and Arabia. A notable account of this phenomenon is to be found in a book by J. F. C. Hecker called *The Epidemics of the Middle Ages*, published in London in English translation in 1859.

One notable epidemic in Metz, which was then a free imperial city, is said to have involved 1100 dancers and a complete cessation of all normal activity in the town. To quote one source:

> Peasants left their plows, mechanics their shops, servants their masters, children their homes; and beggars and idle vagabonds, who understood how to imitate the convulsions, roved from place to place inducing all sorts of crime and vice among the afflicted.

In the epidemic in Strasbourg in 1418 the dancing mania was, for the first time, given the title of St Vitus' dance. Burton refers to the English epidemics in his *Anatomy of Melancholy*, describing the phenomenon as 'chorus Sancti Viti' – communal St Vitus' dance. His account, in the first volume of the *Anatomy*, is worth reading:

> the lascivious dance, Paracelsus calls it, because they that are taken from it can do nothing but dance till they be dead or cured. It is so called for that the parties so troubled were wont to go to St Vitus for help, and after they had danced there awhile, they were certainly freed. It is strange to hear how long they will dance and in what manner, over stools, forms, tables; even great-bellied women sometimes (and yet never hurt their children) will dance so long that they can stir neither hand nor foot, but seem to be quite dead. One in red clothes they cannot abide. Music above all things they love, and therefore magistrates will hire musicians to play to them, and some lusty sturdy companions to dance with them. Paracelsus in his book on madness brags how many several persons he hath cured of it. Felix Platerus reports of a women in Basil [Basle] whom he saw, that danced a whole month together. The Arabians call it a kind of palsy...

Incidentally, the self-styled Paracelsus, properly Theophrastus Bombastus von Hohenheim (1493–1541), called himself Paracelsus to indicate that he was a greater man than the famous Roman physician Celsus. He was, in fact, a complete phoney. But he was nothing if not imaginative. The disease, he asserted with his usual authority, was caused by an 'internal pruriency' in certain vessels which 'produced laughter and set the blood into commotion in consequence of an alteration in the vital spirits, thereby occasioning a propensity to dance'. This, of course, is nonsense. His remedies for the dancing mania were so severe that he probably killed more of his patients than did the mania. It is only fair to add, however, that Paracelsus also stated that some of the cases were due to sexual desire and to imagination. In this latter assertion he came very close to the truth.

The dancing mania was commonly associated with vivid hallucinations, often of the sight of evil spirits who were conjured up by the furious and shameless dancing. Some of the people affected reported that their legs were deep in a lake of blood and that it was this that caused them to leap so high. Another feature was swelling of the abdomen from gas in the intestinal or peritoneal cavity (tympanites). This caused the sufferers to compress or thump their abdomens to get relief. One report recounts how frantic dancing was egged on by an abbot standing high on a tombstone and vigorously 'conducting' the music. As a grand finale, this very agile churchman descended from his vantage point by performing a somersault — an act 'which aroused the onlookers to great enthusiasm.'

Mass hysteria is one of the striking aberrations of the human mind, and numerous instances, other than that of the dancing mania, have been described. It is common to this day and often occurs in relatively closed institutions such as schools, convents, prisons and monasteries. People in close groups of all kinds are very susceptible to suggestion, and each year several minor outbreaks occur in Britain. Most commonly, nowadays, these attacks occur in boarding schools for girls, usually at a time of general upset or stress, and they often originate in a particularly high-status individual such as a head prefect or a senior mistress. The symptoms experienced by this person, whatever they may be, are reported and then others are identically affected in an order that, interestingly, usually spreads down the 'status hierarchy'. Often these minor epidemics have features that make it clear that they could not have been caused by any normal infective agent.

Mass hysteria has its counterpart in mob action of various kinds. People in a crowd or mob behave differently from the way they behave when they are alone (see **The mind in a mob**), as attested by the behaviour of football hooligans. It is a long way from tarantulas to drunken football hooliganism, but the connection is clear. All these instances of mass hysteria reflect human frailty and remind us that we can never count on the supremacy of reason.

The mind in a mob: collective ignorance

Humans generally hate solitude, preferring to form groups. Loneliness, mental isolation and a deep sense of incompleteness are relieved only by human association or religious activity. People will therefore strive to be members of a group of some kind. One can hardly exaggerate the importance of the group to individuals or the strength of the influence it wields upon them. As the English surgeon, physiologist and philosopher Wilfred Trotter (1872–1939) says in his influential book *Instincts of the Herd in Peace and War* (1916).

> He is more sensitive to the voice of the herd than to any other influence. It can inhibit or stimulate his thought and conduct. It is the source of his moral codes, of the sanction of his ethics and philosophy. It can endow him with energy, courage and endurance, and can as easily take these away.

Trotter's next sentence illuminates how the influence of the group, although as strong as ever, has changed since his time, certainly in Britain. It goes:

> It can make him acquiesce in his own punishment and embrace his executioner, submit to poverty, bow to tyranny, and sink without complaint under starvation.

Once groups are formed some people will want to dominate. Most, fortunately, will be content to accept the leadership of another. In making this selection, however, the group is seldom notable for the reasonableness of its choice and is likely to be influenced by the skills of a demagogue, and by appearances, rather than by solid merit. This, of course, is one of the shortcomings of our democratic electoral system. The important point is that the judgment and intelligence of the group, as a whole, is less than that of the most intelligent and more than that of the least intelligent. This is one of many examples of the way in which the characteristics of the group differ from those of the individual members.

Human groups can be loose or cohesive depending on how greatly people value membership. In a highly cohesive group the members strongly subscribe to common opinions, are anxious to participate in the group's activities and want to help it to achieve its goals. Membership of such an group, whether a political party, a masonic lodge, a rotary group club, or a veterans' association, confers a feeling of identity and security and increases the feeling of personal worth. Some groups, as they mature, develop standards or norms for the opinions, attitudes, values, behaviour and even sometimes the dress of the members. These norms are important to the cohesiveness of the group and people who fail to conform to the most important of them are disapproved of as deviants. Conformists are rewarded by acceptance and inclusion; non-conformists may be punished by being ostracized.

Norms are seldom made statutory, but some groups, such as, for instance, private golf clubs, anxious to emphasize them will sometimes become preoccupied with formalization of the rules in print. The uniformity that results from these cohesive pressures has the positive effect of strengthening the group, but often leads to a sterile rigidity of outlook and to chauvinism in its wider sense. Inevitably, certain members of well-established groups tend to assume a leadership role and to establish a hierarchical structure. Functions are allocated, sub-groups formed and formal channels of communication established. The imposition of such structures can insulate the leadership too much from low-status members who may have valuable contributions to make. The result, especially in large groups such as political parties, may be a diminishing satisfaction on the part of lower-status members, a tendency to fragmentation and the formation of splinter groups or factions.

In the wider context of society, certain norms, such as queuing for attention in a bank rather than fighting for it, or using utensils in a particular way at table, become so well established that they are shared by almost everyone. These are then known as 'folkways'. When these become established by common agreement as being essential to society, they are known as 'mores' (singular 'mos'). Anyone who contravenes the mores of a society is deemed at best eccentric, at worse, immoral or wicked.

The psychological and social forces that operate on people in groups are known as group dynamics – a term first used by the German psychologist Kurt Lewin (1890–1947) in the course of a study of group psychology that led him to develop what he called his field theory. This has been influential in social science circles. Lewin recognized that people, with their instincts and desires, do not operate in an indifferent environment. Instead he proposed the idea of the 'life space'. This not just a person's physical environment but the whole complex of the person and the environment, together with the way it is perceived and interpreted by that person. It also includes cultural pressures that determine when a particular form of behaviour is appropriate and when it is not. As John Donne put it: 'No man is an *Island*, entire of it self.'

The interaction of the life spaces of the members of a group produces a field of force containing many different elements, some tending to drive the group in one direction of opinion, some pulling it in another. The resultant of these forces determines the group behaviour. A group might, for instance, contain members who were strongly racially prejudiced and others who saw the necessity to respect the rights of others, regardless of race. If such a group were involved in a situation in which a threat was perceived from a different racial group, tensions would arise and the outcome in terms of behaviour of the group would be determined by the relative strength of these. In any attempt to alter the outcome, little is likely to be achieved by attempts to change individual opinion. Since the life space of each member of the group is subjected to the pressures of the group field of force it is this that must be altered if a change is to be achieved.

The psychology of the mob is one of the most important aspects of this subject and deserves much closer attention and wider understanding than it has received. In a mob – a disorderly or riotous crowd – behaviour is nearly always much worse than that of the individual members would be. Trotter, with animal analogies in mind, says of the man in the mob: 'He is subject to the passions of the pack in his mob violence and the passions of the herd in his panics.'

The difference between the behaviour of people in a mob and their normal behaviour as individuals is so striking that some writers, notably Carl Gustav Jung (1875–1961), have suggested that a mob has a 'collective mind'. In a figurative sense, this may be so, but as a serious proposition it is nonsense. There are far simpler and more plausible explanations for this important phenomenon, and the simplest explanation is usually the right one. For a start, a person in a mob who identifies with it has a lowered sense of personal responsibility for what the mob does. It seems to the individual impossible that so many people could be wrong. Most people are only too ready to accept the leadership of others, to conform to the obvious majority wish. Secondly, people in an excited mob experience markedly heightened emotions, partly because they observe the signs of emotion in others and partly because the normal controlling influences on their behaviour are released. Thirdly, many people – especially the kind of people who are apt to find themselves as members of a mob – harbour deep feelings of resentment which they badly want to express in violence but are restrained from so doing because of fear of punishment. Membership of a mob gives them a sense of anonymity and allows them to express these feelings.

The violence that results is not necessarily directed at the real cause of the resentment but may be vented on any apparent symbol of it. So, for example, if a man who bitterly resents not being able to afford an expensive new car, becomes a member of a violent mob, he may well smash the windows and scratch the paintwork of the first expensive vehicle he encounters. For reasons such as these, mobs have always been recognized as being very dangerous. It is hopeless to try to reason with a mob, so public safety and property can be protected only by physical mob containment, and this may involve force. Inevitably, such attempts will be interpreted by the members of the mob as violence or brutality. The resulting hatred of the police can be relied on to reinforce the sense of resentment.

Another important feature of mob psychology is its unthinking partisanship or prejudice. While even quite unimaginative individuals can recognize that not all members of an alien community are alike, the mob is incapable of such subtlety of thought and immediately identifies any recognizable member of such a community as an enemy to be attacked. This phenomenon is commonly carried to remarkable extremes. As has become only too apparent in Europe in recent years, partisan football hooliganism can make a mob unthinkingly reckless, especially when inhibitions are lowered by too much alcohol. Supporters of one team need no further justification than this to attack the supporters of another.

To the mob, skin colour is a sufficient indication of identification, and the tendency to mob reaction is, of course, aggravated by prevailing social inequality and injustice. As a result, race riots have become a feature of many contemporary urban situations. After the assassination of the black civil rights leader Martin Luther King in 1968, race riots occurred in 150 American cities. The Los Angeles race riots of 1992 were precipitated by the acquittal, by an all-white jury, of white police officers who had been seen brutally attacking a black man on television. To the mob, this elicited an automatic condemnation of the 'white' justice system and the Establishment, resulting in unfocused and widespread violence. It was futile to point out that many of the people injured or robbed had also been outraged by the spectacle.

There is some point in all this. Mobs are, on the whole, composed not so much of stupid people as of ignorant and deprived people. People with the knowledge to be aware of the fallacies and irrationalities in mob conduct are not readily persuaded by demagogues to join mobs. Such people know all about demagogues and can distinguish reason from raw emotion. This is why education, in the wider sense, is so important. Because education in this sense is far less effective and much more difficult after the age of seven or eight, primary school teachers are almost the most important people in society. They should be selected with greater care than is given to the selection of university professors. They require equally high qualifications and should be rewarded accordingly. As Ignatius Loyola (1491–1556), the founder of the Jesuits' Order, put it: 'Give me the child until he is seven, and I care not who has him afterwards.'

The mind of the criminal: sociopathy

Is there such a thing as the criminal mind? Not so long ago, this was generally believed to be the case. So writers could produce stories in which Dr Frankenstein accidentally dropped the normal brain and had to make do with a criminal brain to put in his monster. And people like the highly respected English scientist Sir Francis Galton (1822–1911) could write in his *Inquiries into Human Faculty* (1883):

> The perpetuation of the criminal class by heredity is a question difficult to grapple with on many accounts. Their vagrant habits, their illegitimate unions, and extreme untruthfulness, are among the difficulties of the investigation. It is, however, easy to show that the criminal nature tends to be inherited.

Galton recounts in detail the 'infamous Jukes family in America... which includes no less than 540 individuals of Jukes blood, of whom a frightful number degraded into criminality, pauperism, or disease'. Galton described how the whole Jukes family had descended from a single individual – a 'half savage whose descendants went to the bad, and such hereditary moral weaknesses as they may have had, rose to the surface and worked their mischief without check producing a prevalent criminal type.' In Galton's time many other human activities and attitudes were attributed, on equally slender grounds, to heredity.

Galton thus clearly believed that there was a criminal mind. The difficulty is to say what it is. Galton's idea of 'hereditary moral weakness' is complete nonsense. There is no gene or genes for morality or for criminality, and today psychologists, aware of the enormous effect of environmental influences on the young developing mind, recognize that there is no need to postulate any such thing.

Criminal families certainly exist but early conditioning into their own particular modes of behaviour provides an adequate explanation. In a small proportion of cases, organic brain disorder, chromosomal abnormalities and psychiatric disorder may be associated with crime, but these cases provide no general explanation of the causes of crime.

People wishing to show that a criminal mind is inherent in some people are at once presented with two difficulties. First, there are no absolutes of behaviour against which such a mind could be judged, because the rules and beliefs of societies change with time and differ in different cultures. There are, in fact, no absolutes of right and wrong. A widely accepted definition of crime is that it is behaviour that contravenes the current legal or moral codes of a culture. Apparently, the word cannot be defined more specifically than that. It seems that human beings have no inherent or 'built in' standards by which they can judge whether or not their conduct is criminal. They can do this only by reference to the laws and principles obtaining at the time.

No single act, not even the killing of another human being, can be said, invariably and universally, to be criminal. Many acts, once thought criminal or deviant, are not now so regarded. In the West we no longer hang hungry children for stealing stale bread or put women to death for committing adultery. Even breaking the law is not always now regarded as criminal by the majority. Some of these infractions – such as disregard of parking regulations, or the use of certain drugs of addiction, although they may incur penalties, are no longer generally regarded as seriously criminal.

Much human wrong-doing has, in the past, been considered both criminal and immoral, but, today, an increasing part of it is seen to be either one or the other. In the UK and elsewhere, the law now takes no cognizance of many acts which many people still regard as immoral and which were once also regarded as criminal – acts such as homosexual intercourse between consenting adults in private. Again, such views are a product of the culture of the place and time. In contrast, acts such as, for instance, failing to wear a car seat-belt, are acknowledged to be criminal but are not considered immoral. Essentially, morality is concerned with individually held personal standards of behaviour, while criminality is concerned with more universally applied external principles.

The second difficulty arises from the complete lack of evidence that criminality is a specific disorder with a single physical cause. In deciding the cause of crime, each individual case must, it seems, be considered on its own and the causal factors identified. Clearly, early childhood experience is important and we know that the influences operating then have a deeper and more lasting effect than later influences. A child brought up to believe that successful theft is a matter for congratulation and that violence is an acceptable response to frustration is more likely to resort to crime than a child conditioned from the beginning to obey rules, conform to discipline and respect the rights of others. Absence of authority is often an important precipitating factor for crime.

Many criminals have had appallingly deprived childhood circumstances – not necessarily deprived in the material sense, but deprived of love, affection, discipline, rules, emotional security and a clear and unequivocal programme of ethical principles. Although the childhood family environment is not the only source of programming input, it is certainly the most important. The social status of a person, in real terms, is to be measured only by the wealth and quality of the content of the mind, and the correspondence between that content and currently approved social mores. It is also to be measured by the effectiveness (also a matter of programming) with which that quality of mind is applied in a social context. To continue the computing analogy, the criminal might be regarded as suffering from bug-ridden and poor-quality software. Unhappy or broken families feature strongly in the background of people habitually engaged in crime, as do low intelligence, poor health and low income. Even so, although some families foster crime, many members of such families do not become criminals.

The family is not, of course, the only conditioning influence. At quite an early age the child is exposed to a wider social environment from which other, and possibly conflicting, influences are derived. Primary school influences are immensely important, as teachers are, or should be, regarded as figures of authority. One cannot overstress the importance of the quality of the purveyors of primary education. On the negative side, children at that stage may suffer severely from social deprivation. This is one of the many motivating factors for crime. Envy of the perceived advantages of others may provide the trigger for criminal activity. There is also a general correlation between educational level and the tendency to criminality. This relates to the fact that a high proportion of criminals were unhappy at school and have a record of frequent truancy. Delinquent tendencies commonly appear in school. High educational achievement is not, of course, incompatible with crime, but the well-educated criminals form a small minority.

Abuse of drugs and alcohol is also frequently related to crime. Much crime is committed by drug addicts to get the money to support the habit, but there is no convincing evidence that the immediate physical effect of the drugs is to promote crime. Indeed, drugs like heroin and marijuana have a sedating effect which, other things being equal, is likely to reduce a tendency to criminal activity especially violent crime. Opium addicts in areas where the drug is very cheap do not resort to crime. Unfortunately, in the West, the need to finance heroin addiction counterbalances this sedative effect. The main association in the case of alcohol is with driving offences, which are often serious.

None of this bears directly on the central question of the nature of the mind of the criminal. There are some general points to be made about this. Malefactors differ in their characteristics as much as anyone else and it would be nonsense to suggest that there are people who are *wholly* criminal. Also, many law-breakers break the law for a limited period of their adolescence only, and these, clearly, should not be considered as criminals.

The confirmed adult criminal has a paradigm that differs in some important particulars from that of the law-abiding citizen. Whether many criminals devote much deep thought to their relationship to society is a moot point, but if they did, they would discover that they are operating a complex set of double standards. The rules of conduct that they expect society to apply to them are not the same as the rules they apply to society. Often, however, they will comply with society's rules in their dealings with their own families and friends. In general, however, the exhortation to 'do unto others as you would be done to' cuts little ice with the confirmed criminal.

The term 'psychopath' has become unfashionable, almost politically incorrect, but we still need a succinct word for the person whose behaviour is seriously self-centred and antisocial and who appears incapable of any form of emotional identification with others. Terms such as 'sociopath', 'moral defective' or 'patient with a personality disorder' have been applied, often for reasons of euphemism or displaced sympathy, but these merely diffuse the clarity of the concept. The psychopath is dangerous and the study of his or her (mostly his) characteristics is important. History is full of examples of the enormous harm psychopaths can cause.

Psychopaths have no defect of intellectual function and may be highly intelligent. There are no abnormalities of perception, memory or imagination, no delusions or hallucinations and no signs of organic brain disorder. Psychopaths have normal electroencephalograms. They occur in every level of society and in every walk of life. Although many of them are common criminals, the more intelligent and successful of them do not fall foul of the law. Their behaviour, however, is always, by real human standards, unacceptable. They are to be found in the armed forces, in the police, in the worlds of business, finance and politics – even in the medical profession and, occasionally, in the church. Psychopaths commonly have outbursts of explosive rage and violence or show reckless disregard for the safety or well-being of others. But this is not an invariable sign. Equally often, they may manifest ruthless, cold, manoeuvring and heartless dealings by which they gain a social or commercial advantage over others. It has been claimed that modern social pressures and the emphasis on material factors in contemporary society have brought about a sharp increase in the incidence of psychopathy.

If the problem of crime in modern society is to be effectively attacked at source, far more attention will have to be paid to the real underlying causes – poverty, social inequality, lack of education, lack of respect for the rules of society and the rights of others, and lack of respect for the guardians of the law. Inexplicably, the idea of deliberately conditioning young people into patterns of acceptable social behaviour by laying down firm rules and seeing that they are obeyed, has been seriously opposed and has been thoughtlessly equated with 'brainwashing'. We have allowed woolly-minded educational psychologists to persuade us that any such process is inherently damaging to the child who must, at all costs, be allowed to manifest his or her own individuality in complete freedom. We are now reaping the fruits of this absurd doctrine. (See also **Conformity enforced**.)

Of saints and sexuality: sanctity and self-abuse

Any consideration of the more extreme manifestations of saintliness must inevitably include the role of sex. Indeed, the subject of sex seems to be inextricably bound up with many aspects of organized Western religion. Why is this so? So far as Christian literalists are concerned, the matter is simple. The story of Adam and Eve in the Garden of Eden, from the book of Genesis, clearly implies that sex is a bad thing. Adam and Eve were OK until they lost their innocence and 'knew that they were naked'. At that point they started to look for fig leaves and the whole connection between sex and religion got under way. From then on, things went from bad to worse.

The matter, unfortunately, is no subject for joking. The preoccupation of the religious with sex goes far deeper than simply conformity to the implications of a rather charming legend. There are several possible reasons for the extraordinary importance theologians have given to sex throughout history. Perhaps the emotions aroused by sexual interest and activity were deemed to rival or threaten those that should be directed to more spiritual things. Perhaps the obvious human conflicts that were often promoted by sexual jealousy were seen to be in themselves evil. This, in itself, would be good grounds for proscribing promiscuous sex and for converting it into a sin.

Whatever these reasons, complete avoidance of all sexual activity was early seen to be a religious virtue. Celibacy and rigorous self-denial were the criteria of spiritual worth. Christ, himself, had little to say on the matter and was, in this as in all things, remarkable liberal and understanding. He recognized human sexuality as a fact of life and acknowledged that people would give way to it. His liberal attitude to prostitution and his association with prostitutes shocked many of his

163

contemporaries. It was probably St Paul who was mainly responsible for the prohibitive attitude of the Christian church to sex. It seems that Paul was not satisfied by the mere restriction of sex to marriage; ideally, he believed, it should be banished. For many, even to this very day, the word 'morality' necessarily implies behaviour in relation to sex.

Many people were to learn that deliberate sexual repression, whatever its motives, and however laudable these might be, was a prolific cause of trouble. Among these were many who, by their efforts in this direction, were subsequently regarded as saints. In some, the trouble this caused proved fatal. The courage many people found to face martyrdom was often founded in, and sublimated from, sexual energy.

Among the most remarkable states of mind are those of the early Christian saints of the desert. These were mostly men and were driven by their emotions to repudiate not only sex but even all society and to become ascetics and hermits, devoting themselves to prayer and meditation and, inevitably, to the torturing frenzy of sexual fantasies. Sexual repression in men will lead to erotic dreams and, quite commonly, to spontaneous orgasms in the course of such dreams. To a man who genuinely believed that any form of sexual indulgence was sinful and a threat to the future of his immortal soul, these normal physiological experiences, and the yielding to the temptation to masturbation, must have been distressing in the extreme and the cause of unimaginable suffering.

Ironically, some of these people succeeded in rationalizing their complex motivation in such a way as to believe that they should test their virtue by sleeping with women while still resisting temptation. The apparently complete failure to recognize that sexuality was a natural phenomenon responsible for the continuation of the human species, forced these unhappy people to believe that their recurrent sexual thoughts and experiences were the work of the devil. Their 'temptations' were seldom far from their thoughts. The attempt to control these 'sins of the flesh' led many of them to engage in what may seem to be ridiculous practices, including self-torture, flagellation, binding with ropes, near-starvation, avoidance of washing and near-nakedness rather than seeming to decorate their bodies with clothes.

These and other practices left many anchorites emaciated, with long hair, beards and fingernails, filthy, and covered with ulcers and fungal infections. To the extent that they neglected and abused their bodies they were regarded as saintly. Holiness, it seemed, was next to filthiness. Even this kind of self-abuse was related to sex. The beauty and adornment of the body were clearly the principal stimulus to lustful thoughts, so anything that minimized such a stimulus had to be virtuous.

Perhaps the most remarkable instance of ascetic perversity was that of the stylites (from the Greek *stylos*, a column), a set of Christian anchorites. The best known is St Simeon Stylites, so called because he sat for years, from AD 423 onwards, on top of a narrow pillar. This evidence of theological worth earned him, and some of his imitators, rapid beatification. Simeon was by no means the only stylite, but he seems to have started the vogue. His imitators included St Daniel (409–493) in Constantinople, St Simeon Stylites the Younger (517–592) on Mount Admirable near Antioch, St Luke (879–979) at Chalcedon, and St Lazarus (968–1054) on Mount Galesion near Ephesus. There were also a few female stylites (one forbears even to contemplate the Freudian symbolism of this!). The stylites sometimes allowed themselves a tiny roof as protection from the weather but were otherwise exposed. They remained standing day and night and were prevented from falling off only by a guard rail. They depended on disciples for food which had to be brought up by ladder. The essence of the matter was duration. One of them, the seventh-century saint, St Alypius, earned great virtue by remaining aloft for 67 years.

The founder of the movement did not confine himself to mere altitude. St Simeon the Elder, in addition to standing on one leg, quite literally mortified his flesh by binding it so tightly with cords that they cut into the skin and muscles. The wounds, of course, putrefied, providing an excellent culture medium for fly larvae (always described in the literature as 'worms') which were thus constantly renewed. St Simeon owed more to these maggots than he realized. Fly larvae are excellent scavengers of dead tissue and bacteria and probably saved him from septicaemia. So his habit of insisting that any 'worms' that fell out should be replaced was one of the few sensible things he did in his life. When he eventually died he was universally acknowledged, and officially pronounced, to be the highest possible model of saintliness.

Another extraordinary manifestation of the denial of the body is the saintly preoccupation with deliberate contact with disease in others. The motives in this are obviously mixed and may include, as well as plain charity and sympathy, a desire for self-immolation. Francis of Assisi was notorious for his tendency to kiss lepers. Others went further. St Francis Xavier, St John of God and Margaret Mary Alacoque are reported to have used their tongues to cleanse the ulcers and purulent sores of people in their care. Such extremes are unlikely to be achieved unless the desire to repress the natural instincts of the body has a very high priority.

The fourteenth-century German mystic and itinerant preacher Heinrich Suso or Seuse (c.1300–66) wrote an extraordinary third person autobiography in which he recounted his own efforts at the subjugation of his body:

As a youth he was full of fire and passion that grieved him, and that he made many efforts to subdue. He wore a hair shirt and an iron chain for a long time until they made him bleed. Then he had an undergarment secretly fabricated for him containing strips of leather through which 150 brass nails were driven, the sharpened points turned towards the flesh. This garment, which reached up to his navel, was made very tight, and he slept in it at night so that often he would cry aloud and twist about in his agony. He strove to attain such a degree of purity that he would neither scratch nor even touch any part of his body save only his hands and feet.

He practised rigid poverty and tortured himself by denial of water so that his thirst was extreme.

The preoccupation of the Church with the denial of sex relates to a wider interest in asceticism. This idea was formalized by the ancient Greek philosophical school of Stoics who took the view that we ought to deny our 'lower' sensual desires and emphasize our higher spiritual aspirations. Plato believed that it was necessary to suppress bodily desires so as to free the soul to search for knowledge. This idea sprang from the notion that, unless we train ourselves to resist bodily desires, we shall become slaves to these desires and unable to pursue higher things. The Stoics were much concerned with the repression of the emotions, and their promptings, and considered imperturbability to be a high virtue.

The Roman Catholic church, and especially the Jesuit branch, is notable for its strong impulse to codify anything connected with the faith that is susceptible of codification. Asceticism and its motives have not escaped this tendency. Any number of manuals have been written to assist those seeking Christian perfection. One of the earliest and best known, that of the Jesuit Rodriguez, has been translated into many languages. These books emphasize that sin arises from concupiscence, and concupiscence from the carnal desires and temptations. These must be resisted, and the discipline of self-mortification is the most effective way. St John of the Cross is eloquent on the subject. Believers are exhorted to deny themselves the pleasure of looking at, or listening to, anything that does not promote the glorification of God; they are to turn their souls to what is hardest, most distasteful, most disgusting and most contemptible; they are to despise themselves and wish other to despise them, possess nothing and have no taste for anything.

Religious asceticism, with its emphasis on the repression of sexual desire and its insistence that libido is the work of the devil, has had a hard time retaining imperturbability. Indeed, the lives of the ascetic saints are usually notable for the impossibility of achieving this happy state in a context of almost continuous guilt and fear. Such a state would have been impossible to maintain but for the categorical promise that there was a very much better time coming in the next life. This life was transitory, nasty, brutish and short. The life beyond the grave was eternal and, after proper conformity to the principles of behaviour laid down by the Church, beatific. The other powerful incentive to denying the natural functioning of human physiology was, of course, the fear of hell. Until comparatively recently, the depiction, in lurid detail of the horrors of hell was a major industry. All available channels of communication – the pulpit, the written and printed word, the graphic arts, drama, music, opera and poetry – were exploited vigorously and effectively to this end. St Ephraem Syrus, a Syrian theologian, insisted that monks should meditate on hell, and the likelihood of their being consigned to it, with such ardour that their inner life 'became a burning lava and torment'.

It seems probable that some of the behaviour of the saints may have involved an element of masochistic sexual pleasure. In the book *Deux Héroines de la Foi* by Claparède and Goty (Paris, 1880), quoted, dead-pan, by William James, there is an account by the Huguenot Christian martyr Blanche Gamond of an experience of her persecution:

They shut all the doors and I saw six women with thick bunches of willow rods a yard long. 'Get your clothes off,' he ordered, and I did. 'And the shift,' he said, 'You must take it off too.' But the women were too impatient, so they tore it off leaving me stripped to the waist. Then they tied me with a cord to a beam. They drew the cord as tight as they could. 'Does that hurt?' they asked. Then they fell on me furiously, shouting as they struck me 'Pray now to your God.' But at this moment I had the greatest happiness of my whole life, for I had the honour of being whipped for the name of Christ and of being crowned with his mercy and consolation. I can't describe the peace and consolation I felt inwardly. I was ravished. Only those who have had the same experience can understand it. Where affliction is greatest, there grace is given most abundantly. The women cried 'We must strike twice as hard. She feels nothing and neither speaks nor cries.' How should I have cried, when I was swooning with happiness within?

Chevalier von Sacher-Masoch would have loved this (see **Of Sade and Masoch**).

The French founder of the Order of the Sacred Heart, St Madeleine Sophie Barat (1779–1865), had an insatiable love of suffering and pain. She testified that she could live cheerfully until the Day of Judgment provided she could experience daily suffering for God. A single day without suffering would be intolerable to her. She had, she said, two unassuageable thirsts – one for holy communion and one for humiliation, pain and annihilation. She repeatedly wrote in her letters that only pain made her life supportable.

Another striking manifestation of the mind of the saint is the phenomenon of stigmata. These are marks on the body corresponding to the wounds Christ received in the course of his crucifixion. So they may occur on the palms and back of the hands and on the backs and soles of the feet (vicariously from the nails), on the flank (from the spear thrust), around the forehead (from the crown of thorns) or on the back and shoulders (from the whipping). The appearance of such marks on the body of a religious person, usually during an episode of extreme religious ecstasy, may be regarded by the Church as miraculous and a sign of saintliness.

The phenomenon seems to have originated with St Francis of Assisi. It is related that, about two years before his death, while meditating on the sufferings of Christ in his cell on Mount Alverno in 1224, he was visited by an angel who inflicted on his body the five wounds of Christ. These, apparently, persisted for the rest of his life. Pope Alexander IV and many others testified that they had seen these marks on Francis' body, both before and after his death. This did much for the reputation of Francis and led to his beatitude and to the foundation of the order of Franciscans. From that time to the present, over 330 people are known to have been 'stigmatized' and, of these, 60 have been declared saints. One of the best known was the fourteenth-century Catherine of Siena, an obvious hysteric but a woman of great courage and a prolific writer on religious mystical experience, who got her first stigma at the age of 23.

Although in some cases the appearance of stigmata does seem to be genuine, the majority of cases are probably self-inflicted for the sake of notoriety or to enhance the reputation for piety. Most of such cases will, on investigation, reveal evidence of emotional or mental instability. True psychosomatic stigmatization implies a powerful emotional experience. In such cases spontaneous haemorrhaging into the skin may appear at the appropriate sites. Some cases have been fairly carefully studied. The Belgian woman Louise Lateau had her arm sealed up within a glass cylinder so that there was no possibility of her gaining access to her hand. In spite of this, spontaneous oozing of blood occurred through the skin of the palm. The doctors of the Belgian Academy of Medicine were convinced, and officially recorded that they affirmed the reality of the phenomenon. The influence of the mind on the skin is well documented. These range from the simplest and most commonplace effect of blushing from embarrassment to the production of a large blister by a hypnotic suggestion that a light touch with a finger is actually a burn with a red-hot iron. It has to be said that the latter, although medically accepted, is a very rare occurrence.

It is unnecessary to go on multiplying examples of the pathological extremities toward which people reputed, or officially acknowledged, to be saints have gone in pursuit of their vocations. And nothing that has been written in this vein need be read as other than an expression of a belief in moderation in all things. Saintliness in this sense will never be understood or approved of by those, whatever their religious convictions, who believe that it is a central characteristic of a healthy mind to have a high regard and respect for the health, integrity and normal functioning of that most miraculous of all entities — the human body, including its sexual functions.

Of Sade and Masoch: the S-M story

Although the term sado-masochism is widely known, there is less information around about the minds of the two men from whose names the term was derived. Let us deal first with the lesser evil. Chevalier Leopold von Sacher-Masoch (1836–95) was a lawyer with a taste for writing. His many short stories and novels are trivial and he would have been forgotten altogether but for the fact that he was one of the first writers in modern times to depict the relationship between pain and sexual pleasure. As we shall see, the history of sadism, and its literature, goes back very much further. Sacher-Masoch's best-known work, and one of the few of his books worth reading, is called *Venus in Furs*. Another novel, *The Don Juan of Kolomea*, is concerned with the life of Polish Jews in a small town.

Sacher-Masoch was the middle-class son of an Austrian police chief, who delighted in telling him grisly stories of beatings and murders. Leopold was ready for such stories because his wet nurse had a taste for horrors and regaled him, at an early age, with terrifying German fairy-tales, such as those of the Grimm brothers, Jacob Ludwig Carl and Wilhelm Carl. Many of these stories are quite unsuitable for young children and must have had a deep influence on the boy. Sacher-Masoch grew up with a distinctly unusual personality and a strong taste for humiliation and punishment. He was married twice but also had a number of mistresses whom he required to dominate him in every possible way. He derived great satisfaction from being a slave to these women. It is not clear whether he was able to find women who were willing to enter enthusiastically into these games. This is unlikely, as women are not commonly interested in inflicting physical pain. But Leopold badly wanted to be whipped and, on at least one occasion, drew up a contract with a married mistress, Frau Pistor, in which she was required to treat him as a willing slave and, whenever 'feeling cruel' was required to wear furs. Clearly Leopold was also a bit of a fetishist. We know that, while he was still a student, he had already developed a taste for physical punishment. He was especially fond of 'studded whips'. By present day standards, *Venus in Furs* is a pretty mild book, but Leopold's writing makes it clear that he derived considerable satisfaction from being beaten, subjugated and humiliated.

If by masochism we mean any sexual pleasure related to pain, then masochism is extremely common. In the great majority of cases, however, the amount of pain involved is very small and seldom qualifies as obvious cruelty. Many people are 'turned on' by a bit of rough play during sex, and biting, nail-scratching, slapping and heavy pinching are a common feature of sexual intercourse. In the great majority of cases the participants fully accept and enjoy the minor pain, and some would feel neglected without these expressions of affection. Oddly enough, the infliction of 'love bites' is a common feature of copulation in mammal species other than humans.

Fully-fledged masochism, however, is a different matter altogether and involves the genuine humiliation and often severe punishment of the masochist. Submission is often symbolized by bondage and this, also, may be a means of inflicting pain. The sense of being totally at the mercy of the assailant is an important part of the attraction of the situation for the masochist. The degree of pain inflicted can vary from harmless ritual 'punishment' to severe whipping or beating. Fortunately, the masochist usually retains some control and will terminate the session before dangerous injury occurs. For the serious masochist, pain is the principal element in sexual activity. Between these two extremes is a large group of people for whom sado-masochistic fantasy is an important part of sex. Indeed, it is commoner for people to be sexually aroused by purely imagined sado-masochistic activity or by mutual talk about it than by the physical actuality.

Pure masochism is much less common than a combination of

masochism with sadism – in which pleasure is derived from the infliction of pain on others. Quite often, a person will adopt alternate roles and will achieve sexual arousal both by suffering and by inflicting pain. Sadists, however, often prefer a non-masochistic victim because arousal may depend on the perception of the genuine fear and unwillingness of the victim. Sadism is a much more serious matter than masochism as it often becomes uncontrolled and may lead to the infliction of grave injury or even to murder.

There is a considerable sadist literature and art dating back to the earliest times. Much of the later material is half-concealed in accounts of what purport to be justified chastisement or disciplinary punishment. Such literature is often lavishly illustrated with heavy emphasis on the naked buttocks of handsome boys – which seem to have exercised an irresistible fascination for generations of schoolteachers and others in authority over young people. The sado-masochistic element is also strong in this shady by-way of the literary art. Greek and Roman sculpture and *bas-relief* work often feature such practices. Even the great Aristotle was not spared the humiliation of appearing, in legend, in this genre. Numerous medieval illustrations exist showing the naked philosopher being physically chastised, ridden upon like an ass, and otherwise humiliated by Phyllis, the young wife of Alexander the Great, who was Aristotle's pupil.

The term 'sadism' was introduced by the eminent nineteenth-century German sexologist Richard von Krafft-Ebing (1840–1902), whose textbook on aberrant sexual behaviour, *Psychopathia Sexualis* (1886), was the first serious work in the field. Krafft-Ebing derived the term from the name of a notorious psychopath called Donatien Alphonse-François, Marquis de Sade (1740–1814). De Sade, a member of the French minor nobility, was born in Paris and, as a young man, joined the army and fought in the Seven Years' War. He was fond of prostitutes but they were not fond of him, and their complaints of his cruel treatment of them got him into trouble with the police.

De Sade formulated a 'philosophy' in which he held that vicious behaviour was natural to humans, and that the sexual exploitation of others, and infliction of cruelty on them for personal gratification, were acceptable and even laudable activities. He was a thorough-going sensualist who believed in trying everything in his quest for satisfaction. At the age of 32 he was convicted of sodomy, then a capital crime, and of the attempted murder of a prostitute. He was sentenced to death but escaped from confinement. On application by *lettres de cachet* by his outraged mother-in-law, however, he was locked up in the Bastille. He was there for 17 years during which time he wrote many of his scandalous books extolling the sexual abuse, rape, humiliation and torture of women and children, sexual murder, sodomy, flagellation and obscene degradation of religion. In 1789, just a few days before the breaking open of the Bastille by the Parisian mob at the start of the French Revolution, de Sade was moved to another prison. But with the success of the Revolution he was freed and became a judge in a revolutionary tribunal.

Perhaps surprisingly, de Sade showed extraordinary leniency to those aristocrats who appeared before him, so much so that his revolutionary associates suspected him of partisanship and he was, for a time, in serious risk of being beheaded. In 1801, however, he was again indicted for obscenity in his writings and went back to prison. Two years later his family had him certified insane and locked up in a lunatic asylum at Charenton where he remained until he died. He was not, however, without the comforts that money could buy and he was looked after by two mistresses, a young teenage girl and a middle-aged actress. De Sade enjoys a minor literary reputation and his rather boring novels remain in print, largely because of their titillating content and steady sales. The best known are *The Hundred and Twenty Days of Sodom* (1784), *Justine, or the Misfortunes of Virtue* (1791), *The Bedroom Philosophers* (1793), *Juliette* (1798) and *Crimes of Love* (1800).

De Sade's pernicious 'philosophy' cannot be justified on any terms. Sadism is, at any level, a crime against humanity and, even if physical maltreatment is not involved, should always be regarded as abhorrent.

The mind of the medium:
a conduit to the other world?

Many distinguished people have believed in spiritualism or in psychic phenomena, among them a number of scientists, including the English chemist and physicist Sir William Crookes, who invented the cathode ray tube; the physiologist Professor Charles Richet; the psychologists Professor William James and Professor William McDougall; the physicist Sir William Barrett; the biologist Professor A. C. Hardy; and many others.

One of the most interesting of these, because of his status as a scientist, was the English physicist Sir Oliver Lodge FRS (1851–1940) who made important advances in the understanding of electromagnetic radiation and radio wave propagation. Lodge's interest in psychic phenomena began in about 1883, when he carried out some telepathy experiments that seemed to work. He then proceeded to investigate two well-known mediums, Mrs Piper and Eusapia Palladino. The only way Lodge could explain the results seemingly obtained by Mrs Piper was to assume the validity of telepathy. In the case of Palladino he became convinced that he was witnessing telekinesis – moving matter by the power of the mind. Lodge concluded, on the evidence he had personally observed, that the mind had an existence independently of the body and that it survived the destruction of the brain. He also concluded that he could communicate with the dead.

Now, Oliver Lodge was no fool. He was a trained scientist and observer and had all the scepticism proper to a scientist. He was president of the Physical Society and a Fellow of the Royal Society – an honour reserved only for those who have made substantial contributions to science. He was awarded honorary degrees from thirteen universities. His interest in the supernatural led him to become president of the Society for Psychical Research. He was a prolific writer; the work that, more than any of the others, caught the public imagination was called *Raymond* (named after Lodge's youngest son, killed in the First World War) and published in 1916.

Mrs Piper was a stout and matronly young married lady of Boston, Massachusetts, when, in 1884, her mediumistic powers became apparent. This happened after she sought treatment from a psychic healer and, in a trance, became controlled by a French doctor called Phinuit. Thereafter Dr Phinuit became Mrs Piper's regular control. Oddly enough, Dr Phinuit did not speak French and did not appear to know as much about medicine as the average American housewife. But Mrs Piper's performance while in her trances was amazing. Her fame spread and she was investigated by a number of sceptical people, including William James and the keenly critical Dr Richard Hodgson, who had recently, in India, exposed the fraudulent practices of the Russian spiritualist Madam Blavatsky. William James, a detached, scientific, medically qualified psychologist and author of one of the most influential psychology texts of the time, *Principles of Psychology*, was not particularly impressed with Dr Phinuit's 'tiresome twaddle' and his significant tendency to go on fishing expeditions after information. He decided that the gentleman was entirely fictitious. He was, however, deeply impressed by Mrs Piper's account of some accurate details of affairs in his own family and, being an open-minded man, decided to take her seriously.

Mrs Piper's forte was to make statements about matters she could not have known concerning the families of people present. Hodgson went so far as to employ detectives to check whether she was making private enquiries. Neither then, nor later, was she discovered in any dishonesty. James and Hodgson were intrigued and suggested to the London Society for Psychical Research that they should invite the lady to England. She made the trip in 1889 and was met at the gangplank by Oliver Lodge, who was then Professor of Physics at Liverpool University.

Soon Mrs Piper was settled in the Lodge ménage. Since she was a stranger to England and knew no one there, the circumstances were ideal for psychical research. Lodge made sure that she had no opportunity to meet or communicate with any of the people who came to her seances and he locked up all letters, photograph albums and other biographical material relating to his own family. He even searched Mrs Piper's luggage. Then he decided to try an experiment. He wrote to his Uncle Robert, whose twin brother had died 20 years before, and asked him to send something that had belonged to the dead man. His uncle sent him a watch. In Mrs Piper's next trance, Lodge handed her the watch. Dr Phinuit immediately stated that the watch had belonged to an uncle, whom he called 'Uncle Jerry'. Phinuit then mentioned a number of incidents that had occurred to 'Uncle Jerry' in his boyhood – before Lodge was born. Jerry had nearly drowned while swimming in a river; he had killed a cat in Smith's Field; and he had had a long snake skin.

Lodge checked with his surviving uncle who said he remembered the snake skin but denied the rest. Uncle Robert then wrote to another brother, Frank, who insisted that he remembered every detail of the near-drowning and cat killing and the snake skin. He also identified Smith's Field as a place where the boys used to play. Lodge was convinced that this evidence was to be believed. The circumstance that finally turned him into a confirmed spiritualist was to come later. Mrs Piper, who had taken up 'automatic writing', brought him a message in the form of an allusion to an Ode of Horace – something with which Mrs Piper could hardly have been expected to be familiar. This is known as the 'Faunus message'. Lodge took this to be a warning that a terrible blow was to fall on him. When, soon afterwards, his young son was killed on active service in France he concluded that communication with the dead was an established fact.

Even in today's sceptical climate, there are all kinds of reasons for a person to wish to be regarded as a genuine trance medium – money, fame, status, the admiration of the public, and so on. There are also many kinds of ways in which people purporting to be mediums can fraudulently support their reputations, especially among gullible and uncritical clients. A great many people who consult mediums, desperately want to believe in the possibility of communicating with the dead. So the stage is set for deception. A medium may, for instance, make some very broad general remarks while in a 'trance' and closely observe the reaction of those present. A sharp drawing in of breath is all that is needed to indicate that the medium is getting warm. Often, the most unspecific of messages are interpreted by those present as genuine communication. People will believe what they want to believe and will always latch on to anything they regard as 'evidence'. Equally, they will ignore the numerous instances on which no 'evidence' is produced. The law of averages does not operate in this field.

Many mediums undoubtedly start out by believing that they have genuine psychic powers. Some, no doubt, continue to sustain this belief in spite of many failures. But the pressures on them to produce results are great and they are, after all, only human. So it is not particularly surprising that nearly all mediums have been detected in fraud. Perhaps Sir Oliver was right and some people, like Mrs Piper, do have telepathic powers. Any medium so endowed would have a perfect set-up for proving that he or she could communicate with the dead.

Unfortunately for the mediums, never in the whole history of the spiritualist movement has any information been conveyed from the 'next world' that is other than completely trivial and commonplace. There have been innumerable claims of communications with the dead, many of which have provided comfort to the bereaved and have encouraged people to a belief in the immortality of the soul. Science has nothing to say about the soul, and most certainly is not in the business of trying to disabuse people of their religious beliefs. In fact, most religious belief is perfectly compatible with a strictly scientific approach. But science, in the shape of serious and disinterested research into alleged psychical phenomena, has provided one important opinion: that whatever the truth of the matter of survival of some kind of personal awareness after bodily death, information about it is not to be obtained from the intervention of spiritualistic mediums – who, like all other human beings, are limited in what they can know strictly to the range of human knowledge.

Seeking a better life: the fugue state

The *History of Mr Polly* by H. G. Wells is one of his most endearing and least doctrinaire novels. It is also a brilliant example of an interesting, so-called, dissociative phenomenon – the fugue state. It may be objected that Mr Polly's departure from a detested environment and his adoption of a new and infinitely more pleasant life was an entirely conscious process. But this is to beg the question of the true nature of the fugue. It is also to beg the question of the precise nature of consciousness.

Dissociative phenomena, which include such things as loss of memory (amnesia), multiple personality and depersonalization, are defined as 'altered states of consciousness'. This definition may be just a little presumptuous, perhaps even arrogant, in that it implies a degree of insight into the mind of the affected person that is not necessarily justified by the facts. The truth is that 'a state of altered consciousness' can be inferred only by observation of the behaviour of the subject. There is no other source of information. Who is to say whether the person's behaviour, or claims, are honest?

Mr Polly made no pretence to loss of memory. But if he had, no one – not even the most experienced psychologist – could possibly have judged from his behaviour that he was not in a fugue state. The fugue is a rare and fascinating psychological reaction in which the affected person takes on a completely new identity and wanders away from the old environment, apparently in a state of amnesia for the former life. The word 'fugue' comes from the Latin *fuga*, meaning 'flight' or 'escape'. Such people may take up a new occupation and, indeed, assume a completely new life. They are usually quiet, inoffensive people living a somewhat reclusive existence and, perhaps sensibly, they avoid drawing attention to themselves. Like Mr Polly, fugitives from wives or husbands who by their behaviour have destroyed the fugitive's quality of life and sense of personal worth are well represented in the ranks of the fugue victims. Others include those whose careers have been ruined, those who have lost a beloved child and those who have suffered extreme disgrace in the eyes of their own community.

We have no details of the reasons for the fugue of the Reverend Bourne, reported in the *Proceedings of the Society for Psychical Research* and elsewhere. Bourne was a Methodist minister of Rhode Island who, apparently, wandered away from his home. One day he 'woke up' to find himself in Norristown, Pennsylvania. With no memory of his previous life, he found he had enough money to purchase a small stock of sweets and rent a shop. Soon he was running a thriving candy store under the name of A. J. Brown. This continued for two years. One night, however, he awoke in his former state of consciousness as a minister of religion and was astonished to observe his surroundings. He had, he said, no idea where he was or why he was in a strange house. Terrified that he might be taken for a burglar, he was reassured by neighbours whom he informed of his true identity. His friends were sent for and he returned home.

It is interesting to speculate on the background to this case. Unfortunately, instead of taking a detailed history of social, sexual or theological stress – which may well have thrown light on the matter – the investigators were preoccupied with psychic influences and made much of the fact that the reverend gentleman 'had in early life shown a tendency to abnormal psychic conditions', whatever that means. Apparently he had once been the subject of a stage hypnotist and had been made to assume various characters. This suggested a possible explanation for multiple personality.

The term 'fugue' is well chosen, because fugues always occur as a response to an intolerable situation from which the victim takes flight. The conventional psychological view is that the unbearable pains and stresses of the old life exert such devastating pressures on the personality that there is a mental breakdown manifested by loss of memory so that the affected person has no alternative but to wander away in search of a new identity. The phenomenon has attracted much theorizing and the invention of impressive-sounding terms. The concept of dissociation implies a 'splitting off' of part of the memory from conscious awareness and the implication is that this occurs outside the volition of the victim.

There is a principle, known as Ockham's (or Occam's) razor, that is not always as widely applied as it ought to be. It holds that assumptions should be reduced to the absolute minimum; that generalizations should never be based on other generalizations; and that explanations should never contain any unnecessary detail. In other words, we should always go for the simplest hypothesis to account for anything. In accordance with Ockham's razor, then, it is more reasonable to assume that the fugue is a conscious phenomenon, deliberately adopted as a way out of a desperately painful situation. Looked at in this way, the 'amnesia' can be seen as a mechanism allowing the unfortunate victim to accept a course of action which would normally be considered outrageous.

This proposition is supported by the fact that in no case of fugue does the 'memory loss' make any real sense. There is, for instance, none of the acute anxiety that would normally accompany sudden loss of memory. Even more significantly, the loss is highly selective and does not preclude use of the previous general education or of knowledge necessary for the management of the new life. The part that is not remembered is the painful period; the rest is accessible. If there is recovery from the fugue, there is, perhaps not surprisingly, amnesia for the period covered by the fugue. It is apparent that, for some, the fugue represents a reasonable and logical solution to a major life problem − in effect, a defence mechanism (see **Universal self-delusion**). In cases in which there is 'recovery' from the fugue state, the victim is suddenly restored to awareness of his or her true identity and manifests great distress and wonder as to how he or she came to be in totally strange surroundings. To do otherwise would be unacceptable to all concerned.

To reduce the fugue state to what appears to be no more than malingering is to be unduly harsh to people whose misfortune it has been to fall into appalling and unendurable life situations. No outside person can judge from the available evidence what is unendurable for someone else. Rather than categorize these unfortunate people as dishonest, it might be more just to recognize that each one of us is entitled, within reason, to fight with any available weapons for amelioration of extreme distress and for a reasonable quality of life. For many, the fugue may be the best, or the only available, solution. Or is this attitude too liberal?

Unfortunately, there are difficulties with it. Marital conflicts are never one-sided. To the outsider the fault may seem to be all on one side and, as in the case of readers of *The History of Mr Polly*, the fugue may be felt to be entirely justified. But life isn't like that. When one partner appears to be behaving intolerably to the other, the reason is unlikely to be constitutional malevolence. Fiction writers are aware of the importance of conflict and will often cheat by creating a character whom we all love to hate. But such people are very rare, and what seems to be intolerable behaviour is far more likely to be a function of the relationship. The self that 'victimized' people present to the outside world is often highly at odds with reality. In cases of marital and other personal conflict, it may often be the apparent aggressor who is the more honest of the pair.

Problems may also arise when the escape into the fugue state endangers national security as it may tend to do when fugues are used to escape dangerous military service. Whatever the psychologists may claim, the military authorities are liable to take a pragmatic view of desertion in the face of the enemy. Certainly, attitudes are now somewhat more sympathetic than they were in the days when the penalty for a fugue was to be put against a wall and shot, *pour encourager les autres*. But, under the Army Act, desertion is still considered to be a serious offence, attracting a long period of imprisonment.

The overriding, inescapable fact is, however, that, for many people, occasions occur when life becomes insupportable. When that happens, the options are, short of murder, reduced to a very few. One of these is suicide; another is simply to run away in a completely conscious and deliberate manner. But for many, to do so seems humiliating or cowardly. For these, there is a third and possibly more acceptable course – to adopt, whether by intent or by the labyrinthine workings of the unconscious, what must seem to others an extraordinary state of mind – the fugue.

Divided minds: multiple personality

Probably the best-known account of dual personality is to be found in R. L. Stevenson's novel *Dr Jekyll and Mr Hyde*, which, of course, is entirely fictitious. The interesting question is whether Stevenson was relying solely on his unquestionably vivid imagination or whether he had previously heard of such cases. It is distinctly possible that the latter is true, for the psychiatric literature contains many references to cases of multiple personality. Most of these references make it clear that the psychiatrists and psychologists involved were convinced that these cases were genuine psychiatric abnormalities.

One of the earliest of these, recorded in a paper by a Dr Weir Mitchell in the *Transactions of the College of Physicians of Philadelphia* concerns an 18-year-old girl, Mary Reynolds. Mary was a quiet, reserved, timid girl with a long history of hysterical episodes. In one of these she became, to all appearances, totally blind and deaf and remained so for six weeks. Three months after recovering her vision and hearing, Mary fell into a deep sleep from which it was impossible to arouse her. When she finally awoke, she was a different person. All memory of her previous existence – her name, parents, country, residence – all had gone and she was, as it were, a young and ignorant child.

Mary's education had to be undertaken again almost from the beginning. She had to be taught to read and write. Happily, she proved an apt pupil and a remarkably quick learner. In the course of seven or eight weeks she was restored, once again, to full literacy. The most striking thing, however, was the change in her personality. The new Mary was fun-loving, boisterous, daring and rash. She could hardly have been more different from her former self. She went rushing off into the wild countryside and forests, indifferent to the hazards and, indeed, seemed to welcome danger.

After a few weeks Mary again went into a deep sleep and when she awoke she had returned to her first incarnation. If anything, her personality was even more quiet and timid than before. She strenuously denied that anything untoward had happened and professed to have no memory of the short, happy life of the extrovert. For the ensuing sixteen years, Mary alternated between her two personalities. Each was wholly divorced from the other and in neither, apparently, had she any awareness of the other. In each, however, she retained full recollection of what had happened to her in previous episodes of that particular state. It was, to all appearances, as if she were two entirely different people.

This extraordinary state of affairs lasted until Mary was 36 and then ceased. After that, her personality seemed to be a blend of the two, and was, in fact, a great improvement on either. She was neither rash nor unduly cautious, neither secretive nor over-impetuous. The synthesis of the two personalities had, apparently, resulted in an altogether better version of Mary Reynolds, and in this happy condition she lived to the age of 65 and then died.

The French psychologist Alfred Binet (1857–1911), who invented the IQ test, described a similar case, that of the morose and gloomy seamstress Felida who, almost daily, suffered a severe headache, fell into a deep state of languor, and awoke as a totally different person. In her second state she was cheerful, over-excited and full of vivid imaginings. While in the manic phases – which lasted for only an hour or two – she remembered what had happened to her in previous excitable episodes and also in her normal (original) state. But when in the latter, she could remember nothing of any of the episodes of her jovial phase.

Felida was so much happier in her extrovert state that she came to regard the melancholy periods as abnormal. She called these periods, her 'crisis'. One day, when cheerful, but while attending a funeral, she felt a 'crisis' coming on, passed into a brief doze, and awoke to find herself, allegedly to her astonishment, in a mourning carriage listening to a conversation about a deceased person whose name was unknown to her. Once, while manic, she discovered that her husband was supporting a mistress – a lady whom she knew – and she tried to kill herself. On returning to her sombre phase, however, she was able to meet this lady and relate to her with perfect equanimity and with no seeming cause for complaint against her.

This extraordinary daily cycle of personalities persisted for many years, but, as time passed, the state of cheerfulness gradually assumed dominance. Eventually, it became her normal state. As Binet recorded: 'It is rather satisfactory to chronicle that as between the two *egos* which alternately possess her, the more cheerful has finally reached the ascendant.' At the time he wrote, Felida was still alive.

Multiple personality is far commoner than was previously supposed. Recent reviews of the literature have thrown up hundreds of cases, many of them occurring in the recent past. Analysis of these shows that the multiple personalities of the same person may differ in more respects than had been imagined. They may differ in claimed age, attitudes, handwriting, blood pressure, average pulse rate, date of onset of menstruation in the cycle, moral codes, and even sexual orientation (one may be heterosexual, the other homosexual). Those whose menstrual periods are out of synchronization have the misfortune to spend much of the month menstruating and may be at risk of developing iron deficiency anaemia.

Multiple personality is an example of a dissociative phenomenon and is described as a discrete clinical entity in the American Psychiatric Association's *Diagnostic and Statistical Manual of Mental Disorders* (*DSM* for short), now in its fourth edition. In it, multiple personality disorder is stated to be:

> The existence within the person of two or more distinct personalities or personality states (each with its own relatively enduring pattern of perceiving, relating to, and thinking about the environment and self). At least two of these personality states recurrently take full control of the person's behavior.

To side-track for a moment, *DSM* is remarkably comforting to psychiatrists because it purports to perform what is probably an impossible task – to define and describe all known psychiatric abnormalities. One cannot shake off a certain uneasiness about all this. The whole ethos of *DSM* presupposes that there is a real correspondence between organic disease and mental disease. The unquestioned premise is that, because the symptoms and signs of a psychiatric condition can be listed, and an effective prescription can often be written for its treatment, it follows that it is legitimate and reasonable to refer to any apparent anomaly of behaviour as a 'mental disorder'. The authors of the fourth edition of *DSM* are not indifferent to public opinion on these matters. The third edition, published in 1987, appeared, for example, still to have a lingering inclination to regard homosexuality as a mental disorder. But by the time the fourth edition appeared, homosexuality was no longer regarded as a disease by the American Psychiatric Association.

Multiple personality disorder is also a case in which care must be exercised. Because these cases are bizarre and interesting, they are studied closely and the findings recorded and often published. This, as always, gives them an often unjustified gloss of truth. By including in a textbook a list of manifestations found to be common to a number of different cases of multiple personality, the entity quickly acquires verisimilitude. But it must be remembered that none of the facts recorded have any more objective validity than the say-so of the 'patient' and the observation of his or her behaviour. The psychiatrist has no insight into the mind of his or her subject. And it is easy to forget that people who develop multiple personalities have the strongest possible motives for deceit. There is considerable overlap between multiple personality and fugue (see **Seeking a better life**) and the distinction – that in one case the subject wanders off and in the other that the subject does not – seems rather arbitrary. It seems likely that the origins of the two states are much the same and that they should be considered together.

The case of Sally Beauchamp is strongly suggestive of the need for caution. This case is reported in a book, *The Dissociation of a Personality*, by Dr Morton Prince, who was especially interested in multiple personality and had already published a number of papers on the subject. Dr Prince studied Sally for seven years, from the time she was 23, and during that period she developed three new personalities. The doctor was enthusiastic about hypnotism, and two of Sally's four personalities appeared while she was under hypnosis.

Sally loved to be hypnotized and regularly begged the doctor to 'put her under'. This, she constantly reminded him, was the only thing that helped her. There was a 'hypnogenic point' over her spine and whenever this was touched by the doctor 'a thrill ran through her that weakened her will and quickly induced a hypnotic state'. Fairly obviously, Sally had a strong transference for the doctor, whom she knew to be delighted with the extraordinary material she was providing him. His management of 'the family', as he called the four personalities of Sally, gave him all the information he needed to write a fascinating book about multiple personality. Books such as that of Dr Prince can have a considerable influence on other writers and, as the data are perpetuated from book to book, they gain a sometimes spurious credence.

Oddly enough, the great majority of people who develop multiple personalities are women. We hear of the three faces of Eve, but not of Adam. In the past at least, nearly all the doctors who have reported these cases have been men and, as in the case of Dr Morton Prince, have been older than their subjects. It is hard to exaggerate the power of the desire to elicit praise and gratitude from an older, admired and respected person. Perhaps in more cases than we imagine, the young ladies were more than happy to be able to give their doctors exactly what they wanted. Certainly, this kind of situation is no basis for the determination of truth.

Divided brains:
cutting of the corpus callosum

The cases described in the previous section (**Divided minds**) might lead some people to suppose that they could be due to physical changes, such, for instance, as an actual separation of the two halves of the brain. But the effects of such separation are so striking and so different from those of 'psychological' cases of dual personality as to make it clear that the latter are not the result of organic division of the brain. Physical separation of the two halves of the brain is possible because the two hemispheres are connected by a broad band, consisting of about 800 million parallel nerve fibres, and called the corpus callosum. Cutting of the corpus callosum certainly produces an extraordinary state of mind.

One of the earliest cases to be described of separation of the two cerebral hemispheres was in a 1908 report by the neurologist Kurt Goldstein. This report described the case of a woman whose behaviour was so bizarre that she had been admitted to hospital. This woman complained constantly that her left hand was 'bad' and that she had no control over it. Indeed, this seemed to be the case. Repeatedly, her left hand would jerk up to her neck and the fingers would take a stranglehold. In order to prevent herself from being injured or killed, it was necessary for her to use her right hand to drag the left hand away. To prevent a repetition, she would sit on her evil-doing left hand. This hand had other destructive tendencies too: it would tear at the bed sheets and throw her pillows about. When questioned about this, she would insist that she had no control over the left hand.

Most people would simply have attributed such behaviour to

psychiatric disorder or shamming, but Goldstein was a skilled neurologist who was able to detect other physical signs of dissociation of the two hemispheres of her brain – signs that could not have been deliberately simulated or caused by delusions or hallucinations. So he concluded that the woman's corpus callosum had been at least partially cut. Later, after she died, a post-mortem examination showed that indeed this was the case. Disease processes had effectively divided the structure.

Since Goldstein's time it has been deemed necessary, in a number of cases, to cut the corpus callosum for medical reasons. This has been done deliberately as a treatment for some very severe forms of epilepsy in which the massive electrical discharges are carried by the corpus callosum from one side of the brain to the other. As a result of studies done on such patients since the late 1960s, mainly by the American neurophysiologist Roger W. Sperry (1913–), much more is now known about the effects of hemispheric separation. Interestingly, in nearly all such cases, it has been the left hand that has engaged in bizarre behaviour. It is, of course, well known that although the two halves of the brain have much in common, they also have important differences in function. In nearly all people, for instance, the left half controls most of the functions of language and speech. It is also important to remember that all the major nerve trunks coming down from and running up to the brain cross over to the other side just above the spinal cord. The effect of this is that the right half of the brain controls the left side of the body and the left half of the brain controls the right side of the body.

Cutting the corpus callosum has an extraordinary effect on the state of the mind. This is to be expected, as the corpus callosum is by far the most important channel of communication between the two halves of the brain, so that the separate functions can be coordinated to produce a single mind. When the corpus callosum is cut – in an operation known as cerebral commisurotomy (a commisure is a bundle of nerve fibres, and the suffix '-otomy' just means 'cutting') there is a profound change in mental activity. The most dramatic effect is that the right half of the brain, which is now deprived of access to any language or speech functions, cannot express its feelings or awareness in words. So the only response possible to stimuli that reach the right side of the brain is action, and it is perhaps not surprising that such action should be aggressive or violent, and, of course, expressed with the left hand. Stimuli reaching the left half of the brain have no problem is evoking a verbal response. Objects seen or felt can immediately be described and named.

Many studies have been performed to interrogate the separate halves of the brains of patients who have had a commisurotomy and much has been learned about the differing functions of the two halves, as well as of the relationship of brain function to the mind. If a word stimulus is passed only to the right side of the brain, although its significance cannot be expressed in words, there is some comprehension. If the word describes an object, the object can be correctly picked out from a number of different objects using the left hand (controlled by the right half of the brain). Embarrassing pictures, shown only to the right half of the brain, evoke an appropriate emotion and its physical expression – such as a shamefaced laugh – but the person concerned is unable to account for this reaction.

When non-verbal intelligence tests are applied to the right half of the brain it is found that there are functions, and modes of thinking, in which it is markedly superior to the left side. The right side dominates in the handling of shapes and patterns, in the memory of the appearance of things and in the ability to form conclusions about whole objects from partial data. It is also much better at understanding metaphors than the prosaic and literal left side. Significantly, it is much better at perceiving the emotions behind different facial expressions than the left side.

While the right half of the brain can recognize single printed words from their shape and can match up identical words in this way, it appears to be incapable of imagining the sound produced when a particular word is spoken. The isolated right half of the brain can manage language to a certain extent if it is part of a context of visible and tangible objects and actions that provide additional clues to the meaning of words. When words are separated from such a context, the right side of the brain is in real trouble.

The plight of the right half of the brain in trying to manage verbal information is strongly reminiscent of that of a toddler tackling the new problems of language. It is well known that small children make most rapid progress in learning language when words are used in real-life contexts. The child copes most easily, and learns most quickly, if the word is directly associated with the object or situation it stands for. The inference is that brain function subserving mind involves a close inter-relationship of words, their meanings, the things they describe, the emotions they evoke and so on. Research of this kind has made it clear that full, normal, mental experience requires close cooperative action between the rational, analytical left side of the brain and the intuitive, synthetic right side. The constant inflow of information during consciousness impinges on both sides of the brain and is then coordinated by both sides and conveyed to all parts.

Only in this way are we able to experience the normal state of mind we call consciousness or awareness. The current paradigm of most cognitive psychologists is that the state of mind we call subjective awareness or consciousness is the result of the unceasing need of the left half of the brain to make logical and verbal sense of the mass of incoming data that is being acquired, processed and 'perceived' by the rest of the nervous system. Neurological links between the two halves of the brain can occur only by way of messages sent via the corpus callosum.

It would be wrong to suppose that the functional division into right and left brains is cast in concrete. The whole brain is a plastic and adaptable entity capable of remarkable changes in functional capacity as a result of education and experience. To a limited extent, the special functions of each side can be taken over by the other side. Cultural and educational differences, operating from birth, can bring about remarkable differences in the degree of relative dominance of the functions of one or other cerebral hemisphere. This is why some people's talents are manifested in the visual and plastic arts while others have greater literary capacity.

For his remarkable research into these matters, Sperry was awarded the Nobel Prize for Physiology or Medicine in 1981. Incidentally, these discoveries have rendered worthless, except to historians of human thought, countless volumes of speculative philosophy and psychology on the nature of mind.

Human as machine: automatism

The robot-like human acting without volition, or the mindless zombie stomping with expressionless face through a ground mist in a Caribbean jungle, are common stereotypes of cheap fiction or television. But the truth may be stranger than fiction. Automatism, although fortunately uncommon in its most bizarre manifestations, is a reality. Whether it can legitimately be described as an extraordinary state of mind is a moot point, however, because automatism is often characterized by the absence of what we normally understand as 'mind'.

The condition is defined as the performance of acts, sometimes highly complex, without any awareness of what is being done. Perhaps surprisingly, automatism is a feature of much of normal life. We carry out many actions on 'autopilot' for which we may have no recollection. In certain circumstances automatism may persist for long periods. It is not generally appreciated, for instance, that musicians reading fairly familiar music can play for many minutes at a stretch while thinking of something quite unconnected with music. If they are skilled and experienced musicians, the performance, during automatism, can be quite creditable if, perhaps, lacking in spontaneity and innovation. It is amusing to contemplate an entire symphony orchestra performing Beethoven's fifth symphony for the umpteenth time, with all the members indulging in their favourite fantasies, and returning to reality only to respond to the rapturous applause of the audience.

Cases of abnormal automatism are always the result of brain damage or disease. The condition is, for instance, a common feature of epilepsy, especially epilepsy arising in the temporal lobe of the brain. The movements involved in the epileptic seizure are automatic and involuntary and are due to spread of electrical activity over the brain. But automatic behaviour can also occur during the period of clouding of consciousness that commonly follows the seizure. This is usually short, but if it is prolonged, automatic behaviour, such as undressing or wandering away without volition, may occur. This state of post-epileptic automatism may provide a legal defence for criminal actions performed during it. Fortunately, because of the absence of volition, criminal activity in this state is rare.

Abnormal automatism can also follow what seem to be comparatively minor head injuries. Post-traumatic amnesia may occur without any loss of consciousness and with no apparent change in behaviour. A football player may receive a kick on the head and may briefly be dazed but not knocked out. He may continue to play but may be acting automatically and may later have no memory of events of the game following the injury. Cases have even occurred in which players in this condition have scored a goal and are astonished, afterwards, to receive the congratulations of their team-mates. This phenomenon is known as traumatic automatism and, like other cases, features complete amnesia.

Some quite remarkable cases have been described in people who have suffered permanent brain damage as a result of injury. One of the most extraordinary instances was that reported in the *Gazette Hebdomadaire de Médicine et de Chirurgerie* of Paris, in 1874. The case concerned a young man, a talented concert singer, who had been shot on the left side of his head but had survived. After an initial right-sided paralysis, which must have been due to brain swelling rather than destruction, for it soon passed off, the attacks of automatism began. These lasted for 24 to 48 hours and during them the man appeared to have no conscious volition. He was unable to speak and walked about unceasingly, making chewing movements with his jaw. He appeared to be totally insensible to pain and made no reaction to electric shocks or pin-pricks. If a pen was put into his hand he would write a sensible and well-constructed letter dealing with the topics of the day. This kind of dissociation of the ability to speak and to write, incidentally, is well recognized as a feature of temporal lobe damage and may occur after a stroke.

If given a cigarette paper the young man would seek out his tobacco and would neatly roll a cigarette and light it. If chopped linen threads were substituted for his tobacco, he would still make a cigarette and try to smoke it. A strange feature of his automatism was that he would try to steal anything portable that came his way. Because of his former profession, trials were made to see if he could still sing while in a state of automatism. It was found that if he were given a pair of the white gloves he had been accustomed to wear during his performances, he would carefully put these on and then go though a complex mime of giving a performance. He would appear to look through his music, take up position, bow to an audience and then launch into song.

There is a report of another remarkable case in a Detroit medical journal for 1859. It concerns a farm worker of 55 who, when once started on a job of physical work, appeared to have no power to stop. If sent to the woodpile for a log he would continue to carry in wood until the room was full. If asked to throw down a forkful of straw from the barn loft, he would continue until it was all on the ground. Often, he would drive himself to the point of utter exhaustion and sometimes he had to be restrained from his labours by force.

The fact that automatic action can occur apparently in the absence of awareness forces us to consider the question of the causal link between the brain and the mind – a relationship still denied by many people. This question was first addressed, in detail, by the French philosopher and mathematician René Descartes (1596–1650), who held that a human being consists of a body and a mind. The two ran, as it were, in parallel, working on each other, but were fundamentally distinct. This dualistic view is often known as Cartesian dualism (Cartesian because the 'Des' is a preposition and his definitive surname was Cartes). It holds that these two entities, although somehow related, are believed each to have an existence in its own right.

The problems with this idea are to account for how body and mind are related to each other and for how a mind can exist on its own. A dualistic theory must account for certain observable facts about human beings. Mental events are most certainly related to things that happen to the body. All sensations start as stimuli impinging on the body or occurring in the body; and all emotions give rise to bodily changes — effects such as dry mouth, fast pulse, pallor or redness of the face, a feeling of 'butterflies in the stomach', and so on. Descartes opted for *interactionism* — the view that mind and body are each capable of affecting the other causally. Events in one cause events in the other. One point on which Descartes was incorrect was in his proposal that it was the pineal gland that was the point at which this interaction took place. We now know the function of the pineal gland, and this is certainly *not* what it does.

Interactionism implies that the brain does not function exclusively in terms of neurology, but that it requires the intervention, at crucial moments, of the influences of the mind. But every advance in the understanding of brain function seems to suggest more and more strongly that the brain *does* function exclusively in terms of neurology. To get round this difficulty, the idea of *epiphenomenalism* was evolved. This is the view that the body can affect the mind but not vice versa; mental events are by-products of brain activity, just like bodily indications such as the blush of embarrassment or the grimace of pain.

Those philosophers who accepted the causal relationship between brain and mind but who still believed that these were distinct entities, often found it impossible to see how they could affect each other, causally or otherwise. So they came up with the idea of *parallelism*. This postulates that mind and brain are like two perfectly synchronized clocks, each with its own kind of mechanism but working in perfect coordination with each other. This may have been a brave try, but is much too hard to swallow. Elaborate explanations of this kind are usually wrong. Moreover, this idea still leaves us with a mysterious and invisible entity — the mind — floating about like some kind of ghost.

Until recently, Western medicine has accepted some kind of dualistic notion, usually without much consideration. Advances in neurophysiology and physiological psychology, especially since the start of the era of cognitive psychology, have, however, brought about a remarkable convergence of these disciplines and there are few biological or medical scientists of today who would disagree with the proposition that the mind is solely a function of brain activity. The persistence of Cartesian dualism has more to do with emotion than with logic and comes from the emotional necessity to believe that there is a part of us that can survive death. Since the body obviously cannot do so for long, we are left with the mind, or – as it was usually referred to in this context – the soul. Unfortunately, there seems to be no non-theological way to distinguish the soul from the mind.

Latter-day theologians, unable to gainsay the advances in neurophysiology, still refer constantly to the soul. This they define as 'a principle of being, rather than an entity, which exists for its own sake and has entered into an adventitious union with matter'. A 'principle of being' is defined as 'an intrinsic source of a being, as a result of which the being has characteristics none of which can be adequately explained by its other characteristics, though each one, being part of the whole, is co-determined by the whole'. This definition may satisfy the theologians but is hardly simple to understand.

Some philosophers have challenged the Cartesian dualistic view in a more profound way. Gilbert Ryle (1900–76), Professor of Philosophy at Oxford from 1945 to 1968 and editor of *Mind* for 24 years, suggested that any proposition about, indeed any consideration of, the relationship of the body and the mind assumes, unthinkingly, and unjustifiably, that these two terms – body and mind – are in the same logical class and can be considered in relation to each other. Since, as he insisted, they are not, such a statement is meaningless. The mind and the body, he claimed, are wholly different categories of concept and cannot logically be treated as if they were within the same category.

Ryle illustrated this by citing the category distinction between, on the one hand, the collection of the Oxford colleges – a physical entity – and, on the other, the University – a non-physical entity in the sense used by Newman in his remarkable book *On the Scope and Nature of University Education*. A stranger, unaware of the distinction, might, after being shown all the colleges, say: 'Very nice, but where is the University?' It would, according to Ryle, be logically meaningless to make certain statements about the (non-physical) University which would be perfectly meaningful if made about the (physical) colleges. It would, for instance, be meaningless to say that the University (meaning the non-physical entity) is being worn away by the passage of so many tourists. Such a statement, relating to the physical colleges, is perfectly meaningful.

Whatever the current status of this philosophical idea of categories, Ryle's position has not been contradicted by any advance in the understanding of the effect of bodily processes on consciousness and the emotions. It is clear that every bodily action and every perceived emotion is accompanied by some physical change in the body, whether it be a discharge of impulses along nerves or a change in the levels of hormones in the bloodstream. Changes in the levels of hormones, such as adrenaline or cortisol, are monitored by physical structures in the body and immediately produce changes in the nervous system. In the hypothalamus of the brain, an intimate two-way link exists between the hormonal (chemical) and the neural (electrical) systems. There is now no argument, among scientists, that the performance of the intellectual functions depends wholly on neurological activity and that these functions are progressively diminished by progressive destruction of brain structure.

Ryle's gentle joke was to refer to the Cartesian idea as that of a 'ghost in the machine'. In view of these observations, it is becoming increasingly difficult to maintain any version of dualism. Every advance in neurological and neuropharmacological understanding makes this position less tenable.

Unfortunately, such arguments seem by many to be anti-religious. Emotions are aroused, science is condemned, and logic departs. The solution to this seeming impasse may lie in the recognition that to equate mechanistic physiology with atheism is, if not a category mistake, certainly an error in simple logic. The theological position has nothing to do with science, or with the relationship of the brain and the mind. When theologians attempt, mistakenly, to keep up with scientists by adducing pseudoscientific 'logical' arguments to support their position, they do their cause no service.

Of the deadly dread of disease: hypochondriasis

To the ordinary, healthy, mentally-outgoing person, the mind of the hypochondriac will often seem extraordinary. One of the most notable literary links with hypochondriasis was that of the French dramatist Jean-Baptiste Poquelin (1622–73), who wrote under the pseudonym of Molière, and is generally regarded as the greatest comic writer in French literature. Molière's highly successful plays include *Tartuffe* (1664), *Le Misanthrope* (1666), *Le Médecin malgré lui* (1666), *L'Avare* (1668) and *Le Bourgeois gentilhomme* (1670), but the piece that has for ever associated him with the subject of this chapter was *Le Malade imaginaire* (1673).

There is no reason to suppose that Molière was, himself, a hypochondriac. Hypochondriacs are usually greatly in favour of doctors, and Molière was, in fact, a distinguished doctor-hater. One of his principal characteristics as a playwright was his skill in revealing defects of character – among his targets being hypocrites, misanthropes, misers, hypochondriacs, snobs and poseurs. The court of Louis XIV, to which Molière was attached as a favourite of the King, swarmed with medical quacks and it became a favourite game of his to show up these charlatans.

Molière suffered from pulmonary tuberculosis and the doctors could do nothing to help him – or anyone else with this disease. Early in his career he began to make use of the opportunities as a playwright to ridicule the medical profession, starting with the play *Féstin de Pierre* and continuing with *L'Amour médecin*, *Le Médecin malgré lui*, *Monsieur de Porceaugnac* and, above all, *Le Malade imaginaire*. The latter, unfortunately, although one of his greatest successes, was to be his undoing. It is a comedy of hypochondriasis containing an intermezzo ballet that is one of the most savage and amusing pieces of medical satire ever to appear on the stage. It satirizes the elaborate and lengthy medical graduation ceremonies of the seventeenth century and shows new doctors entering into a mystical union with the medical faculty while the chorus did their bits of stage business with enormous clyster (enema) syringes.

Molière always acted in his own plays, usually taking the principal comic parts, and at the fourth performance of *Le Malade imaginaire* the chest pain from the tuberculosis became particularly severe. His wife and his friend Baron, the actor, tried to persuade him not to appear, but Molière insisted. During the play he had a brief convulsion which he tried to conceal by a laugh. By the end of the performance he was seriously ill and was able to get home only with the assistance of Baron. The disease was eating into a large artery in his lung and soon after reaching home he began to cough blood. This rapidly worsened as the artery opened and the haemorrhage from his mouth quickly increased to the point at which he was asphyxiated – literally drowned in his own blood. It is a dramatic irony, in more ways than one, that Molière should have met his end in this way while representing a hypochondriac.

The fate of the true hypochondriac is usually a more fortunate, although not necessarily a happier one. Hypochondriasis is a defect of personality leading to a constant, but unjustified, conviction of illness. The hypochondriac is convinced that he or she is suffering from one or other of any number of serious organic disorders, and there is a tendency, as time passes, for the nature of the disorder to change.

The derivation of the term deserves mention. '*Hypo*' means 'under' and '*chondro*' means 'cartilage'. The hypochondrium is the area of the abdomen under the lower rib cartilages. The Greeks believed that the spleen, which lies in this area on the left, was the seat of melancholy and pessimism – hence hypochondriasis. Professor William Cullen of

Edinburgh published an excellent, if rather pompous, description of hypochondriasis in 1816:

> In certain persons, there is a state of mind distinguished by a concurrence of the following circumstances: a languor, listlessness or want of resolution and activity with respect to all undertakings; a disposition to seriousness, sadness and timidity; as to all future events, an apprehension of the worst or most unhappy state of them; and therefore, often upon slight grounds, an apprehension of great evil. Such persons are particularly attentive to the state of their own health, to every smallest change of feeling in their bodies; and from any unusual feeling, perhaps of the slightest kind, they apprehend great danger and even death itself. In respect to all these feelings and apprehensions, there is commonly the most obstinate belief and persuasion.

There is no limit to the range of conditions from which hypochondriacs may believe themselves to be suffering. One of the commonest forms of hypochondriasis, however, is the cardiac neurosis. This may take two forms. The first, which may be thought justified, is an excessively high level of anxiety suffered by someone who has had a heart attack and has recovered. Symptoms such as chest pain and tightness, breathlessness and palpitations are experienced, although these are not due to recurrence of the disease, and the affected person finds great difficulty in returning to a normal working life. The second is a mistaken conviction that one is suffering from heart disease. This is notoriously persistent and difficult to treat. Often, there is a family background of heart trouble and a belief that heart disease is hereditary – which it is not. The conviction is usually fortified by various symptoms, especially harmless palpitation, and chest pain, usually arising from heartburn.

Strong medical reassurance, even based on comprehensive examination and investigation, seldom succeeds in dispelling the belief and the unfortunate mental sufferer goes from doctor to doctor almost as if hoping for confirmation of the fears. There is little to be done to help such people. Logical arguments, and demonstration that the patient is capable of physical activity impossible to those with heart disease, do not impress. In most cases, the cardiac neurotic lives a long and medically uneventful life. In some cases, he does not.

Herein lies the doctor's dilemma. In the great majority of cases the complaints are entirely imaginary and to carry out repeated examinations and tests is not only to waste medical time and resources, but also to strengthen the patient's delusion and make his hypochondriasis worse. The wise doctor will take a very careful history before deciding that he or she is dealing with a hypochondriac, and will then offer a comprehensive scheme of examination and tests, with the explicit understanding that these, if negative, are to mark the end of investigation of the current complaint.

Doctors in general practice estimate that from 3 to 14 per cent of their patients are hypochondriacs. This may be a commentary on the doctors as much as on their patients. The peak incidence is said to occur in patients in their fifties and sixties but, as every doctor knows, hypochondriasis occurs at almost every age. It is common in adolescents and not unknown in children. It is thought to be slightly commoner in males than in females. If one identical twin is hypochondriac, it is extremely likely that the other will be so also. Medical students commonly suffer from an impressive form of hypochondriasis in which they are attacked, serially and consecutively, by each disease they study. Fortunately, this form is self-limiting as most students have a sufficiently acute sense of humour to appreciate the absurdity of the situation.

Regrettably, the true nature of hypochondriasis remains obscure, so no logical approach to treatment is possible. It has been thought to be a form of pathological depression, but it does not respond to anti-depressive treatment. The patient has full insight and cannot, by definition, be considered psychotic. It is not a form of malingering; the patient is genuinely convinced of the presence of serious disease. The psychoanalytic movement claims to understand the condition. According to this school of thought, hypochondriasis occurs because aggression towards others is transferred, by repression and displacement, into physical complaints. The anger of the hypochondriac arises from previous rejection and disappointments and is now expressed by demanding help and sympathy from doctors and then immediately rejecting them as ineffective. Hypochondriacs are also said to take on pain and suffering as a means of atonement for past wickedness.

The nearest that sensible doctors can come to a reasonable classification is to view it as an inherent defect of personality characterized by a low threshold of fear, and hypersensitivity to bodily sensation and to the awareness of the normal bodily functions. Some experts classify it as being of a narcissistic character featuring 'excessive concern with self and with the gratification of dependency needs'. It may be that, in some cases, hypochondriasis is used as a way of opting out of disagreeable obligations and duties, but it has to be said that there are many dedicated hypochondriacs who live a highly productive and fruitful life in the arts, literature, business, academia and even, remarkably enough, in medicine. The great majority of cases of the latter group, however, are transient and are experienced only during the clinical training.

With new hypochondriacal patients, the experienced physician soon recognizes that the symptoms do not wholly correspond to those of recognizable organic pathology and are not backed up by objective physical signs. Often they are bizarre, sometimes hilarious, but they are not delusions, and there are no other indications of psychosis. Hypochondriacal neurosis may remain seemingly unchanged for years or may take a varying course. Only a very small proportion of patients – perhaps one in 20 – will recover permanently. The condition is notoriously resistant to all forms of treatment.

Mind manipulated: the hypnotic state

The hypnotic 'trance', while certainly an extraordinary state of mind, is not the strange, mysterious thing that most people imagine. It is a manifestation of one of the properties of the mind -- that of being able to narrow down and concentrate its activities often to surprising, and even dramatic, effect. There is nothing magical about it, nor does it partake of the supernatural.

Around 1772, the Austrian physician Friedrich Anton Mesmer (1734–1815), determined to show how the planets influenced humankind, conceived the idea that there was a strange 'aethereal fluid' linking animate and inanimate matter, by which people were influenced by the stars. Having made this decision he then decided that, by the manipulation of the fluid, it should be possible to influence people in different ways by affecting the operation of their nervous systems. To control the aethereal fluid, Mesmer first tried magnets, which he fixed to the bodies of his subjects. Not surprisingly, this had no effect.

Mesmer then concluded that the magnets alone could not modulate the nervous system and that another principle was necessary. This principle, or power, which he postulated, and called 'animal magnetism', was analogous to physical magnetism between ferrous metals. To control it, Mesmer pointed his finger at his subjects, made strange passes with his hands and stared intently into his subjects' eyes. In many cases the effects were remarkable and Mesmer was able to exert a powerful influence over people, causing them to pass into a trance-like state. Some of his subjects were suffering from hysterical and other conditions and, in some instances, by telling them that they would be cured, Mesmer succeeded in dispelling these disorders.

In 1778, Mesmer treated an 18-year-old blind patient, a Miss Paradis. Mesmer's own accounts of the Paradis case reveal that hers was an obvious case of hysterical blindness and that there were other gross manifestations of neurosis. There is, however, clear indication that he had restored at least some degree of vision. Perhaps as a result of this, she fell for him, but her parents, after their initial delight at their daughter's recovery, turned against Mesmer, partly on the grounds that a pension their daughter had might be stopped, and denounced him. Allegations of improper conduct were made, a scandal succeeded, and he was forced to flee to Paris.

In a short time Mesmer had become famous. His process became widely known as 'mesmerism' and he created a sensation with his *séances* at which he purported to cure all kinds of diseases. He was offered an enormous sum of money for the secret of his remarkable treatment but refused it. In 1785 his claims were investigated by an official commission of doctors appointed by the French Academy of Sciences and he was denounced as an impostor. After that he retired into obscurity. The downfall of Mesmer was a considerable injustice because, although many of his claims were spurious and were easily disproved, and although the theory he proposed for what he was doing was fatuous, he had indeed had some real successes. Much more importantly, he had discovered, and demonstrated, a remarkable property of the mind that could be of some medical value.

A more accurate notion of the nature of the mesmeric state was formed by the Manchester surgeon James Braid (1795–1860), who took up the study of the subject around 1841 and who coined the term 'hypnotism'. Braid demonstrated that the state could be induced by a process of tiring the subject's eye muscles or even by the simple power of suggestion. Mesmer's magnetic passes were unnecessary and the whole idea of animal magnetism began to be seen to be what it actually was – complete nonsense.

Braid, too, had a difficult time. He was, of course, condemned by the supporters of Mesmer's ideas, but was also condemned by the orthodox medical profession, who still remembered the extraordinary claims and theories of the long-dead Mesmer. The *Lancet* talked of 'gross humbug' and a paper Braid wrote for the British Association for the Advancement of Science was rejected.

Braid dissociated himself from animal magnetism and candidly confessed that he was unable to account for the phenomenon which readily enabled him to induce 'cataleptiform rigidity or the extreme opposite condition' in his subjects. He was aware 'that great prejudice had been raised against hypnotism, from the idea that it might be turned to immoral purposes' but was quite certain that it deserved no such censure. He went on to say:

> I have proved by experiments that during the state of excitement, the judgment is sufficiently active to make the patients, if possible, even more fastidious as regards propriety of conduct, than in the waking condition. We have acquired the power of raising sensibility to the most extraordinary degree, and also of depressing it far below the torpor of natural sleep.

Braid stated that hypnotism was 'a simple, speedy and certain mode of throwing the nervous system into a new condition.' Above all, he insisted that it was not a universal remedy, as Mesmer had claimed. Gradually, hypnotism acquired respectability. Many reputable academics, especially in France, investigated the condition and stripped it of its magical and imaginative associations. Twentieth-century studies by Clark L. Hull at Yale, E. R. Hilgard of New York, and many others, put it on a regular scientific footing and clarified its properties and limitations. It was established that there were differences of hypnotic suggestibility and that scales could be constructed to classify different people in this respect. The findings of these researchers include that there is no gender difference in susceptibility; that children are more easily hypnotized than adults, children between about 8 and 12 years old being most susceptible of all; that it is possible to induce selective changes in sensory sensitivity, to abolish pain, for instance, or to produce deafness; and that major illusions and hallucinations can be induced in people of high susceptibility.

Changes in behaviour appropriate to suggested age regression can be induced, but there is serious doubt whether regression to infancy can genuinely be obtained. Regression to 'previous existences' is, of course, sheer fantasy.

Post-hypnotic suggestion, in which the subject feels obliged to carry out certain acts at some time after being instructed to do so during a hypnosis session, is one of the more bizarre aspects of the subject. Only some subjects can be induced to show this effect. The susceptible person can be told to forget that the suggestion has been made but to perform the required act. The question as to why he or she behaves in this manner will usually elicit some elaborate and variously plausible rationalization. The production of blisters and other skin phenomena by pure suggestion, as of burning or other trauma, is an established fact.

The hypnotic state is often described as being one of sleep or drowsiness, but this is a fundamental misconception. There may certainly be diminished awareness of reality, but hypnosis is quite different from sleep. Subjects do not relax their muscles as in sleep; reflexes absent during sleep are readily elicited; and the record of brain waves (electroencephalogram, or EEG) is entirely characteristic of full wakefulness. The subject under hypnosis shows sharply narrowed concentration of attention with greatly reduced self-awareness and self-criticism. It is this property that allows stage hypnotists to make fools of their willing victims and to exploit the phenomenon for the amusement of others and for personal gain.

Hypnotism has a limited value in medicine and dentistry. It has been used to control pain and to allay anxiety. It has sometimes been possible, by hypnotism, to achieve treatments wished by the patient but greatly feared. It is sometimes used by psychotherapists as an aid to treatment. One disadvantage, however, is the greatly varying susceptibility of different people to suggestion, so that the method cannot be relied upon for general use. In itself, it appears to be harmless, but experienced practitioners point out that, in subjects unsuspectingly suffering from psychiatric disorder, the effects of the use of hypnotism may be to induce strong emotional relationships (transferences) of both positive and negative kinds with which the hypnotist may not be equipped, by knowledge or professional ethical restraints, to deal.

Of faith and fossils: what is truth?

In 1586, a man called James Ussher was born in Dublin. He was to become a person of great piety, industry and erudition, a notable scholar, a prolific writer, a Privy Councillor and an Archbishop. Today Ussher is forgotten except for one thing – he worked out the date of the beginning of the world. According to a careful calculation derived from data from the Bible, and published in the book *Chronologia Sacrae*, this took place in the year 4004 BC. In his day, and for over 200 years afterwards, Ussher's reputation was such that this date commanded almost universal acceptance and was hardly questioned.

Another man of great distinction, Charles Lyell, was born in 1797, took a degree at Oxford and, to please his parents, studied law and was called to the bar. He hated the law, however, and turned to science. While at Oxford he had sat in on some geology lectures and found the subject fascinating, so for several years he travelled in Europe studying the geology of all the regions he visited, and writing papers for the *Transactions of the Geological Society of London* on what he had seen. These papers aroused great interest and his reputation rapidly grew. The first volume of his great work *Principles of Geology* was published in 1830, and in 1832 he was appointed Professor of Geology at the new King's College, London. Before his career as a geologist was over he had been knighted for his scientific work and had had an honorary degree from Oxford conferred on him. He died in 1875 and was buried in Westminster Abbey.

During Lyell's lifetime, and to a large extent because of his studies and popular writings, which epitomized his own findings and those of many other geologists, there was a radical change in outlook – a paradigm shift – not only in the scientific community but even in that of the educated lay public. Lyell and others had made plain that the world was enormously older than Ussher had ever dreamt. Furthermore, the things the geologists had discovered about fossils, and the conclusions they had derived from these findings, were the principal stimuli that led Charles Darwin to recognize the significance of his own observations and to propose his theory of evolution by natural selection. This idea, once understood, was immediately seen by many people to be completely convincing. Today, it is accepted in its general principles by all disinterested scientists.

Geochronology, that is, the science of the age of the earth, involves studying the strata of rocks and the fossils preserved within them. Rock outcroppings provide us with information from which we can deduce their age. About 70 per cent of all rocks are sedimentary – formed by the slow settling and compression of suspended particles from the oceans. It is a fairly straightforward matter to work out roughly the length of time it takes for a given layer of sedimentary rock to form. Lower strata are older and those above are more recent. The forms of the fossilized plants and animals that have been trapped in these sediments provide confirmation of relative age. Structurally simpler and more primitive forms are older; more complex forms are more recent. This kind of work makes it possible to construct a relative geological time scale.

These geological discoveries threw the cat right in among the theological pigeons. No sensible person could deny that the scientific facts of geology were true: they were self-evidently so. They were incontrovertible facts and led powerfully to the idea of evolution. Unfortunately, they were in clear contradiction to the first few verses of the book of Genesis in the Bible. What was to be done?

There were a few very ingenious attempts to get round the problem. One idea of the churchmen was to propose the idea that God had created the rocks, complete with fossils just to test people's faith. This one was a bit too rich for most people. Abraham Gottlob Werner, a distinguished and highly regarded scholar of the time, came up with a slightly better suggestion. His idea was that all rocks were the result either of sedimentation in God's primaeval ocean during Noah's flood, or were the result of deposition occurring during the retreat of the flood from the land. These ideas seemed, for a time, to save the theological bacon, but a later and more critical study showed that they would not hold water. Not only did they not conform to many clear geological observations, but, in addition, there were rocks – basaltic rocks – that pushed up through the sedimentary rocks from the interior of the earth and could not have been formed by deposition.

We now know that a flood that covered all the land – which it would have had to do to provide all the sedimentary rocks and to fit with the biblical story – would involve an atmosphere of almost 100 per cent pure water vapour. So Noah and his family and animals would not have been able to breathe. Since the time of Lyell and Werner there have been great advances, especially in the field of radiometric dating, which is based on the known rate of decay of radioactive atoms. These methods have enabled us to determine the age of various rocks that predate the appearance of life on earth. Today, no orthodox scientist believes that the world, to say nothing of the universe, was created in the manner described in the book of Genesis (there are, of course, many scientists who are committed Christians, but not fundamentalists, as will be seen).

There are many other difficulties in the way of a person who holds that every word of the Bible is literally true. Quite apart from the many obvious inconsistencies between the characteristics of the bloodthirsty God of the Old Testament and the loving God of the New, there is the question of the sources and origins of the Bible. The Bible is not the exclusive province of Christianity. A large part of it – the Old Testament – is also a sacred text of Judaism. The versions of the Bible used by the Protestant and Roman Catholic churches are not quite the same. Some of the books and parts of books of the Roman Catholic version of the Old Testament were declared questionable (apocryphal) by the Protestants and were removed from their Bible. The book of Revelation (the Apocalypse) is a selection, officially recognized as theologically acceptable, from a large quantity of apocalyptic literature that was written in the early days of Christianity.

No one knows who originally wrote the books of the Old Testament. We do not even know whether they were written by single authors or by organized groups of scholars. We know, however, that nearly all of the Old Testament was first written in Hebrew, with some parts in Aramaic. Scholars have been able to identify many sources for the Old Testament. Those for the Pentateuch, that is the first five books of the Old Testament, include two books – 'The Book of the Wars of Yahweh [God]' and 'The Book of Yashar [the Upright]'. These books no longer exist but material was taken from them. Most of the New Testament seems to have been written in Greek, again with some Aramaic.

Later, the Pentateuch was translated from the Hebrew into Aramaic, which was the common language of the Mediterranean area at the time. In due course, Aramaic gave way to Greek, and in the third century BC the Aramaic version was translated into Greek. In AD 382 the Pope commissioned the leading biblical scholar of the time, a man called Jerome, to produce a Latin translation of the whole Bible. Jerome only took about a year to complete his translation of the New Testament, but he worked on the Old Testament for 23 years. Jerome based the Pentateuch initially on the Greek version but later decided that this was unsatisfactory, so he eventually went back to the original Hebrew. The result was the 'common version' or Vulgate Bible. Jerome was eventually canonized. There was no printing in those days and copies could be made only by hand. Needless to say, not all the copyists were as careful as they might be and many errors and corruptions of the text occurred. Even so, the Vulgate is the basis of the Bible we have today.

Most of the sources of the New Testament are known. Matthew and Luke are believed by contemporary scholars to have derived their accounts mainly from Mark, but all three also derived material directly from the sayings of Jesus. For these reasons the first three gospels are called 'synoptic' – having a common source. The Gospel according to St John seems to have come from separate sources. The other sources of the New Testament are some five thousand manuscripts in Greek dating from the second to the fifteenth century AD and numerous translations of the early Greek and Aramaic text into other languages. Some of the material also consists of quotations from the New Testament by early Christian writers. Modern translations are based on a selection by the translator from these many sources. Different translators make their selection in accordance with their own views, tastes and styles.

The interesting thing about all this, however, and the relevance to our present topic, is that there are millions of people who still maintain that every word of the Bible is literally true. Many of these people are not aware of the geological evidence or of the origins and history of the Bible, but a great number of them are educated people who know all about the scientific arguments, and about biblical studies. So which is the extraordinary state of mind? That of the rigid unbending scientist who is confined by the limitations of scientific observation and theory and who insists that every belief must be based on strict logic; or that of people to whom religious faith and the comforts and support provided by religion are so fundamentally important that, by comparison, logical inconsistency carries very little weight?

Two things must be said. Firstly, there are many scientists of profound religious faith who are able to regard the Bible, not as a document, every word of which is literally true, but as a metaphorical expression of religious truth – a collection of allegories. Secondly, there are many creationists and literalists who feel compelled to strive to maintain their position by reasonable argument. The human mind cannot rest easy if it has to live with logical inconsistency. Something has to be done to resolve the problem and it is not clear how the solution can ever be logical. Whatever the solution elected, it becomes cherished and will be defended vigorously against all attackers.

Because the adherence to it is primarily emotional rather than rational, strong emotions tend to be raised. So, among the educated, the scientists have the easier time of it because they hold what seems to them a consistent paradigm. This is not, of course, an argument in favour of the truth of the rationalist standpoint.

The creationists believe passionately in their position. They are not stupid, or mad or 'misguided'. Their belief, that the Bible is the literal word of God, is at the foundation of their religion and, like so many of the proselytizers of the past, they see themselves justified in taking extreme measures to promote this belief. For a group without much logic on their side, they have been remarkably successful. Some of them, especially groups in the southern United States, have been promoting a strong movement to provide for the teaching of creationism in schools. Their activities may have led to the wide-spread, but entirely erroneous, public perception in some areas that acceptance of Darwinian evolution is contrary to all religious belief. A textbook called *Of Pandas and People: The Central Question of Biological Origins* has been delivered widely to schools in more than a dozen US states. This book informs its readers that the theory of evolution is incompatible with the complexity of life. What it does not make plain to its readers is that evolution is accepted as true – almost as self-evident – by virtually all biologists and other scientists.

The creationist movement is based on the premise that the whole complexity of life as we know it was created at the same time – in present-day language, the 'initial complexity model'. Their current epithet for the theory of evolution side-steps the actual nature of the theory by referring to it as the 'initial primitiveness model'. The movement is attempting to get its supporters onto school boards and state education committees. From late 1996, all biology textbooks in Alabama must contain an insert that states that evolution is contro-versial and should not be regarded as a fact.

In a democratic country, anyone with a passionately and sincerely held belief is perfectly entitled to express it and to try to persuade others to accept it. This is what the American creationists have been doing, and their success is an impressive commentary on the ease with which reasonable counsels can be set aside. Partly as a result of their activities, a high proportion of American first-year university students have no clear idea of Darwin's evolutionary theory — the idea that unifies the whole of modern biology. Recent polls have indicated that about half of the population of the United States and Canada reject the scientific account of evolution and accept the biblical story of creation. This is not a bad record of achievement in the face of the scientific evidence.

'What is truth?' said jesting Pilate; and would not stay for an answer.

Francis Bacon, *Essays*

Alien abduction: all in the mind?

People who have been abducted by aliens show a remarkable consistency in the stories they tell. The event starts with a sudden paralytic experience, often associated with an intense blue light that seems to be the cause of the paralysis. This usually occurs at night and often out of doors or during a car journey. The paralysis renders the victims completely immobile so that they are at the mercy of the aliens. Sometimes the light is accompanied by a humming sound and a tingling sensation as of intense energy. The victims are then bodily transported, often through a physical barrier such as the roof of a car or a wall, and carried upwards on a beam of some kind into the alien craft. This is almost invariably saucer-shaped and is floating high above the earth. The craft is usually of a silver colour and has a dome on top. In almost all cases it has lights that rotate.

Once inside the alien craft, the victims are subjected to a scientific examination in which all the body orifices are entered and the interior inspected. Commonly, sperm are removed from men and eggs from women. Sperm removal may be achieved by the deliberate induction of an erection and an orgasm with milking of seminal fluid. Successful milking seems to excite great satisfaction in the aliens. Sperm and eggs are used to produce hybrid beings that are usually incubated in the flying saucer in tall tubular transparent plastic containers supplied with suitable nutrients. The hybrids, even in their embryonic stages, radiate a powerful intelligence that is almost palpable. They are destined later to populate the earth. Often, the victims are brought back on later occasions to the alien craft and are shown the progress and development of their hybrids. Sometimes, the motive of the aliens appears to be different and the victims have to undergo the implantation of electronic or other devices – presumably for control purposes – into their brains. Happily, surgery of this kind appears not to be particularly painful.

There is also considerable consistency in the description of the alien beings. These come in various sizes, but most of them are smaller than humans. The majority seem to be about 1 metre tall and their bodies are naked and have a rubbery quality. They do not appear to have jointed limbs but the limbs are capable of flexion. Most are grey in colour, but some are smaller and darker, almost purple. The superior beings, those who conduct the examinations and perform the surgery, are usually taller than average, often as tall as humans. Although the aliens are small and weak-looking, some abductees have reported that they are enormously strong.

Communication is not by normal language but by what seems to be some kind of telepathic process in which the eyes are important. In conversing – or informing – the aliens come very close and stare fixedly at the victim. In external appearance the eyes appear to be identical to human eyes except that they are often larger.

In some cases the victims have been shown previews of the destruction of the earth. These do not appear to be threats of alien aggression but warnings of what will happen if our present course of ecological indifference and environmental damage continues.

Experts in the field of alien abduction tell us that the experience is far commoner than is reported. There is a good reason for this. Public scepticism is so strong that anyone brave enough to admit to such an experience is immediately branded as either mad, a liar or dangerously imaginative. Such people may even be at risk of losing their jobs because they are held to be unreliable. Many of the people who have had abduction experiences are well aware of these dangers and so they keep quiet about it all and just go on living with the secret knowledge of what has happened to them.

Sceptics have suggested that alien abduction is simply a Western cultural phenomenon based on science fiction stories and films, but the experts tell us that this is not so. They point out that these experiences have been reported from all over the world. They assure us that reputable psychiatrists who have examined these victims are convinced that the experiences are genuine. They also assure us that the occasional abduction has been seen by a number of independent witnesses. The case of the woman who was abducted from the twelfth floor of a New York apartment at 3 a.m. was, they say, allowed by the aliens to be witnessed by others. Some of the witnesses were terrified. One of them even saw the alien craft, which was said to be enormous.

The experts claim that many millions of people have had encounters with aliens. Many of them are unaware of it, the experience having been repressed in their minds by the aliens. Many others are only too aware of what has happened but dare not talk about it. Some know that something very strange has happened to them but do not realize the true nature of what it is. The experts tell us that there are very definite signs of a past alien abduction. These include memories of flying through the air; the perception of beams of light; dreams of UFOs; waking up in a strange place or in a strange position in bed; the presence of unexplained scars or indentations on the surface of the body or within the mouth or nose; being pregnant and then not pregnant; having a feeling of being watched; waking with painful or sore genitalia; waking with indications of having had a nose bleed; waking with unusual body stiffness; the experience of telepathic messages; being convinced that you must not get involved in a sexual relationship with anyone; and having had cosmic awareness. Any of these things could be an indication that you have had an unsuspected alien abduction.

So far so good. But there are some other things you should know. Are you aware that there are a great many, probably 200, inhabited planets in our own galaxy – to say nothing of the countless millions of other galaxies in the universe? This is known because some of these planets have been visited by an earthling who has lived on them for several days. Are you aware that it is possible to obtain the help and advice of advanced hermaphrodite people who are billions of years ahead of us in development? Are you aware that these people know the purpose of our existence and the purpose of life on earth? Are you aware that space travel across multi-dimensional space is possible at speeds much greater than the speed of light? Are you aware that planet earth is very near the bottom of the scale of civilized evolution?

The chances are that you are not aware of these things, mainly because you have not read the book *Thiaoouba Prophecy* by Michel Desmarquet, which has gone into four editions and has been translated into Japanese. This book has been described as 'one of the most important books in the last 2000 years'. This is because it contains information vital to our future, provided by people from the planet Thiaoouba.

Now for the other side of the story. There is not a scrap of evidence − of the kind that would stand up in a court of law − that extraterrestrial 'aliens' have ever visited this planet or that they even exist. There is not a scrap of scientific evidence to support the proposition that people can be teleported up into hovering craft of any kind. There is no known physical principle by which a large craft could hover silently overhead. For such a craft to do so would require a tremendous fiery down-thrust from rockets or massive helicopter-like blades on top. There is no physical evidence whatsoever of the arrival of UFOs that could not very much more plausibly be explained by natural forces or events. On the other hand, there are plenty of psychological and other explanations that can account for the unquestioned experiences of many people who have heard of alien abduction, and there are highly plausible reasons why these claimed experiences resemble each other.

Some of the people who claim to have had alien encounters are breathtaking liars, but most of them are perfectly genuine people who believe what they say. These people do not deserve derision; they deserve sympathy, understanding, and often help. In many cases they are very unhappy people with real problems and we should be compassionate rather than censorious.

Of course, debunking of this kind is terribly boring, and journalists and others are simply not interested in it. There is a considerable market for sensational stories of alien encounters, but no market for books that pour cold water on all these stories, and publishers inevitably opt for books they expect to sell well. The result, of course, is that there is a great deal of 'evidence' for alien abduction and little or no defence against it.

Why do humans want to believe in this nonsense? There are several reasons, and they all throw light on the extraordinary state of the human mind. For most people there is simply too much science around – too many explanations and not enough mystery. For many people, explanations are cold and tedious and seriously lacking in excitement. The possibility of visitation by beings from outer space so far ahead of us that they can be supposed to have special insight into our perennial philosophical questions, provides excitement and interest comparable to that given by the explorers of the remote corners of the globe 150 years ago. There really is not enough of the unknown left to us these days.

Perhaps a deeper reason is that in a mechanistic age when even the greatest wonders can readily be explained away, there is a serious lack of spiritual sustenance. For many, there is a kind of spiritual hunger that only the amalgamation of some kind of mystical experience with science can satisfy.

The absent mind:
persistent vegetative state

This section is not about absent-mindedness but about something far more serious — the complete absence of the mind. The so-called persistent vegetative state can occur in a person who has suffered a particular form of severe brain damage. In most cases of severe brain damage the whole of the brain is injured and the affected person either dies or is left severely disabled. In the persistent vegetative state, the victim retains what might be called the 'lower' functions of the brain — the automatic brain mechanisms that keep the heart beating and the lungs breathing — but no longer has the higher functions. These higher functions operate in the fairly thin outer 'rind' of the brain, the part called the cortex.

The cortex of the brain is the most advanced part and, in evolutionary terms, the most recently developed. It contains the mechanisms for seeing; hearing; smelling; tasting; feeling touch, pressure, pain and other sensations; remembering; speaking; formulating language and understanding words; thinking; engaging in artistic and creative pursuits; and so on. In human brains, the cortex is thicker and more highly developed than in the brains of any other species. The further down you go in the evolutionary scale, the less prominent become those parts of the cortex concerned with what we consider as our higher functions — the activities of the mind and intellect — and the relatively more prominent become those parts concerned with matter such as smelling, seeing and hearing.

The lower brain functions, those common to all vertebrates, are in the stem of the brain, just above the point at which the spinal cord starts. These lower functions have nothing to do with volition or awareness and most of them operate automatically. We do not have to breathe deliberately to keep breathing, and we do not have to take thought to keep our hearts beating.

Probably because they are so complex, the parts of the brain concerned with the higher functions are more easily damaged than the lower. They are, for instance, much more sensitive to oxygen deprivation than the parts in the brainstem. It is this difference in resistance to damage that leads, in a small proportion of cases of severe head injury, to the persistent vegetative state. In people in this condition the lower parts of the brain are working normally, but the higher parts are not working at all. Because the brainstem functions are preserved, the person concerned breathes spontaneously and does not require mechanical ventilation. Since voluntary movement is initiated in the cortex, this is totally abolished and there is complete paralysis of all four limbs. Eye movements are, however, controlled from nerve centres in the brainstem and so the eyes can still move. The eyes will often open spontaneously and remain open for long periods. They may even follow a moving object. Similarly, the head may be turned and facial movement is possible. The head may turn suddenly in response to a strong stimulus and there may be grimacing. Sometimes the affected person will groan and make other sounds. He or she will never, however, speak any words or make any kind of meaningful response. There is no indication of any kind that conscious mental activity is present. If a person in a persistent vegetative state is fed and nursed, he or she may remain, in the crudest physiological sense, 'alive' for many years.

Most cases of the persistent vegetative state are caused by cutting nerve connections between the cortex and the lower parts. Unfortunately, although many human tissues can regenerate and join up, brain nerves cannot. So, once cut, these vital connections cannot be re-established. Cutting of the nerve links results from the kind of massive shake-up of the brain that is involved in severe head injuries. The living brain is not hard like the ones you may have seen preserved in jars in a museum: such brains have been soaked in formalin, which has a powerful hardening effect. The real, living, brain is very soft, almost jelly-like. So you can imagine the degree of distortion that occurs in severe injury, such as the kind of thing that happens when a person comes off a motor cycle at high speed, or goes through a car windscreen in a crash. The whole brain swings and twists.

Most of the other cases of persistent vegetative state are due to damage to the brain from bleeding inside the skull or from temporary loss of the blood supply to the brain. This means that the vital oxygen and glucose fuel are unavailable. The metabolism of brain tissue is very high – it uses far more oxygen and glucose than an equal weight of any other tissue. Deprivation of these supplies will cause damage within a few minutes. At normal temperatures, if the blood supply to the brain is cut off for more than about five minutes, the brain is likely to be fatally injured. Such deprivation may result from heart stoppage (cardiac arrest), near-drowning, asphyxiation or a long period of very low blood glucose (hypoglycaemia) in a diabetic person. There are several other possible causes of the persistent vegetative state. Probably the next most common is Alzheimer's disease and other forms of dementia, such as that caused by repeated strokes. The condition can also be caused by brain infection (encephalitis), poisoning and congenital brain defects.

Doctors are extremely careful to avoid assuming wrongly that a person is in a persistent vegetative state. There are, in fact, several other conditions that may be mistaken for it. It could be confused with profound sedation by drugs; total muscle paralysis by curare-like poisons; hypothermia; simple dementia and blindness; and a night-marish condition known as the 'locked-in state', in which the affected person is fully conscious but paralysed and unable to communicate in any way except by moving the eyes and blinking.

Is recovery possible? This, of course, depends on the degree of damage. If there is severance of all the cortical connections or destruction of the cortex, there is no question of recovery; such cases should be described as 'permanent vegetative state'. There have, however, been quite a number of cases in which people have come out of a persistent vegetative state. Most of these have been children and almost all of them have recovered within a year of onset. Most doctors would agree that after a year, the cortex must be assumed to be dead. There are some objective signs that the case is hopeless. Brain scanning, for instance, may show actual loss of cortical and other tissue with enlargement of the normal fluid spaces in the brain (the ventricles).

One of the great difficulties that lay people have in coming to terms with a relative with persistent vegetative state is that the affected person appears to be alive. When strong physical stimuli cause crude responses, such as turning of the head or movement of the eyes, it is difficult not to interpret these as signs of consciousness. So how can we tell that a person in this state is not conscious? How can we be sure that, although the cortex may be cut off from the rest of the body, it may still not be the seat of consciousness? Do we really know enough about the relationship between the brain and the mind to be sure about our assertions that such people have no awareness and thus no possibility of feeling pain or of suffering in any other way, and are incapable of experiencing anything?

The problem here is that many people, both inside and outside the medical profession, have serious misconceptions about the meaning of the word 'death'. This difficulty goes back a long way. From earliest times life was equated with breathing. An old test for whether someone was alive was to hold a cold mirror to a patient's face to see if it clouded as a result of condensation from the breath. More recently, life was equated with the presence of a heartbeat. Indeed, this criterion of life was widely accepted until comparatively recently. When it was shown that respiration could be maintained artificially by an air pump, the criterion of the heartbeat displaced the idea of breathing. But we now know that the heart is even less sensitive to oxygen lack than the brainstem and that it can go on beating long after the brain has been destroyed.

In any real sense, death means death of the brain. Since loss of spontaneous respiration and loss of heartbeat can occur in sequence, sometimes with long intervals between them, death is not an event but a process. In many cases the exact time of death can never be accurately established. Until effective resuscitation was developed, people who suffered brain death seldom survived long. The large number of people who, in recent years, have passed into a persistent vegetative state is largely an unhappy consequence of scientific advance. This poses a dilemma for the doctors. Their responsibility is to do everything they can to save life. Advances in first aid and medical technology have put powerful tools into their hands and these tools have saved countless lives and restored many people to full health. The doctors' problem is that they cannot, in the early stages, distinguish those in whom the outlook is hopeless from those who may recover. The result is that many people who should be left to die are kept artificially 'alive'.

This book is about the mind. The big question for many non-scientific readers is whether people in this condition have a mind. Here we run into another difficulty arising from long-held habits of thought. We have all become accustomed to thinking of the mind and the body as if they were quite distinct and separate entities. Almost all neurophysiologists and most biological scientists agree, however, that the mind, however we define it, is a function of the brain. Every component of the conscious mind has its corresponding area, or set of areas, of the brain. When any one or more of these areas is destroyed, the corresponding mental faculty – whether it be memory, emotion, volition, the experiences of seeing, hearing, smelling, tasting, and so on – is lost. Memory is not, like many of the other faculties, located in any one place in the cortex of the brain. It is a comprehensive faculty requiring access to almost all parts of the cortex – for verbal memory, visual memory, olfactory memory, tactile memory, and so on. The areas for registration and recall of memories and for short-term memory (like holding a telephone number in the mind until we make a call) are localized and are known, and destruction of these deprives us of the power of storing memories or recalling them or of keeping items in the mind for even a few seconds. If the whole of the cortex has suffered global damage, as in severe dementia or late Alzheimer's disease, all aspects of memory may be lost.

Thinking, entirely in the abstract, is impossible. We can only think either by talking internally to ourselves or by visualizing internally. Abstract words, like 'understand', have been derived from concrete ideas like 'standing under'. All thinking is thus closely linked to sensory experience and to memory. In addition, there is clear evidence that, in order to be put to work, the cortex requires sensory input. In other words, the brain has to be stimulated into action. People who are experimentally deprived of sensory input – by being placed in a environment of total darkness, perfect silence, appropriate temperature and minimal skin contact sensation – do not engage in deep philosophical thought. They tend to lose all touch with reality and then to drift into a kind of mindless state almost like coma. It is, of course, impossible to arrange total sensory deprivation. Considerable sensory input, for instance, comes from the interior of the body itself. But even an approximation to it can show its effects. In the waking state the cortex needs a great deal of information input coming up to it by way of the sensory nerves connected to the sense organs and the skin. All this adds up to one very clear conclusion. If the cortex is dead, or its input and output connections from and to the outside world are severed, the mind no longer exists.

This is the view taken by most scientists. But there are others who refuse to accept what they consider to be the 'reductionist' view that the mind is 'nothing more' than a by-product or epiphenomenon of brain function. To such people, the destruction of parts of the brain does not destroy parts of the mind; it simply cuts these parts off from our consciousness or awareness. The whole of the mind still exists but bits of it are no longer accessible. To these people, followers of the French philosopher René Descartes (1596–1650), the mind has an existence of its own remote from the body. This idea, known as Cartesian dualism (see **Human as machine**), was almost universally believed until the twentieth century. It is now gradually being eroded and few people who understand the facts of the matter now hold to it.

Some modern philosophers have even proposed that it is meaningless to ask such a question as 'does the mind exist?' because the words 'mind' and 'existence' belong to quite different categories and cannot rationally be related to one another.

It is, of course, impossible to make scientific statements about a matter that is right outside the province of science. The idea that the mind has an existence independently of the brain is in the realm of theology and has to be a matter of faith rather than of something that can be proved or disproved. In this context, the word 'mind' tends to be equated with the word 'soul'. For most people, the idea of a conscious mind that is somehow linked to a body but that is incapable of moving or otherwise affecting the body, or expressing itself through the body, is as frightening as it is implausible. People who fully understand the facts outlined in this chapter are likely to take the view that, although this possibility cannot be wholly discounted, consciousness without a brain is a contradiction in terms.

Incidentally, many doctors believe that once the diagnosis of the persistent vegetative state is positively and unequivocally established, it is unethical to persist in maintaining physiological life – that to do so is, in fact, an unwarranted interference with nature. They believe that, if the relatives and others concerned agree, it is proper to end all efforts to maintain this meaningless form of life. A number of cases have been the subject of detailed legal argument both in the UK and USA, and this belief has been upheld in law.

The creative mind:
inspiration or perspiration?

There is something truly extraordinary about the creative mind. The ability to produce something completely new is, in a sense, antagonistic to conventional logical thought. This is especially so in the production of new science. Normal scientific thinking tends to be convergent – a process of synthesis in which causally related phenomena are put together in a conventional way. Creative thought is divergent and often appears irrational – a leap in the dark, a process of 'lateral thinking', of dreaming or fantasizing or engaging in analogies or in free associations. Creativity is the realm of those whose minds are not necessarily restrained by logic but who are, nevertheless, capable of logic when logic is appropriate.

It is impossible to generalize about creativity or to provide a ready recipe for the process. Creativity is a mysterious activity and the ways in which creative artists and scientists go about their business vary greatly. People producing work of comparable creative status appear to create with greatly varying degrees of difficulty. As a classic example, Mozart composed his numerous masterpieces at top speed, with no hesitation and few amendments. He could see every note in the score in the mind before picking up his pen. Brahms, in contrast, would get into a dreadful state of distress, weeping and groaning in the agony of his composition. Some composers write, like Mozart, at a table, hearing the music in their heads; others cannot work without an instrument such as a piano.

Much experience has shown that important problems are often solved, not at the height of concentrated thought, but in the period of relaxation afterwards. Solutions are often apparent on waking from a night's sleep, especially if the matter has been dwelt on beforehand. It seems that once the unconscious mind is supplied with the necessary data and given time to work on it, it may come up with a surprising answer. Einstein, noted for the extreme originality of some of his most important ideas, pithily remarked that the really creative scientists are those with access to their dreams. To produce something completely new, it is often necessary to forget conventional wisdom.

No one really understands the nature of the creative process. It is said that the difference between a craftsman and an artist is that the craftsman knows exactly what the outcome of his effort will be before he starts, while an artist must wait until the work is complete before discovering what has been achieved. Many artists would dispute this, but many would agree. There are, of course, those who know in advance exactly what they want to achieve and appear to be concerned solely with the means of doing so. Some artists find that the production of a work of art involves recognizable successive stages such as preparation, incubation, inspiration and elaboration. Others experience all these stages repeatedly in the same act of creation, or describe other stages. Some begin in a state of confusion with many fragmentary ideas competing for attention in the mind. For these people, the nature of the new creation appears very gradually. As ideas are put together or rejected, some kind of definitive entity solidifies from the mist.

Freudian and Jungian psychologists have had plenty to say about the creative process, but their theories have been no more enlightening than those of other schools. Freud initially saw creativity as the working out of unconscious desires. He called this 'wish fulfilment'. Later, as his ideas changed, he came to see the creative act as a process of defence by the ego against indictments by the superego. In ordinary language, this means that the superior, ethical and censorious part of the mind was being so critical of the ordinary part of the mind that the latter felt it had to produce something to justify its existence and behaviour. Like many of Freud's 'explanations', this one no longer commands much respect. Jung, in his life-long preoccupation with symbols, saw creativity as an unconscious symbol-making process.

While it would be unreasonable to expect to be able to understand the creative process at a mechanistic level, one can say, with some assurance, that nothing can come out that has not previously gone in. Inspirational ideas and images do not appear magically from thin air, although they may often seem to do so. What causes this illusion is the fact that in the mind of the creative artist there are infinite possibilities of synthesis, by the interaction between new data and stimuli and his or her fund of selected stored data. The various components, before synthesis, may be familiar; but once they are incorporated into a new creation they may no longer be identifiable. In this way it may seem to the artist that something completely new has been made.

Creativity is not universally accepted as being a component of intelligence. This may, of course, merely reflect the difficulty in adequately defining intelligence, but many people make an intuitive distinction between the two qualities. Studies that have attempted to correlate intelligence and creativity have produced conflicting results. This suggests that the originators of different trials may have had different ideas of the nature of creativity – or of intelligence. The consensus of opinion, however, is that the two correlate well at low and average levels, but that, when exceptionally gifted people are studied, intelligence and creativity are often mutually incompatible. We know that many adults of great originality – people like Albert Einstein and Isaac Newton – were unremarkable as children. We also know that the highest achievers in science – those who make the major advances and win Nobel Prizes – do not, in general, have exceptionally high IQs. They tend to be people of high average ability whose interest and imagination is caught by a particular subject, and who then concentrate very hard on it.

No account of creativity can omit some reference to cerebral lateralization – the fact that the two halves of the brain have different overall functions. In over 95 per cent of people, the left hemisphere of the brain contains the nerve centres for speech, language and language-related functions such as rational thought. It also controls movement of the right side of the body, including right-hand activities. Because speech, language and writing are so central to our higher activities, the left hemisphere is called the dominant hemisphere. In a small proportion of left-handed people the *right* hemisphere is dominant in this way. In most people, the right side of the brain is concerned with a wide range of non-verbal activities — things like spatial relationships, patterns, styles, design, data synthesis, metaphors, new combinations of ideas, and so on. The right brain is intuitive rather than logical, holistic rather than specific, and relational rather than factual.

What all this adds up to is that nearly all the important functions fundamentally concerned with creativity are centred in the right side of the brain. This illuminates the distinction between the truly basic internal creative acts and the physical processes and manual skills required for their expression. Using a paintbrush or a pen or word processor is not a creative act; these are simply the tools that can be used to realize the result of the creative process. This might also suggest that literary art is a less pure form of artistic activity than some of the others. Verbal ability and command of the language, which seem to be inextricably linked with literary art, must, of course, substantially involve the left side of the brain. But most critics would agree that language, too, is simply a tool of the literary artist and that facility with language is, artistically, of comparatively little importance.

Since the relative development of the different parts of the brain determines our abilities, we can infer that highly creative people have outstanding development in certain parts of the right side of their brains, relative to other parts. It is not then surprising that, in groups of such people, there may sometimes be a divergence between creativity and intelligence — assuming the definition of intelligence is restricted to linguistic and logical abilities. High levels of development in certain parts of the brain do not happen by chance. We know that innate abilities, or the structural basis for the development of such abilities, are often inherited. In such cases there are often also powerful early environmental influences operating to encourage the constant use and development of these faculties – a process associated with the development of the part of the brain concerned.

Children who show outstanding early ability – child prodigies – are of special interest to those studying creativity. They are also of great interest to the general public in their power to evoke wonder and amazement. Most child prodigies seem to have been very one-sided geniuses and very ordinary in other respects. A clear distinction should be made between prodigies who are otherwise normal and the so-called *idiots savants* who are retarded in other respects (see **The intelligent mind**).

The commonly-held opinion that child prodigies achieve their remarkable success without great labour is almost certainly wrong. Studies of many young composers have shown that most of them worked intensively for at least ten years before producing anything of merit. Even Mozart was drilled ruthlessly in composition by his father before, at the age of 12, he showed the first signs of his supreme mastery of the art. There is probably more truth than we imagine in Thomas Edison's witty remark: 'Genius is one per cent inspiration and ninety-nine per cent perspiration.' It seems probable that in many child prodigies, unusual achievement is the result of an exceptional quality of mind that allows single-minded concentration on the recording and organization of experience so that great achievement is possible without help or even against opposition. When the seventeenth-century French mathematician Blaise Pascal (1623–62) was a child, his father, anxious that he should study the classics, deprived him of the mathematical textbooks in which he was showing interest. So young Pascal secretly worked out his own geometry. Genius has been described as 'an infinite capacity for taking pains'.

Is it possible to measure creativity? One suggested way is to assess what is sometimes called ideational fluency – the number of different ideas a person can generate in a particular context. One might, for instance, ask a test subject to suggest as many uses as possible of an empty champagne bottle. Other tests might involve interpretation of Rorschach ink blots, made by folding a sheet of paper in half over a pool of ink; or writing an account of the story behind various posed photographs. A major difficulty in such testing is the highly subjective nature of the examiner's response to the subject's answers. Some answers might seem highly original to one examiner but banal to another.

Of course, the most obvious way of assessing creativity is to look at what the person has actually achieved in the way of creation. The fact that critics may disagree about the artistic worth of a poem, book, painting, piece of sculpture, string quartet, opera or symphony is neither here nor there. Status as a creative artist demands both quantity and quality. Quantitative creativity can be easily assessed by the number of poems, books, paintings, etc. that have been produced. Qualitative creativity can safely be left to the judgment of time. Any created thing worthy of preservation will, barring accidents or the acts of the philistines, be preserved.

The chromatic mind: colour associations

Francis Galton had an acquaintance, Baron von Osten Sachen, a Russian diplomat and insect expert, who perceived of numbers as being coloured. The number 1 was black, 2 yellow, 3 pale brick red, 4 brown, 5 blackish grey, 6 reddish brown, 7 green, 8 bluish, and 9 reddish brown. The Baron explained to Galton that the colours appeared very distinctly when he thought of the numbers individually, but were less obvious in compound numbers. The most remarkable thing about the Baron's colour associations appeared when he recollected historical events. Whenever he thought of an occurrence in a previous century, it appeared to him against a background that was coloured according to the principal numbers in the date of the century concerned. All major eighteenth-century events were perceived on a green background because of the prominence of a 7 in the date.

Today there are many people to whom the sequence black, brown, red, orange, yellow, green, blue, violet, grey and white will instantly call up the numbers from 0 to 9, as this was the standard colour code for resistors and small capacitors. The growth of integrated circuit digital electronics on silicon chips has somewhat reduced the number of people to whom this sequence is vital, but many will still recognize it.

There is a link between these two examples. The only explanation that the Baron could suggest for the colour association phenomenon was that, when he was a child, his tutor had taught him history using diagrams in which each century was represented by 100 squares, with a coloured border for each century. Associations of this kind are likely to have been formed early in life, as many readers who were electronic hobbyists in childhood will agree. Much depends, of course, on the significance of colour to the individual. The 10 per cent or so of males who have difficulty in distinguishing brown from green and who soldered in 100 ohm resistors instead of 1,000,000 ohm resistors will recollect the emotion but probably deny the pleasure in the matter.

Colour associations are very common. In addition to associations with numbers, people may associate certain colours with the days of the week, the months of the year, the vowel sounds, the letters of the alphabet, various odours and perfumes, tactile sensation, and tastes. In short, experiential links can occur between colour vision and other senses.

One of the most striking and prevalent colour associations is that with musical sounds. Note that we are not referring here to what musicians describe as 'tone colour': in that context the word 'colour' is used metaphorically to refer to the timbre or tonal quality of instruments or combinations of instruments, and has nothing to do with the visual sense. The association of sound with real colour is quite another matter. Some musicians have strong and permanent associations between sound and colour. Synaesthesias of this kind have been deeply important to some composers, especially those of a highly sensual nature. One of the most striking of these was the Russian pianist and composer Scriabin (1872–1915). Scriabin, like Wagner, was a hypersensualist who was even affected by the sensation of running his fingers caressingly along the top of his piano. Scriabin's most impressive manifestation of his colour associations was in the symphonic work *The Poem of Fire*, or *Prometheus*, first performed in 1913. The orchestral score contains a stave for a keyboard which, instead of producing music, projects a play of various colours onto a screen.

To Scriabin, every key had its own colour. For example, C major was red, D major was brilliant yellow and E flat was a metallic steel colour. The association between keys and colours appears to be entirely arbitrary. Rimsky-Korsakov also associated keys with colours, but his associations were entirely different from those of Scriabin. Arnold Schoenberg (1874–1951) was another composer who believed that tones had colours.

The association of colours with tones goes back a long way. The earliest account of the matter appears to be that of the Egyptian astronomer Ptolemy, Claudius Ptolemaeus (*c*.90–168), who turned his thoughts to a great range of subjects. The Jesuit musical theorist and mathematician Athanasius Kircher (1602–80) believed that for each musical sound there is a definite, fixed corresponding colour. He also believed that everything visible could be heard. He was, in short, slightly round the bend. Another Jesuit, Louis Bernard Castel (1688–1757) wrote a book called *Music in Colour*. This priest must have been reasonably sane because he was a Fellow of the Royal Society. In spite of living at a time when the only sources of artificial light were candles and other burning objects, such as oil lamps, he nevertheless designed a keyboard instrument which produced a different projected colour for each key pressed. Since then there have been a number of proposals for 'colour organs'. What is significant, however, is that each designer seems to have a different idea of which colours correspond to which notes.

There have even been attempts to translate sounds directly into colours. For modern electronic technology this is a trivial task, and a variety of formulae can be devised to establish and realize the relationship between pitch, timbre, harmony, rhythm, key change, etc., and colour. Such formulae are, however, decided upon in an entirely arbitrary manner. To try to find a real association, based on physical characteristics, is doomed to failure.

People who experience sound in the same way as Scriabin are usually convinced, however, that there is an absolute, if mystical relationship between musical elements and colour. As Scriabin's musical development progressed, he became more and more engrossed in philosophical, or theosophical, speculations. These led him to use 'programs' for his great tone poems. The program for the third symphony (*Le Divin Poème*) was 'the evolution of the human spirit from pantheism to unity with the universe'. Eventually, Scriabin was to carry synaesthesia to greater and more outrageous lengths than any other artist. He planned a great work that was to combine liturgy, colours, scents, dance, poetry and music into an all-embracing whole. This work would require those attending to become 'worshippers' and to acknowledge Scriabin as the new Messiah. Its effect on participants would be to reunite them with the spirit. Perhaps fortunately, the great work never got beyond some preliminary sketches.

Few musicians went this far, but many will agree that, to a greater or lesser extent, they associate keys and timbres with colours. In the case of keyboard musicians it is especially extraordinary that the sense of colour association between musical keys and colours should have persisted long after it became routine to tune pianos and other keyboard instruments in equal temperament. In this method every semitone is the same interval so, apart from pitch, all keys are physically the same.

It is also remarkable that the phenomenon survived changes in the standard frequency on which the tuning of instruments is based. This standard, now set so that the pitch of the note A is 440 hertz (cycles per second; abbreviated to Hz), has, in the past been wholly unstandardized. For example, Handel used a tuning fork (A = 422.5 Hz) that gave a pitch lower than today's, while Mozart's piano was tuned to A = 421.6 Hz. If there were any real link between particular notes or keys and colour, it would, logically, have had to change with each change in standard of pitch. That it did not do so indicated that the link is not a logical or physical one.

Different emotional effects may be associated with different instruments, and – since colours often do seem to be associated with particular emotions (sombre black, brilliant yellow, moody blue, upbeat red, and so on), perhaps different instruments could come to be associated with certain colours. But caution is required here. One instrument can produce all sorts of different music, with a whole range of emotional effects. Also, the emotional impact of a piece of music often depends not only on the music itself: for example, in a piece based on a particular story, listeners who are aware of the emotions of the characters at these points in the story will find it very hard not to be influenced by the literary associations. Perhaps it is in ways such as this that colour associations arise. The extraordinary diversity in the colours perceived in relation to any given musical entity suggests that it is.

The mind of the writer: doing it in the unconscious

Writers come in all literary shapes and sizes, from the towering genius to the Grub Street hack. Their interests, and the kind of things they like to write about, are as varied as humankind. So any attempt to write about the mind of the writer must concentrate on what writers have in common. Even this can be difficult. Take the question of motivation for writing: this might seem to be something writers have in common, but a little study shows that this, too, ranges widely.

Many writers start writing because they want to be writers. They may have an oddly mistaken notion that people who have written a book are, for that reason, admired, and they wish to be admired. This is probably not the world's best motive for writing. Would-be writers in this group also tend to have the even quainter notion that writing books brings in immense amounts of money.

Some write for the simple satisfaction of being able to have a book in their hands that they have written themselves. There is nothing wrong with this kind of motivation except that the realization of it is likely to be a bit of an anticlimax. There is, of course, a momentary thrill in handling one's first book, but then it must go into a bookshelf. One really can't keep on taking it out to show people. Some people even go in for vanity publishing and pay to have their books printed. As Lord Chesterfield is said to have remarked to his son about sexual intercourse: 'The pleasure is momentary, the position ridiculous and the expense damnable.'

Other people want to write because they feel a necessity to tell the world about something that they think is of great importance. This is a slightly better motive, but a book may not be the appropriate medium for conveying the message. An idea of this kind will usually be fairly fully expressible in a page or two, but the attempt to expand the idea to the 50,000 to 100,000 words required to make a respectable book, may prove difficult. Writer's block may supervene and dogged attempts to overcome it may make for dull reading.

Some people want to write because they are natural story-tellers. This is a better reason. There is an insatiable demand for good stories at all levels, and such a person, with practice, may well make a success of it. Or they may not: there are other necessary qualifications.

Fortunate indeed are those whose motive for writing is the simple one, that they like doing it. Perhaps this is why so many of them take to drink. Isaac Asimov (1920–92), one of the most prolific writers of all time, loved writing and continued to pour out books right up to the time of his death. He made a point of writing as simply as possible, partly because he wanted to be understood, but also because the simpler and clearer his text the less he had to revise it. Another prolific writer, Gore Vidal, also enjoys writing. If he did not, he says, he wouldn't do it. However, many writers, even highly successful ones, hate writing and find it a painful, lonely, harrowing business.

Writers also vary in the mechanics of how they write. The enormous power of the word processor as a tool has now been appreciated by most writers. Only a few now try to hold out and persist with the rationalization – usually based on a humiliating fear of technology – that word processors actually interfere with the creative process. Those who still prefer paper and pen may be very particular about the kind of paper on which they write and the kind of pen used. Some may have an obsessive-compulsive necessity to sharpen a dozen pencils before starting, or to arrange the writing desk in a particular way. Some are helpless without a supply of yellow, legal-size paper; some must work in hard-covered books, writing on the right side only and leaving the left page for insertions.

Some writers can only concentrate when immersed in silence. Joseph Heller, author of *Catch-22*, is unusual in that he can write while playing tapes of music (he prefers Bach's choral music but will often settle for Beethoven). Incidentally, he started writing *Catch-22* – the first book he had ever tried – because he thought it might be a useful way to kill time.

Successful writers with a reasonable output are usually quite well disciplined. This is because they regard writing as a routine job that must be approached in a professional manner. Even so, the hours of work vary. The majority will do three or four hours every morning and then apparently stop for the day. But this is not as lazy as it seems: few creative professional writers ever really stop working. Whatever they may seem to be doing, they are probably living with their current microcosm. Anthony Burgess said that the morning is the conscious period of the day, while the afternoon is for the unconscious mind to assert itself. Others, once they are into the swing of writing, only stop when quite exhausted, perhaps leaving off in the middle of a sentence or paragraph that leads on to another idea, so that they can more easily get started the next day.

Anthony Trollope (1812–82), a highly successful and still enormously popular writer, had a rigidly disciplined approach to writing. Although he was a busy professional man with a full-time appointment with the Post Office, and was also an enthusiastic huntsman, he found time first thing every morning between 5.30 a.m. and breakfast to write. He worked with a watch set up in front of him and would stop when his time was up, regardless of whether the writing was going well or not. In this manner he was able to produce 47 excellent novels and many other works of travel, biography, drama, literary criticism and short fiction. Interestingly, when Trollope revealed these working methods in his autobiography, many members of the public stopped buying his books – a revealing commentary on their romantic notions of the life of a writer.

The next aspect of the mind of the writer to be considered is how he or she sets about the business. Many novelists, on being asked about the creative process, will tell you that they have no idea, in advance, how a book is going to evolve. One thing they do know is that momentum is everything. They need an idea to get them started and then, if all goes well, the characters take over. A surprising number of novelists work in this way. Many will say that, unless this happens, the book never comes to life. The starting point need not be important and, in many cases, having served its purpose, will be discarded. Openings are obviously important and the original one may well turn out in the end to be quite unsuitable.

A few scorn the idea of allowing characters and plots to evolve. Vladimir Nabokov (1899–1977) referred to it as a 'trite little whimsy that is as old as the quills'. 'My characters,' he said, 'are galley slaves.' When Gore Vidal started writing he would plan every book meticulously, but later he started improvising. 'I began with a mood,' he said, 'A sentence. The first sentence is all-important.' Like many other writers, Vidal may not know the ending of a book until he gets there. Talking of *Messiah*, he said 'When I got to the last page ... it was all at once clear to me that the hidden meaning of the story was the true identity of the narrator, which had been hidden from him, too.' Burgess, too, insisted that it is dangerous to work from more than a sketchy plan. 'So many things.' he said, 'are generated by the sheer act of writing.

To the late Kingsley Amis the creation of characters was a mysterious and largely inexplicable process. He quoted other writers as saying that the thoughts and works they produced were not their own; and he agreed with them. In some strange way, characters were, he said, a 'by-product of the development of the central idea.' Once the broad situation in the novel becomes clear, the range of possibilities for the important characters narrows. Their features are, as it were, determined by the way the plot develops. This interesting remark throws a good deal of light on the creative process as experienced by some writers.

John Steinbeck said that the craft or art of writing 'is the clumsy attempt to find symbols for the wordlessness. In utter loneliness a writer tries to explain the inexplicable.' Steinbeck, for all his apparent articulateness and fluidity, found writing very difficult. He often spent weeks in what he rationalized was the 'planning stage' but was really a period of working up the courage to begin writing. 'I suffer always from the fear of putting down the first line. It is amazing the terrors, the magics, the prayers, the straitening shyness that assails one.' And even when he reached the end of a book he always had a deep fear that he had failed to achieve what he had set out to do. In his day, John Steinbeck was one of the most popular and successful novelists and, in spite of the disapproval of the critics, was the winner of the Nobel Prize for Literature.

Jorge Luis Borges had an interesting comment on the minds of some writers. 'I have known many poets,' he said, 'who have written well – very fine stuff – with delicate moods and so on – but if you talk with them, the only thing they tell you is smutty stories or speak of politics in the way that everyone does.' These were not, he thought, real writers, but just people who had learned a few tricks. They had learned to write as a person might learn to play chess. Significantly, he added that most of these writers 'seemed to think of life as having nothing poetic or mysterious about it.'

The state of mind of the creative writer is truly extraordinary. It is nothing without mystery. It operates partly within and partly outside consciousness. It needs to be nourished and provided with conscious stimuli so that it can do its work quietly without further prompting. The results of its efforts are, if it is successful, invariably surprising. Unless they are, creative work has probably failed. The best-laid plans of mice and men are of little interest to the unconscious creative mind, which wants to proceed along its own unpremeditated path. The writer can effect only a little gentle guidance. Apart from that, all he or she has to do is to get the words down on paper.

What could be simpler?

The prejudiced mind:
shades of Chauvin

Nicolas Chauvin, who flourished in the Napoleonic era, was a soldier of great physical courage – or possibly great stupidity – who came to the notice of the Emperor because of his exploits and because he was severely wounded in battle. Napoleon presented him with a red ribbon, a sword and a pension for life. Thereafter, Chauvin's enthusiasm for Napoleon, for the military life and, indeed, for all things French, knew no bounds. His expressions of militant patriotism and of hatred for anyone who was not French became so extreme that even his partisan military colleagues laughed at him. His reputation spread and his name became associated with this kind of nationalistic prejudice. Chauvin has become proverbial and his particular state of mind is now known as chauvinism.

The prejudiced mind is a narrow mind. It is often, but not necessarily, a stupid or simple mind, as in the case of Chauvin, but it is always a dangerous mind. The word 'prejudice' may call up racial prejudice, but this is only one aspect of a much wider matter. Prejudice is essentially a state of mind based on inadequate information or unawareness. In most cases prejudice is unfavourable, and its principal effect is to damage human relations and prevent the development of human links. Prejudice can exist over race, religion, sex, sexual orientation, social status, age, wealth, poverty, possessions, accent, educational status, appearance, skin colour within ethnic groups, obesity, manners, political affiliations and many other matters.

None of us is free from prejudice but some are freer than others. Anyone who claims to be prejudice-free is either unaware of the nature of prejudice or is remarkably lacking in insight into his or her own mind. The fact is that human beings cannot operate without putting things – and people – into categories. So much happens to us in the course of day-to-day living that unless we classify events, our situation becomes too complex for us to deal with. Categories help us quickly to identify things and situations, and are very useful. There was a time when the Army's official view of the private soldier was highly prejudiced in favour of the proposition that he was a pretty stupid chap. This view was unconsciously satirized in the standard joke: 'If it moves, salute it; if it doesn't move, paint it.'

The simpler our minds and the less we know, the fewer and broader are the categories we use. We have to make assumptions about the way these categories will operate, and our tendency is often to do so in a simplistic way. This can lead to gross over-generalization and to false assumptions. Unthinking categorizations can, for instance, lead to the prejudiced opinions that all lawyers are in it for the money; all people with a posh accent are haughty and contemptuous; all the people who go to football matches are lager louts; all educated people despise those who are less well educated; all Jews are money-grubbing misers; all Chinese are inscrutable; all Mexicans are lazy; all Arabs are terrorists; all black men want to rape white women; all white people despise black people; all members of the National Front are thick-headed Nazis; all Irish Catholics are anti-Protestant and want to see Ireland united; all Irish Protestants are anti-Catholic and want to be independent of Ireland; all scientists are atheists; all religious people are more moral than non-religious people; and so on.

Most of our gross categorizations are quickly seen, even on superficial inspection, to be irrational. Unfortunately, experience and research have shown that the formation of irrational categorizations is easier than the formation of rational ones. This is because categorization is more readily based on emotional than on rational factors. However enlightened and open-minded we think we are, we still apply far too broadly general ideas and emotional reactions to our categories. And we tend either to like or to dislike the subjects of our categories. The danger, of course, is that we are liable to apply the same criteria unthinkingly to all members of a category. It is this kind of process that gives rise to racist attitudes.

Many life-damaging prejudices are not the result of personal observation but of information received in childhood. Unfortunately, data acquired in childhood are not only accepted uncritically, readily assimilated and believed, but are also far more difficult to shift than information received later in life. This is because the young child is avid for information, trusting and deeply impressed with what is new. Even when, with years of discretion, the early data are seen to be wrong, the effect of the misinformation, at an emotional level, will often still persist. Many people, of course, never reach years of discretion.

One of the most extraordinary and widespread manifestations of prejudice is anti-semitism. Dislike or hatred of the Jews, resulting in discrimination against them, goes back a long way. In the first century BC, Jews were segregated by Greeks because they refused to worship their gods. They were persecuted by the Romans because they refused to worship the Roman Emperor. With the spread of Christianity, Jews were persecuted even more strongly because they were accused of being the crucifiers of Christ. A people who could do that were capable of any atrocity and the most outrageously improbable stories about them were widely believed.

During the Middle Ages, Europe was a dreadful place for Jews. They were automatically denied the normal rights of citizenship and had the frustration and humiliation of being prohibited from engaging in any of the professions or from holding government and other official appointments. They were excluded from the military and were not even allowed to join the trade guilds. As a result, just about the only thing they could do to make a living was to provide financial services. So many Jews became money-lenders and bankers; although their services were in great demand, they were scorned for engaging in this despised activity. As Shakespeare eloquently expressed it in *The Merchant of Venice*:

> Signior Antonio, many a time and oft
> In the Rialto have you rated me
> About my moneys and my usances:
> Still have I borne it with a patient shrug,
> For sufferance is the badge of all our tribe.
> You call me misbeliever, cut-throat dog,
> And spit upon my Jewish gaberdine,
> And all for use of that which is mine own.

One of the most savagely prejudicial and widely held beliefs about the Jews appeared in the twelfth century. This was the claim that Jews engaged in ritual murders of Christian children during Passover to get blood to make unleavened bread. There was, of course, not a hint of truth in the matter, but this is just the kind of proposition that prejudice accepts and thrives on. Jews were herded into ghettos and were made to wear a yellow Star-of-David badge; thousands of them were murdered by thugs who felt justified in killing them.

Envy of their economic success, coupled with religious prejudice, led to repeated compulsory expulsion of Jews from England, France, Germany, Portugal and the Papal States (1569). Some of the worst persecution was that of the notorious Spanish Inquisition which, in the name of Christianity, burned Jews at the stake and drove out of the country all those who refused to convert to Christianity.

Gross episodes of persecution continued until the end of the eighteenth century when, for a time, the new spirit of enlightenment and tolerance allowed the Jews to acquire some civil rights in Europe. Strong anti-Jewish prejudice remained, however, and, with the growth of nationalistic fervour in the nineteenth century what had been primarily religious prejudice changed to racial prejudice. Persecution again intensified and millions of Jews emigrated to the United States.

The force of prejudice and its underlying dangers are not diminished by the passage of time, and the worst acts of anti-Jewish prejudice were to occur in Russia in the early years of the twentieth century and in Hitler's Germany in the 1930s and 1940s. The Russian secret police forged documents called *Protocols of the Learned Elders of Zion* purporting to be plans for a Jewish plot to dominate the world. The publication of these led to violent pogroms in which many Jews perished.

The plight of the Jews in Germany under the Nazis was pitiable. But German atrocities and their 'Aryan racial purity' propaganda also inspired anti-semitism in France, Britain and the USA. In 1938 almost every synagogue and many other Jewish institutions in Germany were destroyed. By 1940, Jews had lost all rights as citizens and were forced to wear the yellow badge and live in ghettos. They were not allowed to own land. They were not allowed to use the telephone or public transport or libraries. Their children were barred from attending public schools. Anti-Jewish prejudice culminated in the almost unthinkable events of the Holocaust, in which at least six million Jews were systematically murdered in the death camps of Auschwitz, Treblinka, Belzec, Majdanek, Sobibor and Chelmno or were shot, starved or beaten to death in other concentration camps.

Horrors of this kind are possible only because of the ability of the human mind to set aside rational thought and yield to prejudice.

Every aspect of the received reasons or justification for anti-Jewish conduct is irrational. The physical stereotypes of the Jews promoted by Nazi and other propaganda − for instance that they all have big noses and certain other facial characteristics − are emotionally induced and do not correspond to reality. That they are an inferior race in any sense, is irrational. That a whole race should be condemned and deemed blameworthy because a handful of them may have cooperated with the Romans in the crucifixion of Jesus Christ, is totally irrational. Many simple-minded people are unable to grasp this important point or to see that this is one of the principal mechanisms by which prejudice becomes so dangerous.

When prejudice is manifested in religion, as in the conduct of the Inquisition in Spain and elsewhere, rational thought processes become submerged in dangerous emotion and the results are appalling. The same applies to prejudice manifested in political dogma as in Nazi Germany or elsewhere. Unhappily, the world is full of people who are incapable of seeing this. Nicolas Chauvin's spirit remains alive, well and enthusiastically active.

Conformity enforced:
the brainwashed mind

The term 'brainwashing' is a journalistic term, a translation of a Chinese phrase, that became current at the time of the Korean war in the 1950s when it became apparent that the Chinese communists in North Korea were using deliberate techniques of persuasion on prisoners of war. The purpose of these techniques was to induce in the minds of their victims apparent convictions that differed radically from their former beliefs. This was done for political and propaganda purposes.

Unfortunately, the term 'brainwashing' is seriously misleading. The implication of the term is that all previous memories are 'washed away' and are replaced by new ideas. This is nonsense. A system of memories, acquired almost from birth onwards, is fundamental to the functioning of our minds. This system is built up over the course of years and is the basis of our whole cultural being. To wash it out would be to reduce us to vegetables.

Another objection is the established fact that, other than by widespread physical damage to the brain, memory cannot be destroyed. Major local damage in the area concerned with registration and recall of memory can also effectively remove memories (see **The ageing mind**) but not psychological techniques, however ingenious and sinister. But the fact that brainwashing is impossible does not make the methods used to try to achieve it, and the results of these methods, any less terrible.

The most publicized example of brainwashing was that of Colonel Frank H. Schwalbe of the US Marine Corps. The Colonel was a prisoner of war who, for months, was subjected to degrading and humiliating treatment, severe cold, hunger, sleep deprivation, solitary confinement, filthy living conditions, long interrogations from teams of questioners and tremendous psychological pressure to conform to the wishes of his captors. As a result of this treatment he eventually reached a stage at which he was apparently willing to believe the suggestions that were being made to him. He produced a 'confession' in which he admitted that the United States forces were conducting bacteriological warfare against their enemies. The Colonel's statement was detailed and circumstantial. It gave dates and named names.

Full propaganda use was made of this 'confession', which was broadcast to the world. The Chinese must have been confident in the long-term efficacy of their methods for they allowed the Colonel to be repatriated. At the ensuing enquiry, Colonel Schwalbe testified that he had never really believed that his compatriots were using germ warfare, but that all the surrounding details of his 'confession' had become completely real to him.

Colonel Schwalbe and others who were similarly treated were not, as was widely believed, subjected to any mysterious process related to the establishment of Pavlovian conditioned reflexes (this idea probably arose because evidence appeared that the Chinese communists had been instructed in brainwashing by the Russians). In fact, the methods used were centuries old and had been used both by Russian secret police and the Chinese for many years. There was no hypnotism. No mysterious drugs were used. The method was simply one of constant fear of death or serious injury; of reducing a human being to a state of abject humiliation, total isolation and confusion, devoid of any kind of moral support; placing him in a situation in which heroic resistance seemed pointless and would never be known; and making him so desperately unhappy that no price seemed too high to pay to bring the torture to an end.

It does not take much of this kind of thing to force the average person into conformity, and it is not surprising that one third of the American prisoners of war collaborated, in one way or another, with the enemy. One American officer, only 48 hours after he had been captured, made a broadcast on Seoul radio urging his fellow soldiers to believe that the American intervention in Korean 'internal affairs' was a barbaric act of aggression.

Few people would agree that these Far Eastern prisoner-of-war camps had anything in common with British Public Schools, but there is a link – and, from the point of view of the theoretical background to brainwashing, quite an important one. Brian Inglis, Editor of the *Spectator*, wrote an article in 1961 in which he referred to his own experience of indoctrination on joining his public school. He related how, by the end of the first term, the code of the school had been imprinted and assimilated. At the start of the next term he was ready and willing to impose this code on new boys and was already so brainwashed that he was actually looking forward to watching the new boys having their own values despised, rejected and, if necessary, beaten out of them, and replaced by the school's own pupils' mores. Looking back, Inglis recognized that these enforced schoolboy values were 'a very ugly set ... elevating dishonesty into a virtue provided it was used against masters, and stressing conformity.' He comments: 'The craft of the brainwasher has never been a mystery to me, since.'

This observation by Inglis brings to our notice the important point that brainwashing, in the sense generally understood, is a ubiquitous feature of modern society. Many of the opinions we form, or at least express, are imposed on us, sometimes without our being aware of it, sometimes in a painfully obvious manner, by the techniques of persuasion implicit in our group or social environment. In childhood, conformity to the mores of the group is so important that failure to achieve it can lead to desperate unhappiness. Wearing the right kind of trainers and riding the right kind of mountain bike are seen to be essential to contentment and social acceptability. Brainwashing intensifies with adolescence, and young people – whatever their personal tastes – soon learn that peer acceptability implies acquiescence in the kind of clothes they wear, in the language they use, in the drugs they take and in the sexual activity they allow. At university, the pressures are more subtle but are equally strong. And in the work environment, brainwashing must either operate or all hope of advancement is lost.

The methods applied to modify our opinions may not be so brutally obvious as those inflicted upon prisoners of war, but in principle they are the same. 'Your ideas, attitudes, tastes and beliefs are wrong. Here are the correct ones. Adopt them and we will like you and help you. Reject them and you will be an outcast.' In response to these pressures, people everywhere are behaving, speaking, appreciating, even thinking in a way that may be quite foreign to their natural inclinations or early upbringing.

Fortunately, as we have seen, the effect of brainwashing is usually superficial. People's fundamental natures are not changed by such processes. The human mind is far more resistant and resilient than is dreamt of by the brainwasher. Once the pressures are removed we can, in time, almost always, as the saying goes, be ourselves.

The mind of the mathematician:
uncertainty rules

Like other large disciplines, mathematics is a broad subject and individual mathematicians have to become specialists in a particular field: topology, arithmetic, geometry, algebra, and so on. This makes it difficult to make any generalizations about the mind of the mathematician. One thing we can say about mathematicians, though, is that they are extraordinarily subtle in their thinking. They are also remarkably imaginative and creative, often to the point of artistry. Like other creative artists, some of the most important mathematicians have, on producing new work, been considered mad by their colleagues.

However, mathematicians are not creative in the sense that Bach, Shakespeare or Picasso were creative. Mathematical creativity is bound by very strict rules that may not be broken. Mathematics is the language of science and so is a description of the world. Its logic must be consistent with all the rest of mathematics – free of contradictions – and consistent with objective observation. The creative mathematician reaches out in imagination into the unknown in the same way as the artist does, but what he or she comes back with must fit with unassailable logic into the existing corpus of mathematics.

The mathematical mind has, therefore, to be extraordinarily well-disciplined. It must also be capable of thinking in symbols, whereas most non-mathematicians are used only to fairly simple ideas expressed in words; we are also used to thinking in a kind of linear manner, with one thing leading to another. But the mathematical mind deals routinely with a complex set of relationships between symbols, many of which are themselves shorthand for pretty complex ideas.

This is why a page of mathematics looks completely incomprehensible to the average lay person. Even if he or she knew what each symbol stood for, the chances are that it would be impossible to follow their relationships and how the conclusions are derived from them.

Another difficulty about getting at the mathematical mind is that, oddly enough, mathematicians, or at least philosophers of mathematics, cannot agree amongst themselves about whether mathematics is real or whether it is purely synthetic. The classic Alexandrian and Greek mathematicians, who flourished 2000 years ago, had no doubt on this point. As far as they were concerned, mathematics was the absolute and unchangeable truth behind everything. It was the ultimate reality.

There is something to be said for this opinion. When you compare mathematics with science, you will see that, although science is constantly having to amend and revise its ideas as it advances, mathematics, once it is established and its limitations have been defined, does not change. Euclid's famous theorems were limited to figures on plane surfaces and were thought for centuries to be a fairly complete description of relationships on all surfaces. For centuries people inferred that this was the only possible geometry. The inference was wrong but, within its own context of a plane universe, the theorems of Euclid are permanently valid and very useful. Euclid might have speculated on the fact that if you draw a triangle on the inside curve of a horse's saddle, the sum of the angles is equal to less than two right angles. But if he did, he probably thought that this was a trivial observation.

Another reason for taking this view is the notion that the idea of number is quite independent of people. Threeness, for instance, is something that can easily be conceived as existing in some abstract realm, because there can be an infinite number of sets of three things. The class of all triads is an infinite class. The same applies, of course, to any other number, and this is true regardless of the name or symbol used for the number. These ideas were, according to Plato, eternal truths that exist independently of space and time. This concept is hence often called Platonism. Its supporters believe that mathematics has always existed, and that the job of the mathematician is to discover the facts, not to invent them.

Another class of mathematicians are those that believe that mathematics is purely a human invention. According to this group, the idea of number is derived from experiences such as that of a succession of events or the observation of several different objects in the same general class. Members of this group, the 'constructivists' or 'intuitionists', believe that mathematics is constructed from these basic ideas of number. They hold that mathematics must be put together very carefully from number, in a series of logical steps each one of which must contain clear instructions for the next step.

Among other things, the constructivists came up with the useful idea that they were not going to be limited by the belief that a mathematical statement had to be either true or false. A statement could also be such that one could not know whether it was true or false. This struck a distinct chord with quantum physicists who had been bothered for some time by bizarre observations that seemed to require an extension of the old idea that if a thing was not true it must be false. Three-fold logic, however, causes the constructivists a different problem in that it denies them the right to use the classic logical proof method called *reductio ad absurdum*. This is a long-used method of disproving a statement by an analysis that shows that its consequences would be absurd. Alternatively, the method can be applied to proving a proposition by assuming that it was false and then showing that this assumption leads to an absurdity.

There is another class of mathematical thought that holds that, far from being an accurate description of the real world, mathematics is a wholly synthetic construct that people find so compelling that they change their conception of the world to fit the mathematical construct. A lot of mathematicians do not like this idea, but belief in it is growing, partly as a result of the growth of applied mathematics and an interest in fuzzy logic and computer modelling of just about everything. Utilitarianism of this kind is anathema to many strictly disciplined mathematicians, but there are some, mostly the young ones, who think it is acceptable. If it works, it is worth using. That, of course, is not the only, or even the principal, reason to subscribe to this view. Partisans point out that when minds observe and contemplate phenomena, they can do so only in a mathematical manner. It is the properties of the mind that determine the mathematical construct. Mathematics is a purely cultural concept.

There are, however, problems with this idea of mathematics. Some mathematical concepts have proved to be very useful while, at the same time, being quite unrelated to human experience. Take the idea of the square root of −1. This is an entirely imaginary number. Worse than that, it is inconceivable. The square root of the number x is the number which, multiplied by itself, gives the number x. So 5 is the square root of 25. But every schoolchild knows that a negative number multiplied by a negative number gives a positive one: −1 multiplied by −1 gives +1. So there is no possible number that can be the square root of −1. Even so, mathematicians and engineers are using the square root of −1 all the time.

Another objection to culturally-based mathematics is the difficulty of knowing whether the logic that applies to sets containing a finite number of things can also apply to sets containing an infinite number of things. Infinity is a useful idea but it is not one of which any of us has had, or can have, practical experience. This objection gave rise to the formalist school of mathematics, which defines mathematics as no more than the manipulation of symbols in accordance with a strict set of rules. Formalists do not have to worry about natural phenomena as a source of experience. They just construct a logical system, note the rules of usage and get on with it. It is really a kind of game that someone has invented. There are no axioms − 'self-evident truths' in the Euclidean sense − just starting points that are self-consistent.

A pair of mathematical philosophers (or philosophical mathematicians), Bertrand Russell (1872–1970) and Gottlob Frege (1848–1925) tried to prove that all mathematics was derived from logic. Russell and his former teacher, Alfred North Whitehead (1861–1947), expounded their attempt to demonstrate the truth of this proposition in the massive book *Principia Mathematica* (1910–13). For a time it seemed as if they had succeeded, but, although this book has been described as 'the greatest single contribution to logic since Aristotle', the American logician Kurt Gödel (1906–78) published in 1931 a proof that they were wrong. Gödel's paper showed that it was impossible to prove the consistency of a system such as that presented in *Principia Mathematica*. For if such a proof could be found using only the methods of *Principia Mathematica* then the latter would itself be inconsistent.

Gödel's idea, which completely shattered the mathematical world, came about as a result of his consideration, in mathematical terms, of an ancient paradox, the Epimenides paradox. This is the story of the Cretan man Epimenides, who said: 'All Cretans are liars.' We are to understand that everything Epimenides, being a Cretan, says is false. So is the statement of this Cretan true or false? You can, if you like, simplify the paradox to the statement: 'This statement is false.' If you accept this statement as true you are forced to believe that it is false; if you accept that it is false, you are forced to believe that it is true. Thinking about this led Gödel to the idea that there were undecidable propositions. By an ingenious method using a code of numbers to stand for symbols and sequences of symbols, he was able to show that a statement of number theory could, itself, be about a statement of number theory. In this way he was able to translate the Epimenides paradox into mathematical language and apply it to *Principia Mathematica*, or to any other consistent formulation of number theory.

This is not a complete list of the class of all possible mathematical philosophies. But it is enough to demonstrate that the spectrum of the mathematical mind is broad. It is also enough to make the interesting point that a group that must be among the brainiest and most subtle of all the thinkers of the world are unable to decide the ultimate nature of their own discipline.

The intelligent mind:
the *savant* phenomenon

The most extraordinary thing about intelligence is that we have no idea what it is. This may surprise you. You may think you know what intelligence is. But what you probably mean is that you can recognize intelligence when you come across it, usually by comparing it with your own. That is quite a different thing from knowing what intelligence is. Intelligence manifests itself obviously enough. It shows itself in various abilities, such as the speed with which a person grasps the essence of difficult ideas, or forms conclusions from observations. But to describe what something does is not the same as defining it, and, even after more than a century of psychological thought and research, there is still no general consensus among psychologists as to the definition of intelligence.

When people first began seriously to consider the nature of intelligence, it seemed obvious that it was a matter of inherent brain power. Different people inherited brains of different quality. Some people were quick, others were slow, and that was that. Intelligence obviously ran in families. Every now and then an exceptionally powerful brain turned up and the possessor became a genius. Sometimes people were born with very low-grade brains and these unfortunates were deficient in intelligence.

It soon became clear, however, that matters were not quite so simple as that, and that this scheme was inadequate. The idea of innate brain power, independent of educational and environmental factors, did not fit the facts. A mass of evidence showed that the development of intelligence depended less on heredity than on the input to the brain *after* birth. Children of highly intelligent parents were not automatically intelligent. They only *became* intelligent if their environment was conducive to the development of intelligence. The kind of intelligence that developed was very much determined by the children's environment, in particular by the way in which they were educated. It seems clear that two factors are necessary for the development of intelligence – the inheritance of good 'hardware', and the subsequent provision of good 'operating software' and data.

The early idea that intelligence was a power of the mind independently of its separate abilities, had to be dismissed because many attempts to find this inherent power failed. It seems that intelligence – in the sense of a power in its own right – does not in fact exist. The best that the psychologists could come up with was that mental power was a large complex of different abilities or skills present to different degrees. None of these could be unequivocally selected as a central, innate entity we could call intelligence. Even reasoning power, on analysis, turned out to be the ability to perform one or other of the special skills.

There are lots of these different mental skills. The list includes such things as verbal comprehension, word fluency, numerical ability, the ability to detect significant associations, the power of spatial visualization, speed of perception, the ability to acquire and memorize information, the power of recall, the ability to adjust to change, planning ability and the ability to chose between alternative courses of action. One psychologist claimed that human intelligence comprises no fewer than 120 distinguishable elementary abilities, each one involving an operation on something to produce a product. The difference in the degree to which these skills may be present in any one person is remarkable. Two people can both be generally acknowledged to be intelligent yet may have few abilities in common.

Psychologists argue about how many distinguishable mental skills constitute intelligence. Most of them are still not convinced that there is nothing more to intelligence than the totality of these skills. Many claim that there is a general factor in human intelligence, but are rather vague as to its nature. They cannot seem to be able to agree on a definition of intelligence. Some years ago, fourteen top psychologists were asked for their definitions. They all produced different answers. These included such ideas as the ability to learn by experience, to adapt to changing environments, to think in abstractions, to perceive truth, to acquire skills, and so on. One expert defined intelligence as the ability to do well in intelligence tests. This is not such a disingenuous answer as it may seem.

One definition, formulated many years ago but still fairly widely accepted, is that of Charles Spearman (1863–1945), who was Grote Professor of Mind and Logic at University College London. Spearman taught that there *is* a general ability, which he called 'g', and that this general ability is necessary for the performance of all mental tasks. Surrounding this general ability is a cluster of separate specific abilities, present to different degrees and capable of being separately measured. Spearman's concept has been widely discussed and many modifications suggested, but it has not been seriously challenged, even by modern cognitive psychologists who try to understand intelligence in terms of information processing.

Even Spearman's attempt fails to tell us what intelligence really is, and the nature of his 'g' has been a source of much argument. Perhaps the most widely accepted account of 'g' is that it is the ability to detect new and non-chance (and hence significant) associations. If this is really what intelligence is, then it would follow that a supremely intelligent person, in whom the 'g' factor was much more prominent than other mental skills, might be of very little use.

The idea that intelligence has to do with the speed of perceiving non-chance associations has given rise to intelligence tests. The intelligence quotient, or IQ, is the mental age divided by the chronological age and multiplied by 100. When mental and chronological age are equal, the IQ is thus 100. This, of course, begs the question of how to find fair, realistic and reliable ways of measuring the mental age. The difficulty relates closely to the difficulty of defining intelligence and of trying to find abilities to test that are independent of educational and cultural influences. Intelligence tests compiled without due regard to these factors have, rightly, been condemned as being unfair to those candidates who do not share the educational and cultural background of the testers. Such criticisms have tended to bring all intelligence testing into disrepute.

The whole business started when the French government wanted to know which children were worthy to receive education. So they commissioned the French psychologist Alfred Binet (1857–1911), working with Théodore Simon, to put together some tests. In the course of this work, Binet originated the idea of the IQ. These tests were later repeatedly modified at Stanford University in California by Louis Terman and others, and the original Binet–Simon test of 1908 became the battery of Stanford–Binet tests. These are available for various ages from two years to adulthood. Very young children are asked to draw copies of objects, to string beads, build with blocks and answer questions on familiar activities. Tests for older children involve such things as detecting absurdities, finding what various pairs of words have in common, completing sentences with omitted words, explaining proverbs, and so on. Such tests are, of course, strongly educationally oriented and really test scholastic ability. To try to overcome these short-comings, matrix tests were devised in which the subject was required to look at sets of abstract diagrams and to see which fitted in where, or how he or she should draw a diagram to fit a gap in a series.

The most widely used intelligence tests today are the Wechsler tests, compiled by the New York psychologist David Wechsler. These are of two basic kinds – the Wechsler Adult Intelligence Scale (WAIS) and the Wechsler Intelligence Scale for Children (WICS). The tests involve progressively increasing difficulty. Each test has verbal and performance parts, and these can be applied independently for those with language difficulties, or combined to give an overall score. The verbal parts test vocabulary, verbal reasoning, verbal memory, arithmetical skill and general knowledge. The performance sections involve completing pictures, arranging pictures in a logical order, reproducing designs with coloured blocks, assembling puzzles, tracing mazes, and so on. Again, these tests cannot be said to assess much more than the general educational level.

Intelligence tests are not, except in the most general way, accurate predictors of achievement. Scholastic achievement depends on a number of factors other than intelligence, especially the quality of instruction, parental expectations and a rich early educational environment. Achievement later in life is even less accurately predictable on the basis of intelligence tests, and is determined by many other factors, including quality of personality, physical appearance, opportunity, luck and the possession of special skills. Good motivation can compensate for restricted intelligence, while low motivation can result in little effective use being made of high intelligence. In spite of all that, there is, in general, a fairly strong positive correlation between intelligence, as measured by tests, and material and professional success in life.

The so-called *idiot savant* phenomenon is one of the more extraordinary states of mind. Technically, an idiot is a person with a mental age of not more than two years or an IQ of 25 or below. A very small proportion of people in this category have an extraordinary talent of some kind – often for music or for the ability to memorize certain categories of fact or to perform incredible feats of mental arithmetic. Some are able to play chess to a high standard or to produce drawings or sculpture with great skill. Such people have been called *idiots savants*. In some cases the 'intellectual' powers are so affected that the '*savant*' may have little appreciation of his or her capabilities or their uses. In many cases, however, these extraordinary people clearly understand and appreciate their abilities.

The power of mental arithmetic shown by some of these people is almost unbelievable. One particular ability common to quite a number of these *savants* is to work out details of the calendar over a wide period of the past or the future. They will, for instance, be able to tell you almost immediately which day of the week any date was in the past, or what it will be in any date in the future. One pair of identical twins, both of whom had suffered brain damage from prematurity, could perform this feat for many thousands of years in either direction. Some *savants* can calculate, or remember, scores of prime numbers. They will provide all the factors of any large number, often in a matter of seconds, or multiply three-digit numbers by three-digit numbers with complete accuracy as quickly as they can be spoken.

Extraordinary feats of memory are another feature of the *savant* phenomenon. Some can remember and recite, both forwards and backwards, enormously long numbers. One man was able consistently to reproduce a 54-digit number he had studied for just over a minute. There are map memorizers who have committed to memory detailed maps of whole countries. One 18-year-old *savant* had memorized the entire highway atlas of the United States. Another had committed to memory the official population figures for every town in the United States with a population over 5000, together with much ancillary detail such as the names and locations of 2000 leading hotels with the numbers of their rooms.

Some *savants* have astonishing musical ability: beginning when young, they quickly acquire both technique and repertoire. They do not read music but have the uncanny ability to transform what they hear into a performance, often on a range of musical instruments. This is not simply a matter of remembering a melodic line. *Savants* can reproduce rhythmic, harmonic and contrapuntal complexities apparently without effort. Often only a single hearing is necessary. In some cases the standard of performance is musically creditable, while in others it is mechanical, brash and noisy. One musical *savant* was able, after hearing an opera tape that ran for three quarters of an hour, to reproduce not only a piano version of the orchestral music, but simultaneously to sing the artists' parts in the foreign language they had used.

The artistic ability of *savants* can produce remarkable works of visual art. Drawings, paintings and sculpture of extraordinary complexity and detail are turned out, one after the other, quickly and in an endless stream. The faculty seems to be, initially, one of precise and detailed copying in which every element of perspective and line is observed and reproduced. Often the observed detail is remembered so that the same work can later be reproduced from memory. The meticulous detail of some of these drawings, such as the architectural drawings of the British *savant* Stephen Wiltshire, are breathtaking. When, as a child, he was seen on television making a drawing, from memory, of the complicated architecture of St Pancras Station, London, the public response, and demand for his work, was so strong that it led eventually to the publication of a book of his drawings. Stephen's status as a real artist has been confirmed by the experts.

There are other *savant* abilities. One *savant*, who was barely able to read a watch, could tell the correct time to within a minute at any period of the day. Some have remarkable mechanical ability. These people can be given a complex mechanism that has been disassembled and they will put it together correctly, almost without hesitation. In his book *Extraordinary People*, the American psychiatrist Dr Darold A. Treffert provides a detailed exploration of this remarkable phenomenon, including accounts of many historic and contemporary 'savants', details of some of the cases he has personally investigated, and a study of the neurological and psychiatric background to the matter.

Since all the people concerned are seriously deficient in powers of the mind, other than those in which they excel, the *savant* phenomenon seems to be in some sense a matter of narrow concentration on one particular range of abilities. It is almost as if all the mental and sensory resources, normally spread over a wide spectrum of faculties, are, in these cases, concentrated on one kind of activity. Cerebral dominance seems to have something to do with it. In nearly all people, the left side of the brain is concerned with verbal and general intellectual activity while the right side handles creative and artistic matters. It has been suggested that, in *savant* phenomena of the artistic type, there may be, by chance, damage to the left side of the brain but not to the right. The human nervous system is so adaptable in early life that congenital damage to one part of the brain that precludes its function can result in compensatory overdevelopment of other parts.

While we are still unable fully to explain the *savant* phenomenon, it does seem likely that some such mechanism is behind it.

Seeing into the mind: introspection

Throughout this book, there has been what may seem to be an implicit assumption that we are able, in some way, to see into the many extraordinary minds that have been described. The idea that it is possible usefully to do this has, indeed, been the basis of a school of psychology — that of the introspectionists. This school — a subset of the structuralist school — flourished in the early days of modern psychology in the last two or three decades of the nineteenth century. Its leader was the German psychologist Wilhelm Wundt (1832–1920), who was the first to try to apply scientific methods to psychology and who established a psychological laboratory in Leipzig. Wundt believed that information about the mind could best be obtained from the accounts of people 'looking into' their own minds and into those of others — a process known as introspection. He and his colleagues proceeded to do just this.

Unfortunately, there are major snags with this method, as soon became apparent. Most of these were pointed out by the American psychologist and founder of behaviourism, John B. Watson (1878–1958). In his early days as a psychology researcher, Watson was required to practice introspection. He soon recognized the disadvantages and unreliability of the process, and came to dislike it intensely and to regard it as a waste of time. It was not so much that people are liars as that it is extremely difficult for them to know what is really going on in their own minds in terms of motivation. As we have seen, it is only too easy for people to fool themselves (see **Universal self-delusion**). The examination by introspection of one's own mind is wholly subjective and offers little opportunity for checks. Science, to be reliable, must be wholly objective. Watson decided that psychology could never become a science, in the sense that physics and chemistry were sciences, unless it ignored introspection, 'consciousness' or even mind itself, and concentrated exclusively on behaviour.

B. F. Skinner (1904–90), on whom the mantle of Watson fell when the latter was thrown out of the psychological community after a sex scandal, went much further in his analysis of thinking – far too far, in the opinion of many. He suggested that thinking often meant 'behaving weakly', as when the incoming stimuli are not strong enough to motivate positive action. Thus, the statement 'I think I will go to the opera.' really means 'I haven't yet decided whether or not I will go to the opera.' The word 'think' is commonly used in this kind of way to represent indecision, as if the person concerned were waiting for stronger reasons to occur to prompt behaviour. Skinner's view, in his own words, is:

> Mental life and the world in which it is lived are inventions. They have been invented on the analogy of external behaviour occurring under external contingencies. Thinking is behaving. The mistake is in allocating the behaviour to the mind.

The extreme position of the behaviourists in denying the reality of all subjectivity is really rather ridiculous. The extraordinary thing is that this doctrine succeeded in dominating psychology for about 50 years. During the whole of this period psychologists were using their minds to contemplate the mind as a black box that must never be opened, into which stimuli passed and from which the promptings to behaviour emerged. It is one thing to show that introspection is an unreliable tool; it is quite another to try to deny the existence of the mind. The conversation of these people must have been weirdly confusing and full of contradictions.

There is no denying, however, that we have to be extremely careful when using introspection as a tool for investigating the mind. The state of the mind is not a static entity. It is highly dynamic, constantly changing and full of contradictions. One researcher might derive some data from a study of a person and record it, only to find that another researcher immediately derived conflicting material from the same subject. In addition, the nature of the data being obtained is susceptible to different interpretations by different workers. Subjectivity is manifest in both subject and researcher. Behaviour, on the other hand, is public and can be objectively observed by anyone. The mind, as viewed by introspection, is also capable of atrocities of unreason which will often generate ideas that come to be regarded by the person concerned as manifest truths.

Then there is the question of motivation. It seems obvious to many people that introspection enables us to discern our own motives. Surely we can be completely honest with ourselves and say 'I am doing this because...' Regrettably, it is not enough simply to resolve to be completely honest. Our defence mechanisms (see **Universal self-delusion**) will invariably persuade us that we are being honest with ourselves while objective outsiders may be smiling at our apparently unconscious hypocrisy.

Many people believe that insight can be obtained into a state of mind by processes such as psychoanalysis. But if such procedures reveal anything useful it is that human motivation is as complex as it is obscure and that most of it is hidden from us. Psychoanalysis introduces so many layers of introspection and is susceptible to so many different and arbitrary interpretations as to be quite useless as an objective guide to states of mind and their origins.

As a young doctor, I was keenly interested in introspective investigation of the mind. I noticed, during the stage of recovery from a nitrous oxide anaesthetic, that I had a sense of omniscience. This led me to conduct a series of foolish experiments with the gas, and I found that the phenomenon was reproducible. Nitrous oxide was inhaled to the point at which consciousness was just lost. As awareness returned there was an overwhelming conviction of complete understanding of all the mysteries of the universe. Nothing remained concealed. All previous philosophies were swept aside as worthless because all was now known. Interestingly, and significantly, the experience of omniscience was associated with the complete loss of the desire to consider the answer to any question. When one knew everything, there was really no point in asking oneself any questions. As a consequence, of course, the total sum of knowledge derived from the omniscience experience was exactly zero. With the return of the 'real world' and, presumably, of normality, the sense of omniscience quickly faded and all that remained was the desire to repeat this dangerous experience. It was not long before it became clear that the experience, remarkable though it might seem, was an illusion resulting from defective functioning of the brain. Had there been any break-through into new knowledge – spiritual or otherwise – the conclusion would have been different.

The significance of this is that if defective brain function can produce such effects, how much reliability can we ever attribute to unusual states of mind involving great 'insights' of this kind? Does it not seem probable that such experiences usually, if not invariably, result from defective brain functioning? How often might the beatific visions of the saints have been the result of defective brain function from hypoglycaemia or ketosis resulting from self-imposed starvation of fasting?

Our knowledge of the 'outside' world is derived solely from data coming in through our sense organs. We are aware of this but we are not aware of how the resulting states of mind come about. Introspection cannot help us here. It does not enable us to understand how these incoming sensory data, and the brain cortical excitation they cause, give rise to the subjective experience of seeing. Even the most learned of neurophysiologists cannot explain this. There is no way that we can, by 'looking inwards', discover how spontaneous thoughts come about or how creative mental activity is possible. All we know is that we can voluntarily explore the outside world and, as a result, experience various states of mind. Indeed, there is good reason to believe that the totality of the content our conscious minds comes from the outside. If you try to set up a state of mind, or even to have a thought, that is not based on data you have previously had from outside, you will find that you cannot do it.

Shut your eyes and think of a human face. You are not seeing a face, but you have a clear mental image of one. What you have done is somehow to construct this mental image from a great deal of data stored in your brain. You cannot become aware of how this synthetic process comes about; all you know is that it happens. You do not know whereabouts in your brain you store the information that allows you to synthesize the mental image of a face. All you know is that at some prior time you took in and stored information about what faces look like. You can easily dream up the appearance of a face different from any you have ever seen, by taking a bit from this and a bit from that. This is creativity and it indicates that the brain does not store 'photographs' of individual faces. But that is about as far as introspection can take us. As Francis Galton said of consciousness as early as 1883 after a long study of his own mind by introspection, 'Its position appears to be that of a helpless spectator of but a minute fraction of automatic brain work.'

When we try to examine the nature of a particular state of our own mind – such as an emotion – we do have some data to work on because we have some contact with other parts of our bodies by way of the autonomic nervous system. If we are angry, we know that our hearts are beating fast, that we have 'butterflies in our stomachs', that we are breathing fast and that muscles are tense. We may be aware that our faces have turned hot and are probably red. Some psychologists suggest that these autonomic effects are the essence of the emotion. It seems likely that the addition of these effects (which are caused by hormones) is what turns a purely intellectual entity into a 'real' emotion. The somatic effects can easily be abolished by drugs, such as beta blockers, that prevent the hormones from acting, and the result is that, although the original intellectual content of the causes of the emotion remains, we no longer feel emotional. This may be why, when we try to describe what we perceive about our emotions, we often resort to bodily metaphors, such as 'I haven't the heart to tell you this' or 'It really makes my blood boil.' We have investigative contact with these remoter parts of our bodies but we have no such contact with the parts of the brain concerned with thought, visualization, imagination, and so on.

There is no problem about deciding about the *causes* of particular emotions. These always derive, immediately or after a delay, from the outside world via the sense organs, or from bodily dysfunction. But the intellectual content of emotions – the factual knowledge of their causes – like that of all other states of mind, arises as a result of brain activity, and we know nothing of these processes. The only knowledge we have of brain function, other than of sensory experience, is of its results – our consciousness.

Modern psychologists – who are now almost all of the 'cognitive' persuasion – look on thinking as information processing interposed between stimulus and response. Information processing, however, need not manifest itself, and, indeed, could not continuously manifest itself, as any form of conscious experience. It does have a result, of course, which we call awareness or consciousness, but we are not aware of the process by which this is produced. So there is little or nothing that introspection can inform us about our brain function.

As a result of these considerations, introspection has long been abandoned as a scientific means of obtaining information about the state of the mind. So what are we left with? How is it possible to write a book about states of mind if we cannot obtain reliable information about them by questioning the people concerned? The answer is that the state of the mind is accurately reflected in behaviour and that an enormous amount of information can be obtained by observing behaviour. In this context, the word 'behaviour' is used in the widest possible sense and includes both speech and conduct calculated by the subject to mislead about the current state of his or her mind. Of course, the subject's own comments on the state of his or her mind are to be regarded with profound suspicion for the reasons already given. They will usually require interpretation. With that proviso, behaviour should be regarded as the only valid source of insight into the state of the mind.

That is why the accounts in this book are primarily accounts of how people behave, or have behaved, rather than what they have told us about what is going on 'inside their heads'.

The ageing mind: eugeria rules

The word 'senility' comes from the Latin *senilis*, meaning aged. There was a time when old age was honoured as the repository of wisdom; in fact our words 'senate' and 'senator' come from the same root as senility, namely the Latin *senex*, meaning old man. Strictly speaking, the term 'senility' refers only to old age, but it has, unfortunately, come to mean something close to 'dementia'. Except in the law and a few other learned professions, it is common today for the old to be despised as useless and even seen as a bit of a nuisance. This is partly due to the considerable emphasis society places on youthful vitality, sex and machismo, but it is also due to shameful ignorance on the part of many young people.

An ageist stereotype has developed in contemporary Western society. It holds that there is a pattern to which all people of a particular age conform. According to this viewpoint, people who have reached a certain chronological age, say 60 or 65, become unemployable, useless, sexually incapable and possibly demented, and should retire from everything.

If this stereotype is true, we are all going to be in real trouble before very long because our populations are ageing rapidly. Average life expectancy has increased greatly, for example because of medical advances. Even as late as 1950, the world-wide average life expectancy at birth was only 46 years, but by 2050, it is calculated to be 76.6 years. Especially in our pampered Western world, most of us are living to a ripe old age. At the same time, birth rates are falling. Because of all this, the over-65 population of the world is expected to come close to doubling by the year 2020.

Happily, the ageist stereotype is nonsense. The ancients were right about old people. They have experience, and wisdom and experience are inseparable. Knowledge only becomes wisdom when it has been tried out in the real world.

The main plank in the ageist platform is the assumption that, just as our hair turns white and our skin wrinkly and sagging, so our brains deteriorate with age. This is not true. Of course, some old people do develop senile dementia or Alzheimer's disease, but there is no reason to believe that intellectual ability must necessarily decline with age. In the absence of diseases that damage the brain, mental processes show only one confirmed characteristic with increasing age – a degree of slowing. As expressed in the highly respected textbook of psychiatry, *Companion to Psychiatric Studies*, 'The major change with ageing is the decline in psychomotor speed, while other cognitive functions show little in the way of consistent change.' The size of the vocabulary remains constant or increases with age and, apart from the factor of speed, verbal learning shows little or no decline with age.

Even in advanced age there is only limited loss of brain cells and a minor reduction in the connections between them. We have hundreds of billions of brain cells, so loss of a small proportion of them has negligible effect. It is the richness of the brain cell interconnections that equates with mental ability and knowledge. It is only in conditions like Alzheimer's disease, in which an enormous proportion of the brain cells are destroyed, that mental functioning is significantly affected by loss of neuronal tissue.

It is hard to overestimate the significance of memory as a measure of the quality of a human being. Of course there are some people with a rich memory store who never do anything with it, but, in many contexts, the possession of a large amount of accessible information determines the effectiveness and usefulness of a person. Status in the professions, academic fields, etc. is, largely, a matter of memory status. However unkind it may seem, society in general treats those people whose memories have been destroyed – that is, people with dementia – as being of greatly reduced significance as persons.

An unfortunate recent development is the introduction of the term 'age-associated memory loss'. The fact that some drug manufacturers have put a lot of money into research into 'age-associated memory loss' does not mean that there *is* such a thing. Is there any evidence of such a phenomenon? To answer this question, we need to look a little more closely at human memory. The processes involved in memory — defined as the ability to store and retrieve information — are much more complicated than those involved in the processing and storage of data in a computer. Nevertheless, much has been discovered in recent years, and the precise nature of human memory is gradually being uncovered. All biological and medical scientists agree that memory is a function of the brain and that memory data are actually stored in the brain. Unlike the arrangements in a computer, there is no one place in the brain which can be described as the memory. Brains certainly do have structures analogous to read-only memory (ROM), random access memory (RAM), shift registers and other computer parts, but they do not have gigabyte hard discs.

We do have gigabytes of data but, perhaps fortunately, it is not all stored in the same place. There is no single part of the brain which, if damaged by disease or injury, would destroy our whole memory store. There are, however, certain known parts of the brain that, if damaged, can deprive us of *access* to the memory store. This is how *real* loss of memory, as distinct from psychological loss, occurs. These parts, called the hippocampus and the amygdala, are concerned with the temporary storage, registration, processing and recall of information that is to be permanently stored.

Information enters our bodies by way of our eyes, ears, noses, mouths and skin, and this information is very complex. The incoming data to be memorized are never presented in simple form. We do not get bits of information serially in the computer sense, in the way information comes off a floppy disc as a stream of binary ones and zeros. Our information input takes many different forms — pictorial, verbal, numeric, and so on and these complex masses of information are analysed by our sense organs and converted into streams of frequency-modulated nerve impulses. There is good reason to believe that there are many different kinds of memory – visual, auditory, olfactory, gustatory and tactile.

The brain is able to put these nerve impulse data into their context because it 'knows' where they come from – because of the part of the particular sense organ that is stimulated. The brain 'knows' that it is perceiving blue sky because it 'knows' that blue-sensitive cones on the lower parts of the retinas are the ones sending it messages. Light coming from above hits the lower parts of the retinas. And the brain 'knows' that it is seeing sky because a large amount of other information has already been received that 'tells' it that if we are out of doors and we look up and see something bright and blue, the chances are that we are looking at the sky.

So data always arrive as part of a complex matrix in which they are embedded. The context of the data is likely to form part of the memory; indeed daily experience shows us how important context and associations are for effective memorizing. For example, a single item of information conveyed to us by way of speech will be accompanied by a considerable context of other data – the appearance of the speaker's face, its spatial relationship to other things, the quality of the voice, the indications of emotion, and much other information. It is thought that, rather than being stored all in one place, this information is distributed to those parts of the brain known to be concerned with the different sensory functions. Visual information, for instance, always goes right to the back of the brain, while olfactory information is perceived near the front. All the areas of the brain concerned with the many modalities of sensation are known and have been mapped out.

The storage capacity of the human brain is immense, but there is no way in which complex perceptions of this kind could all be stored separately at each moment of perception. If this were happening the brain would soon be filled up. So some kind of analysis and selection must be necessary to determine what should be registered and stored. The probability is that familiar contexts are stored and that only significant *changes* in them are registered. But this kind of analysis and selection can only be performed if the data are temporarily stored so that they can be operated upon. This implies the existence of short-term stores or 'buffers' that are constantly in use.

In fact, individual experience suggests that there are several short-term buffer stores for different types of memory – speech sounds, non-verbal sounds, touch, vision, and so on. There is, for instance, a short-term store that codes for the articulation of a sequence of words that we intend, shortly, to use in spoken conversation. Most people are only too well aware of the annoyance of having forgotten what they were about to say. This is because delay has led to the loss of the content of the short-term store or because something else, usually trivial, came along to be stored and overwrote the earlier pearl of wisdom. We also have a short-term memory for small items of new data that need only be remembered briefly. This buffer, or shift register, has to be constantly refreshed. Most of us can look up and remember a new telephone number if we repeat it internally until we dial it. But if someone speaks to us or we think of something else, the number will be lost as new incoming data displace the current contents of the buffer.

There is also a strict limit to the length of any item of new data if it is to be held in this short-term buffer. Most of us can readily hold a seven or eight-digit number, but not a 12 digit number. Buffers of this kind are extensively used in computers and these, too, have a strictly limited capacity. The human buffer can also be emptied by a blow or an electric shock to the head. Scientists still do not know the actual form in which data are stored in the brain, but it is thought that short-term memory operates via some kind of dynamic neuronal circuit, almost certainly of circulating nerve impulses.

One possible explanation for the increasing forgetfulness of the elderly may be seen by returning to the brain–computer analogy. If computer software has to search though a database before it can come up with what is wanted, the time it takes to do so increases with the size of the database. The more items that have to be looked at the longer it takes. Since older people have been accumulating data for much longer than young people, they have a great deal more to be processed. So is it surprising that older people find that their mental processes have slowed?

All of us have a huge quantity of data stored in our brains, initially recorded via short-term memory and then preserved for a lifetime in permanent storage. This mass of data is highly organized in terms of meaning and association; and the better it is organized the more accessible it is to us. The efficiency of retrieval is heavily dependent on clues, mnemonics and, in particular, cues, all of which seem capable of addressing the appropriate part of the memory store. If someone asked you to recite the beginning of Hamlet's celebrated soliloquy, you might be stuck. But if you were asked for the three words that follow the cue: 'To be or ...' the chances are that you would come up with the continuation: '...not to be'.

The difficulty almost all older people have in remembering names is a case in point. If you are presented with the name of a person you know well, your brain reviews the relevant data and presents you immediately with a flood of data about that person. But the linking associations do not work nearly so well in the opposite direction. You can run over in your mind numerous details about a person but still fail to come up with the name. This is probably because the memory system does not operate by applying labels. To the brain, a name is, neurologically, a less efficient way of identifying something or somebody than the mass of sensory data the brain 'prefers' to deal with.

Efficient and reliable registration for long-term storage demands good organization and strong association. Scholarly people with a deep grasp of their subject assimilate new information on their specialty with the greatest of ease, so long as it can be related to existing stored data. Entirely new matter, unrelated to any previous experience, is much harder to memorize.

It would be ridiculous to deny that many old people do lose their minds. This is what the word dementia means. The important point is that this does not happen because they are old but because they have been unfortunate enough to suffer disease of, or damage to, the brain. This has to be pretty severe and general to cause dementia. Local damage to a small part of the brain could, depending on the site, cause blindness, loss of hearing, loss of the sense of smell, loss of the ability to form words, and so on. This is called focal loss and it results from injury or interference with the blood supply. The commonest cause of such brain damage is a stroke – the result either of bleeding into the brain from a burst artery, or the blockage of an artery so that the vital blood supply with its glucose fuel and oxygen is cut off.

There are several other causes of dementia. Alzheimer's disease is a specific neurological condition causing widespread destruction of brain cells. Very heavy drinking can destroy enough brain cells by straight poisoning to cause dementia. Partial drowning, cardiac arrest or any other cause of deprivation of oxygen to the brain for more than a few minutes can have the same effect. One of the commonest causes of dementia is a long succession of, sometimes unsuspected, mini-strokes. This phenomenon, like major strokes, is certainly age-related, but that is because a lot of older people have so neglected their health (for example, never had their blood pressure checked, lived on unsuitable diets, taken no exercise, etc.) that they develop the common artery disease atherosclerosis, which is the cause of strokes and heart attacks.

'Age-related memory loss' certainly occurs in this sense, but it is not the age that causes the loss. The distinguished biochemist and neurologist Professor Steven Rose acknowledges that mental processing slows with age but insists that there are no grounds for the belief that normal ageing brings memory loss.

Older people have plenty to contribute to society. Here are some examples of some of their achievements. The Spanish cellist Pablo Casals, one of the most distinguished exponents of the instrument, had a public life that lasted for 70 years. When he was 81, Casals married his 20-year-old pupil Maria Montanez; and in 1961, at the age of 84, he gave a cello recital before President of the United States, John F. Kennedy. The pianist Artur Rubinstein was giving virtuoso piano recitals, entirely from memory, when well into his nineties. He died at 95.

The Californian newspaper proprietor Hal Wright is unusual in that he is also the reporter, the writer, the editor and the advertising manager. Not content with that, he also delivers copies to outlying subscribers by his private plane, which he pilots himself. Hal is 93.

The brilliant comic writer P. G. Wodehouse published his final Jeeves book at the age of 90, having published no less than 13 books in his eighties.

At the age of 70 the French musical-comedy actor and singer Maurice Chevalier starred in the film *Gigi*, at 72 in *Can-Can*, and at 73 in *Fanny*. At the age of 77 Mae West made a successful appearance in Gore Vidal's *Myra Breckinridge*, and at 84 she starred in the film *Sextette*.

Antonio Stradivari, the Italian luthier, who made over 1000 violins, violas and cellos, was still working and producing superb instruments at the age of 94. Some of the instruments he made after the age of 90 show subtle indications of loss of his highest abilities – there is, for instance, some just perceptible irregularity in the inlaying of the purfling strip near the edges of the plates – but even these instruments stand high in comparison with those of the best other makers in their prime.

Leopold Stokowski was co-conductor with Toscanini of the NBC Orchestra from the age of 59 to 61, and then, sequentially, conductor of the New York City Symphony Orchestra, the New York Philharmonic, the Houston Symphony Orchestra (when aged 73 to 78) and, from the age of 80 to 90, the American Symphony Orchestra.

At the age of 101 American physician Dr W. L. Pannell was still practising medicine in East Orange, New Jersey.

The Japanese artist and printmaker Hokusai Katsushika, celebrated for his remarkable work *Hundred Views of Mount Fuji*, entered his great period at the age of 75. Although he had been studying his art throughout his life and started to publish at the age of 50, he believed that he had done nothing of much value before he was 70. According to his own account, he began to understand the structure of living things at the age of 73 and expected to achieve real depth at 90 and to be divinely inspired at 100. In fact, he died at a mere 89, having achieved perpetual fame.

British journalist, author, and broadcaster Alistair Cooke has for many years masterfully interpreted the American scene to Britain in his weekly BBC feature 'Letter from America'. This valued and cultivated contribution to Anglo-American understanding continues to run to the time of writing and, Cooke, at 90, shows little sign of flagging or of losing his sharpness of mind, sense of humour, or remarkable memory.

The dying mind: the cortex gives up

During the Malayan campaign in the 1950s in which British and colonial forces were engaged in a bitter jungle struggle against the Chinese Peoples' Liberation Army, a 25-year-old doctor was medical officer to a Scottish battalion, the Gordon Highlanders. He was a very inexperienced young man and should have known better than to try out on himself a very toxic drug that had, in fact, been removed from the pharmacopoeia because of its dangers. The results, however, were not wholly bad. They provided him with an experience that he was to remember for the rest of his life and that was to have a profound effect on his attitude to the experience of dying. The things he learned at that time remained with him, and nothing that he later observed or experienced, in the course of a varied clinical life, caused him to modify the conviction he formed at that time.

Battalion headquarters, where the doctor had his Medical Inspection Room, was in an isolated area in Negri Sembilan and, because the Army was engaged in a war against the communist guerrillas, there were severe restrictions on movement. So when he succeeded in poisoning himself, there was not much to be done. For three days he lay on his narrow bed in the *atap bashah* – the walls and roof made of dusty woven nipa palm leaf thatching, and as he lay there he knew that he was dying.

It was not a matter of thinking that he might die, or that, in his medical judgment based on his own symptoms, he thought he was likely to die. He *knew*, with clear, unequivocal, conviction that he was dying. Many times, during the course of these three days, he lapsed into unconsciousness and between the periods of coma he had a series of amazing hallucinations with grotesque distortion of space and time.

But the important thing about this extraordinary preview of dying was that he accepted the fact with perfect composure. Each time he felt himself slipping into coma he believed that this was the end, and he accepted it easily. There was no struggle, no attempt to hang on to life, no horror, no pain or sense of loss, no regret for the loss of his life. Just complete acceptance.

The doctor thought of his young wife and recently born child back in England and was sorry that he would not see them again, but even this regret was mild and passing. He was 25 years old, just at the beginning of his medical career. One might have expected bitterness or resentment at having to die so young. But there was nothing of that.

Later, of course, when he was recovering, he saw, to his intense surprise, that he had been mistaken – that the conviction that he was dying was the result of an abnormal state of brain function, brought on by the depressant effect of the drug. Nevertheless, his response to that conviction at the time remained, ever after, as a source of great consolation to him and, to this day, he is convinced that, when he comes to die, his last moments of consciousness will be as easy and as accepting.

Since then this doctor has learned much about the physiology of brain function and has studied the changes occurring during the final approach of death. He now knows the reasons for the acceptance and easy resignation. But academic knowledge is one thing and direct experience is another, and this doctor believes that he has been extremely fortunate to have had prior personal experience of dying.

When brain function is dangerously dampened, as it is just before death, or as it is by a variety of poisons and drugs, two important things happen: there is a clear conviction of dying, and there is no distress. This is not to suggest that the whole process of dying is easy, particularly not in young people. If there is early knowledge that death is coming soon, there is, inevitably, a great deal of suffering. The above-mentioned alteration in brain function does not usually occur a long time before the actual moment of death. That depends on the type of the illness from which the person is dying. Sometimes it does, so that for days or even weeks before death, there is peace of mind. But in most cases, this comfort comes fairly late.

The great Canadian physician Sir William Osler (1849–1919), one of the fathers of modern medicine, wrote in his book *Science and Immortality*, that he could hardly remember a dying patient who, at the last, was afraid of death. Osler, in a study of 500 dying patients, found that only 11 were afraid during their last illness. Osler was writing at the turn of the century and it may be that the widespread religious faith of the time was a factor in producing this low incidence of anxiety. More recent studies suggest that in the stage of acceptance, fear or deep anxiety are now much commoner than that, and that those with religious faith show least fear.

The difficulty about these figures is to be sure that one is comparing like with like. It is true that at least a quarter of seriously ill people are deeply anxious about their condition. But most of these are, in fact, at an earlier stage and are anxious at the *possibility* that they might die. People who have accepted that they are dying and have reached the stage at which the brain is beginning to be affected show a much lower incidence of anxiety – nearer to Osler's figures.

This bring us to the question of what are called 'near-death experiences'. Many people who have come very close to death, but have been saved at the last moment, have reported their experience. The most interesting thing about this is how closely their experiences correspond. Common to nearly all of them was a strong sense of peace, contentment and acceptance. About 40 per cent had a feeling of spiritual detachment from the body and about one quarter felt they were moving into an area of darkness. About 10 per cent were convinced that they were passing on into an area of bright light.

There are medical explanations for these experiences. The sense of tranquility comes from a decrease in the rate of neural activity in the brain – the same sort of thing that happens with tranquillizers, or when we are falling asleep – and this results from decreased blood supply to the brain. Next, natural substances called endorphins –

morphine-like chemicals produced by the body itself – act increasingly on a part of the brain called the limbic system to produce a feeling of happiness and of separation from the physical body. As the blood supply to the brain declines further, the part at the back responsible for vision is damped down and we 'enter the darkness'. Before this visual area ceases to function altogether, it commonly has a burst of abnormal activity causing a sensation of bright light. And, briefly, just before the brain blacks out altogether, abnormal activity in other areas may produce a strong hallucination of bodily movement. All voluntary bodily movement is mediated in the brain and the accompanying awareness of the movement is experienced by way of the brain.

Near-death experiences have caused many people to attribute some religious or spiritual significance to what they have gone through. Some have even taken it as a proof of life after death. They believe they will walk into the light and then into the next life. For many, this is a comforting belief. But it is important to understand that when we pass into coma we are never aware of the moment of passage. We are never aware of the moment of loss of consciousness, and our experience proves it every night of our lives. So, if the brain is undergoing these progressive reductions in function, and has reached the stage of hallucination of bright light, we would then, if we are actually going to die, pass, without any awareness at all, into whatever follows. And there is no way we can ever know what does follow.

Bibliography

Allport, G. W. (1954). *The Nature of Prejudice*. Doubleday Anchor Books.

Blakemore, C. and Greenfield, S. (eds.) (1987). *Mindwaves*. Blackwell.

Briggs, R. (1996). *Witches & Neighbours*. HarperCollins.

Brown, J. A. C. (1963). *Techniques of Persuasion*. Penguin Books.

Burton, R. (1932). *The Anatomy of Melancholy*. Dent Everyman.

Cohen, D. (1977). *Psychologists on Psychology*. Routledge & Kegan Paul.

Critchley, M. and Henson, R. A. (eds.) (1977). *Music and the Brain*. Heinemann.

Dally, A. (1991). *Women under the Knife*. Hutchinson Radius.

Dennett, D. C. (1991). *Consciousness Explained*. Allen Lane.

Doerner, K. (1981). *Madmen and the Bourgeoisie*. Blackwell.

Dollimore, J. (1991). *Sexual Dissidence*. Clarendon Press.

Drinka, G. F. (1984). *The Birth of Neurosis*. Simon & Schuster.

Enright, D. J. (ed.) (1989). *Ill at Ease*. Faber & Faber.

Ehrebwald, J. (ed.) (1991). *The History of Psychotherapy*. Jason Aronson Inc.

Enoch, M. D. and Trethowan, W. H. (1979). *Uncommon Psychiatric Syndromes*. John Wright & Sons Ltd.

Eskapa, R. (1987). *Bizarre Sex*. Quartet Books Ltd.

Eysenck, H. J. and Sargent, C. (1982). *Explaining the Unexplained*. Book Club Associates.

Eysenck, H. J. (1964). *Crime and Personality*. Routledge & Kegan Paul.

Feldman, M. D. and Ford, C. V. (1994). *Patient or Pretender*. Wiley.

Galton, F. (1883). *Inquiries into Human Faculty and its Development*. Macmillan.

Gelder, M., Gath, D. and Mayou, R. (1994). *Oxford Textbook of Psychiatry*. Oxford University Press.

Gottesman, I. I. (1991). *Schizophrenia Genesis*. W. H. Freeman.

Gregory, R. L. (ed.) (1987). *Oxford Companion to the Mind*. Oxford University Press.

Haggard, H. W. (1925). *Devils, Drugs and Doctors*. Heinemann.

Hahnemann, S. (1913). *Organon of the Rational Art of Healing*. Dent.

Harrington, A. (1972). *Psychopaths . . . .* If Books.

Hume, D. (1903). *Essays, Moral, Political and Literary*.

Huxley, A. (1952). *The Devils of Loudun*. Chatto & Windus Ltd.

Joubert, L. (1989). *Popular Errors*. University of Alabama Press.

Kaplan, H. I. and Sadock, B. J. (1988). *Clinical Psychiatry*. Williams & Wilkins.

Kendell, R. E. and Zealley, A. K. (ed.) (1988). *Companion to Psychiatric Studies*. Churchill Livingstone.

Leahey, T. H. and Leahey G. E. (1983). *Psychology's Occult Doubles*. Nelson-Hall.

Mackay, C. (1932). *Extraordinary Popular Delusions and the Madness of Crowds*. Farrar, Straus & Giroux.

Medvedev, Z. and Medvedev, R. (1971). *A Question of Madness*. Penguin Books.

Meerloo, J. A. M. (1957). *Mental Seduction and Menticide*. Jonathan Cape.

Miller, J. (ed.) (1983). *States of Mind*. BBC Publications.

Moore, B. (1970). *Reflections on the Causes of Human Misery*. Allen Lane.

Porter, R. (ed.) (1996). *Cambridge Illustrated History of Medicine*. Cambridge University Press.

Read, C. (1995). *Man and His Superstitions*. Senate.

Rose, S. (1973). *The Conscious Brain*. Weidenfeld & Nicolson.

Russell, J. B. (1980). *A History of Witchcraft*. Thames & Hudson.

Sacks, O. (1973). *Awakenings*. Pan Books.

Sacks, O. (1984). *A Leg to Stand On*. Pan Books.

Sacks, O. (1986). *The Man Who Mistook His Wife for a Hat*. Duckworth.

Schopler, E. and Mesibov, G. B. (eds.) (1992). *High-Functioning Individuals with Autism*. Plenum Press.

Seashore, C. E. (1967). *Psychology of Music*. Dover Publications Inc.

Showalter, E. (1997). *Hystories*. Picador.

Skinner, B. F. (1974). *About Behaviourism*. Jonathan Cape.

Sperry, R. W. (1966). In: *Brain and Conscious Experience*. Springer.

Summers, M. (1994). *The History of Witchcraft*. Senate.

Sutherland, S. (1992). *Irrationality – The Enemy Within*. Constable.

Szasz, T. S. (1961). *The Myth of Mental Illness*. Dell Publishing.

Szasz, T. S. (1971). *The Manufacture of Madness*. Routledge & Kegan Paul.

Szasz, T. S. (1974). *Ideology and Insanity*. Penguin Books.

Taylor, G. R. (1979). *The Natural History of the Mind*. Secker & Warburg.

Taylor, J. (1980). *Science and the Supernatural*. Temple Smith.

Treffert, D. A. (1989). *Extraordinary People*. Bantam Press.

Trotter, W. (1916). *Instincts of the Herd in Peace and War*. Ernest Benn.

Van Sommers, P. (1988). *Jealousy*. Penguin Books.

Vincent, J.-D. (1990). *The Biology of the Emotions*. Blackwell.

Webster, R. (1995). *Why Freud was Wrong*. HarperCollins.

Wiltshire, S. (1987). *Drawings*. Dent.

Youngson, R. M. (1994). *The Guinness Encyclopedia of the Human Being*. Guinness Publishing.

Index

8917